SOCIAL ALARMS TO TELECARE

Older people's services in transition

Malcolm J. Fisk

First published in Great Britain in June 2003 by

The Policy Press
University of Bristol
Fourth Floor, Beacon House
Queen's Road
Bristol BS8 1QU
UK

Tel +44 (0)117 331 4054
Fax +44 (0)117 331 4093
e-mail tpp-info@bristol.ac.uk
www.policypress.org.uk

British Library Cataloguing in Publication Data

A catalogue record for this book is available from the British Library

ISBN 1 86134 506 2 paperback

Malcolm J. Fisk is a social scientist with expertise on the support needs of older people. Currently he is Managing Director of Insight Social Research Ltd.

Cover design by Qube Design Associates, Bristol.
Front cover: photograph by David Cahn supplied by Eshel, the Association for the Planning and Development of Services for the Aged in Israel.
Printed and bound in Great Britain by Bell & Bain, Glasgow.

Contents

List of tables and plates

Tables

Plates

Acknowledgements

Acknowledgements are due to a large number of people. Most importantly thanks are due to Dr Kevin Doughty of Technology in Healthcare (formerly of the University College of North Wales, Bangor) and Dr Bob Smith at Cardiff University. Their insights, challenges, advice and encouragement in particular helped bring this work to fruition.

Among the many others to whom thanks are due and who have helped in a myriad of ways, a special note of appreciation is extended to Chris Allen, Ian Bruce, Kevin Cullen, Tom Duncan, George Hough, John McKelvey, Kevin McSorley, Evelyn Maloney, Annalisa Morini, Britt Östlund, Moyra Riseborough, Drago Rudel and Frank Vlaskamp.

Thanks are also due to various agencies who financially supported, directly and indirectly, some of the work undertaken by the author that has been germane to this book. These were the Abbeyfield Society, the American Lifeline Foundation, the Association of Social Alarms Providers (ASAP), Cooperation Ireland, Dundalk Planning Partnership, the Esmée Fairbairn Foundation, Fold Housing Association, the ExtraCare Charitable Trust, Help the Aged, the Joseph Rowntree Foundation, Liverpool Housing Trust, the London Borough of Hillingdon, North British Housing Association, Oldham Metropolitan Borough Council, Telford and Wrekin Council and Touchstone Housing Association.

Thanks are also due to the following who undertook interviews or made translations on behalf of the author: Ann Breslin, Amina Dar, Hayley Fisk, Tineke Fitch, Lorna Fitzpatrick, Margit Gaffal, Nia Hopkins and Una Marron. Aside from these the full list of individuals to whom acknowledgement is due is as follows. The affiliations noted are those that last applied when their information or other help was given.

Kevin Alderson	Tunstall Telecom, Whitley Bridge	England, UK
Kate Allan	University of Stirling	Scotland, UK
Chris Allen	University of Salford	England, UK
Nigel Appleton	Technology for Living Forum, Oxford	England, UK
Mike Atherton	Telford and Wrekin Council	England, UK
Paul Billingsley	Oldham Metropolitan Borough Council	England, UK
Sidsel Bjørneby	Human Factor Solutions, Oslo	Norway
Brendan Brassil	Age Action Ireland, Dublin	Ireland
Hans Brønfeld	Horsens Kommune, Horsens	Denmark
Ian Bruce	DKTOB Pty, Brighton	Australia
Dave Buckner	Glasgow City Council	Scotland, UK
Robin Burley	Eskhill & Co, Musselburgh	Scotland, UK
Roger Burrows	University of York	England, UK
John Butler	Dundalk Planning Partnership	Ireland
Pacey Cheales	London Borough of Hillingdon	England, UK

Lawrence Chomsky	Lifeline Systems Inc, Watertown	United States
Neale Chumbler	Marshfield Center for Health Services Research, Marshfield	United States
Mary Ciantar	Department for the Welfare of the Elderly, B'Kara	Malta
Michel Conan	Centre Scientifique et Technique du Batiment, Paris	France
Jacqueline Couture	St Joseph's Community Health Centre, Hamilton	Canada
Alberto Cristoferi	TESAN, Vicenza	Italy
Kevin Cullen	Work Research Centre, Dublin	Ireland
Dick Curry	University of Sussex	England, UK
Andre Danis	Elcombe Systems, Kanata	Canada
Andrew Dibner	American Lifeline Foundation, Watertown	United States
Margret Dieck	Deutches Zentrum für Altersfragen eV, Berlin	Germany
Kevin Doughty	Technology in Healthcare, Menai Bridge	Wales, UK
Andrew Downing	Flinders University, Adelaide	Australia
Gerard Egan	Dublin Corporation	Ireland
Jane Endersby	London Borough of Hammersmith and Fulham	England, UK
Lindsey Etchell	Ricability, London	England, UK
Paul Fathers	Telford and Wrekin Council	England, UK
Les Fawsitt	Cooper Security, Mitcheldean	England, UK
Anne Finnegan	Glasgow City Council	Scotland, UK
Finbarr Fitzpatrick	CallCare Ireland, Clones	Ireland
John Ford	SureCare, Chester	England, UK
Magnus Fritzen	Swedish Handicap Institute, Stockholm	Sweden
Henrik Friedeger	Ministry of Social Affairs, Copenhagen	Denmark
Roberto Giampieretti	TESAN, Vicenza	Italy
David Gordon	Hanover (Scotland) Housing Association	Scotland, UK
Jan Graafmans	Eindhoven University of Technology	The Netherlands
Chris Greathead	Places for People Group, Preston	England, UK
Jackie Grannell	Liverpool Housing Trust, Liverpool	England, UK
David Grigor	Glasgow City Council	Scotland, UK
Robert Grigorjevs	Oldham Metropolitan Borough Council	England, UK
Denise Hanley	Solihull Metropolitan Borough Council	England, UK
Nancy Harding	University of Leeds	England, UK
Heike Heinemann	University of Dortmund	Germany
John Hennock	Association of Social Alarms Providers, Rochester	England, UK

Afke Hielkema	KBOH, Woerden	The Netherlands
Jean Hillier	Oldham Metropolitan Borough Council	England, UK
Pieter Huijbers	Nederlands Instituut voor Gerontologie, Nijmegen	The Netherlands
Janet Hoffman	Cardiff County Council	Wales, UK
George Hough	Ministry of Housing (Ontario), Toronto	Canada
Steve Iliffe	University College, London	England, UK
Ian Jardine	Institute of Health Services Management, Abingdon	England, UK
Alan Jephcott	Touchstone Housing Association, Coventry	England, UK
Chris Jones	Tunstall Telecom, Whitley Bridge	England, UK
Hans Ketelaars	Estafette BV, Susteren	The Netherlands
Satoshe Kose	Building Research Institute, Tsukuba	Japan
Pauline Leishman	Sunderland City Council	England, UK
Bertie Lewin	Home Care Technologies, Stockholm	Sweden
Sarah Lindley	Tunstall Telecom, Whitley Bridge	England, UK
Guillen Llera	EULEN, Madrid	Spain
Doug Loveday	ExtraCare Charitable Trust, Coventry	England, UK
Jan Lynn	London Borough of Hillingdon	England, UK
Tony Lyons	Age Concern Calderdale, Halifax	England, UK
Kevin McCartney	University of Portsmouth	England, UK
Finbar McDonald	Fitzpatrick Associates, Dublin	Ireland
Catherine McGuigan	CallCare Ireland, Clones	Ireland
Tom McGuirk	Age Action Ireland, Dublin	Ireland
Andrew McIntosh	Tunstall Telecom, Whitley Bridge	England, UK
John McKelvey	Places for People Group, Preston	England, UK
Laura McKenna	Department of Social, Community and Family Affairs, Dublin	Ireland
Donal McManus	Irish Council for Social Housing, Dublin	Ireland
Lucinda McMurran	Oaklee Housing Association	Northern Ireland, UK
Ian MacPherson	Comhairle Nan Eilean Siar, Stornoway	Scotland, UK
Linda MacPherson	Falkirk Council	Scotland, UK
Kevin McSorley	Fold Housing Association, Holywood	Northern Ireland, UK
Evelyn Maloney	Sisters of Charity Ottawa Health Service	Canada
Paul Mifsud	Planning Authority, Floriana	Malta
Pam Mills	Durham County Council, Durham	England, UK
Frank Miskelly	Charing Cross Hospital, London	England, UK
Isabel Moore	Age Concern Scotland, Edinburgh	Scotland, UK
Annalisa Morini	Consiglio Nazionale Della Ricerche, Rome	Italy
Mary Morrison	Newcastle upon Tyne City Council	England, UK

Hans-Aage Moustgaard	International Security Technology, Helsinki	Finland
Derek Nally	Emergency Response, Wexford	Ireland
Joan Nankervis	Department of Human Services, Melbourne	Australia
Stuart Naylor	Jontek, Stockport	England, UK
Deida Nicholls	Silver Chain, Osbourne Park	Australia
Joyce O'Connor	National Institute for Higher Education, Limerick	Ireland
Anne O'Reilly	Help the Aged (NI), Belfast	Northern Ireland, UK
Christine Oldman	University of York	England, UK
Vijay Oliver	Hyde Housing Association, London	England, UK
Britt Östlund	Verket För Innovationssystem, Stockholm	Sweden
Tudor Owens	Wolsey Comcare, Tonypandy	Wales, UK
Eddie Passmore	Sunderland City Council	England, UK
Jean Patel	Lifeline Systems Inc, Watertown	United States
David Phillips	Insight Social Research, Newport	Wales, UK
Peter Phippen	PRP Architects, East Molesey	England, UK
Tony Platten	Tynetec Electronic Engineering, Blyth	England, UK
Pauline Poole	Birmingham City Council	England, UK
Jeremy Porteus	Anchor Trust, Oxford	England, UK
David Powell	City and County of Swansea	Wales, UK
Moyra Riseborough	University of Birmingham	England, UK
Hugh Risebrow	BUPA Dental, Bournemouth	England, UK
Luis Rodriguez	Canada Mortgage and Housing Corporation, Ottawa	Canada
Robert Roush	Baylor College of Medicine, Houston	United States
Marco Roverano	TESAN, Vicenza	Italy
Drago Rudel	University of Ljubljana	Slovenia
Luis Ruiz	Centre Suisse d'Electronique et Microtechnique SA, Neuchâtel	Switzerland
Paul Rushton	Hyde Housing Association, London	England, UK
Jim Sandhu	Inclusive Design Research Associates, Sunderland	England, UK
Karin Scharfenorth	Institut Arbeit und Technik, Gelsenkirchen	Germany
Sarah Shiffman	ESHEL, Jerusalem	Israel
Peter Shirley	Attendo Systems Ltd., Rotherham	England, UK
Andrew Sixsmith	University of Liverpool	England, UK
Carl-Johan Skovsgaard	Århus Kommunes Socialog Sundhedsforvaltning Ældresekforen	Denmark
Steve Smith	Cirrus Communication Systems, New Milton	England, UK
Adrian Sowden	Tunstall Telecom, Whitley Bridge	England, UK
John Steel	Specialist Alarm Services	England, UK
Bob Smith	Cardiff University	Wales, UK

David Thew	Guildford Borough Council	England, UK
Patricia Thornton	University of York	England, UK
Mats Thorsland	Uppsala Universitet	Sweden
Malcolm Tyler	Cirrus Communication Systems, New Milton	England, UK
Frank Ursell	Registered Nursing Home Association, Birmingham	England, UK
Ad van Berlo	Smart Homes Foundation, Eindhoven	The Netherlands
Jan van Boxsel	TNO, Leiden	The Netherlands
Frank Vlaskamp	IRV, Hoensbroek	The Netherlands
Ray Walker	Association of Social and Community Alarms Providers, Rochester	England, UK
James Watzke	Simon Fraser University, Vancouver	Canada
Robert Webster	Elcombe Systems, Kanata	Canada
Ines Weidhase	Evangelisches Johanneswerk eV, Bielefeld	Germany
Hannah Weihl	JDC Brookdale Institute of Gerontology, Jerusalem	Israel
Caroline Welch	Help the Aged, London	England, UK
Janet Whitehead	Oldham Metropolitan Borough Council	England, UK
Diane Whitehouse	European Commission DG XIII, Brussels	Belgium
Jane Wilde	Touchstone Housing Association, Coventry	England, UK
Andrew Williams	Liverpool Housing Trust, Liverpool	England, UK
Gareth Williams	Technology in Healthcare, Menai Bridge	Wales, UK
Peter Wilson	Stockport Metropolitan Borough Council	England, UK
Robin Wilson	Dundalk Planning Partnership	Ireland
Mark Wrigglesworth	WanderGuard (UK), London	England, UK
Margaret Wylde	ProMatura Group, Oxford	United States
Richard Wootton	Queen's University of Belfast	Northern Ireland, UK

Thanks are also due to Eshel, the Association for the Planning and Development of Services for the Aged in Israel, for the photograph used on the cover (taken by David Cahn).

ONE

Introduction: what are social alarms?

This book explores the topic of social alarms. It does so mainly in relation to services in Great Britain and Ireland. However, it also provides an international overview and comparison of such technologies and related services.

The international perspective includes the United States, the country within which, along with Great Britain, social alarm technologies initially developed. It also includes more than 20 other countries throughout much of Europe, North America and most of the developed world.

A number of key issues regarding social alarms are addressed and social alarm service provision internationally is mapped. No other study has attempted to do this or has brought together such an extensive range of material on the topic.

First of all it is necessary to state what social alarms are. In all countries they can be seen, at their simplest, as devices that can help to support the independent living of their users. This is the oft-quoted primary aim of social alarm services. Indeed, the words independent living and independence feature in much of the literature concerning social alarms and are very prominent in publicity material produced by social alarm manufacturers, suppliers and service providers. The main competing perspectives are those that are concerned with the more specific roles of social alarms in offering security and in providing help in emergencies.

The affirmations concerning supporting independent living, offering security and providing help in emergencies have been and are frequently accompanied by imagery associated with such objectives. This, on the one hand, offers pictures of healthy and happy older people that are suggestive of active and independent lifestyles; and, on the other hand, feature the frailest and most vulnerable. The latter most typically portray older women, lying prostrate on the floor having suffered a fall (see Plate 1.1).

Definitions of social alarms and the objectives of this book are set out below. First, however, some of the terms used and which are, in some cases, considered to be a source of confusion, are explained.

Terminology

In all parts of the world, the vast majority of users of social alarm services are older people. The term older people is, therefore, commonplace throughout this book, but such terms as elderly people, the elderly, the aged and seniors do appear when the works of others are quoted.

Plate 1.1 *Social alarms: a negative image*

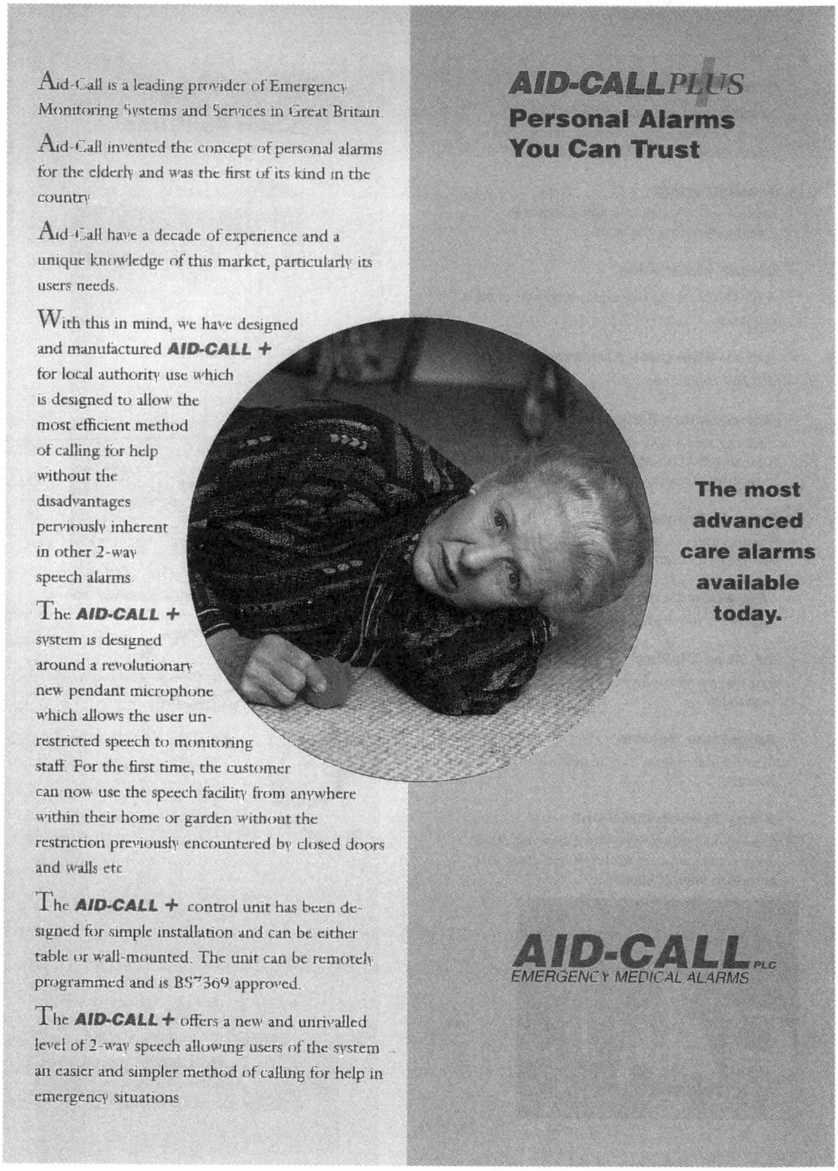

Aid-Call is a leading provider of Emergency Monitoring Systems and Services in Great Britain.

Aid-Call invented the concept of personal alarms for the elderly and was the first of its kind in the country.

Aid-Call have a decade of experience and a unique knowledge of this market, particularly its users needs.

With this in mind, we have designed and manufactured **AID-CALL +** for local authority use which is designed to allow the most efficient method of calling for help without the disadvantages previously inherent in other 2-way speech alarms.

The **AID-CALL +** system is designed around a revolutionary new pendant microphone which allows the user unrestricted speech to monitoring staff. For the first time, the customer can now use the speech facility from anywhere within their home or garden without the restriction previously encountered by closed doors and walls etc.

The **AID-CALL +** control unit has been designed for simple installation and can be either table or wall-mounted. The unit can be remotely programmed and is BS7369 approved.

The **AID-CALL +** offers a new and unrivalled level of 2-way speech allowing users of the system an easier and simpler method of calling for help in emergency situations.

AID-CALL *PLUS*
Personal Alarms
You Can Trust

The most advanced care alarms available today.

AID-CALL PLC
EMERGENCY MEDICAL ALARMS

Source: Aid-Call marketing literature

Older people may generally be taken to include those who are over a designated statutory retirement age. It is recognised, however, that this age varies according to gender and from country to country. It is acknowledged, furthermore, that any retirement age is arbitrary and can only be loosely related to physical ageing. But by virtue of the association of older age with certain infirmities and sensory impairments, and because of the fact that many service frameworks are specifically directed at this group, older people probably comprise over 90 per cent of all users of social alarms.

The association of social alarms with older people is particularly strong in Great Britain and Ireland. This is a result of the presence of such technologies within certain forms of housing. Notable among these are sheltered housing and grouped dwellings designated for older people. The latter includes what is known as amenity housing in Scotland.

Sheltered housing comprises groups of flats and/or bungalows occupied by older people that are linked by a social alarm system to a warden or other designated person who has some responsibility for their well-being, typically a good neighbour who is able to respond in the event of an emergency. More recently, however, the role has evolved to cover tasks relating to the coordination of support services. The name warden is, in addition, being gradually replaced by other titles that better reflect the new role. That role is likely to change more substantially as reforms in funding frameworks aimed at encouraging the delivery of services more flexibly are implemented throughout the United Kingdom (see Fisk and Phillips, 2001).

Other countries have accommodation similar to sheltered housing, but know it by different names. It is usually characterised by different staffing frameworks and generally can cater for higher levels of support need than is normally the case for sheltered housing. Social alarm systems are, nevertheless, a common element.

The manufacturers of social alarms are important. That they have had a major influence on the way in which social alarm services have developed and now operate will become apparent. Where referred to, their full names are not normally given. Rather, companies such as Tunstall Telecom Ltd and Lifeline Systems Inc (respectively the leading companies in Great Britain and the United States) are referred to as simply Tunstall Telecom and Lifeline Systems.

While social alarms are used in different contexts in different countries these generally fall within the arenas of housing, social welfare and health. In Great Britain the emphasis is on public sector housing though some social welfare authorities are involved. In the Republic of Ireland there is substantial emphasis on security. Other than in specific national contexts, the term social welfare is used throughout as a convenient shorthand to embrace the functions of social services authorities in England and Wales and social work authorities in Scotland.

Technical terms relating to the equipment that features as part of social alarm systems are also in use within this book. These include call systems, room units, pull switches, portable triggers, dispersed alarms and carephones. Where necessary such terms are summarily explained when they first appear.

Table 1.1: Social alarms: terminology

Social alarm services and systems		
Call systems	**Dispersed alarms**	
(Hard-wired)	Carephones	Radio units

At the outset, however, it is necessary to point out that the term social alarms may itself be a source of confusion. In this book the term is taken to include those technologies and services which are: (a) hard-wired and installed within groups of dwellings, typically call systems in sheltered housing; and (b) dispersed alarm devices used in other types of accommodation (see Table 1.1). Dispersed alarms, it can be noted, include both carephones (that is dispersed alarm devices that generally operate via the public telephone system) and radio units. Radio units were a feature of many early social alarm systems but are now less common.

Social alarm services generally monitor and provide a response to calls from both of these types of equipment. They may operate throughout communities, counties or regions. A minority of services operate nationally and a few cross international boundaries.

The term social alarms is in common usage among equipment manufacturers and service providers throughout Great Britain and Ireland. An alternative term is community alarms. Other terms are used in other countries. In some parts of Europe, for instance, the term safety alarms is used. The most commonplace alternative terms for social alarms are personal response service (or system) or emergency response service. These are normally abbreviated to PRS or ERS. Such labels are used throughout North America. Occasionally PERS will be encountered for personal emergency response service.

Users of such technologies may know social alarms by such terms, by the titles of the services or by some proprietary names. Notable among the latter is the term Lifeline, a familiar product name in Great Britain and Ireland by virtue of the carephone manufactured by Tunstall Telecom, and in North America through products manufactured by Lifeline Systems.

Social alarms: a definition

Social alarms can be defined as devices (with or without some intelligence) located in the home which, when activated, facilitate communication with a responder and the sending of information, relevant to the user's well-being. They may be part of hard-wired systems or individual devices referred to as carephones or dispersed alarms. In Great Britain and Ireland, social alarm systems normally comprise both call systems and dispersed alarms (almost always carephones), which are linked to a monitoring and response centre. In other countries systems often provide a link only from dispersed alarms.

It should be borne in mind that call systems sometimes stand alone. In other words there is no link to any monitoring and response centre. Such systems are often installed in residential or nursing homes or other forms of accommodation associated with relatively high levels of on-site staff provision. This is not normally the case for sheltered housing schemes where there is a warden or other designated person on site for at least part of the time and who is able to respond to calls on the system – which is switched through to a monitoring and response centre at other times.

Different elements of the above definition of social alarms warrant further attention. The notion that devices might have intelligence, for instance, reflects the fact that social alarm equipment is increasingly designed to enable, with the aid of linked sensors and switches, the gathering of information about the user's environment. There is, in other words, a growing potential for activity and lifestyle monitoring and for users to benefit from proactive rather than reactive interventions.

Facilitating communication acknowledges that, while the primary operational function of social alarms might be seen by most service providers and users as opening a two-way speech channel with a responder after a cord has been pulled or a portable trigger activated, this is not always the case. On establishing contact with a responder, some devices, though not part of social alarm systems or services, simply leave a recorded message. Other devices communicate a code or digital signal that might need to be recorded or will require the recipient to call back, usually via the public telephone network, to the dwelling from which the call originated. In addition it should be noted that, in technical terms, the opening of two-way speech channels, where this does take place, is not normally initiated by the social alarm device itself but rather by the receiving equipment. It is, therefore, dependent on appropriate action being taken by staff at the monitoring and response centre with the operator of the receiving equipment normally having control of the speech channel.

The notion of devices sending information to the monitoring and response centre that is relevant to the user's well-being as part of activity and lifestyle monitoring points to the need to recognise the fact that social alarms are poised to enter what has been referred to by Doughty et al (1996, p 73) as a 'second generation'. The somewhat simple devices and systems that characterised services up to the 1990s will be gradually superseded. It needs to be noted, however, that there are a number of ethical questions that arise when such new technologies and their applications are considered. These include issues about their intrusiveness and the extent of consent, choice and control exercised by the user.

Finally, implicit in the notion of a responder is that some response will be necessary. This follows from the role of social alarms being concerned with both supporting independent living, offering security and enabling help to be obtained in emergencies. Social alarms are not just communication devices. This is a point strongly argued by Thornton (1993a, p 19). Social alarms are communications devices with a wider purpose.

The nature of the response will, of course, vary according to the manner of communication and the nature of information conveyed. In some cases the information will simply need to be recorded and noted as part of a broader monitoring process. In other cases an immediate response may be required, possibly involving one or other of the emergency services.

Putting social alarms into context

Social alarm services are increasingly recognised as important to housing and social policy in Great Britain and Ireland. The first service in Great Britain was established in 1975 (see Chapter Four) and the first in Ireland in the early 1980s (see Chapter Seven). However, alarm and buzzer systems in some forms of housing for older people date back at least to the 1940s. These old technologies gave rise to speech-based warden call systems in the 1960s and, together with dispersed alarms, to today's social alarm systems.

Having peaked in about 1990 at around 300, the number of social alarm services in Great Britain has now reduced to around 270. The reduction in number is a consequence of service rationalisation. This has sometimes taken place in the context of local government reorganisation or stock transfers from local authorities to housing associations. A further reduction in the number of services is anticipated as service efficiencies are sought and more effective controls are exercised in order to raise service standards.

Paradoxically, while the number of services in recent years has decreased a little, the number of users has increased. Extrapolating from earlier figures (Fisk, 1990, p 4; Calling for Help Group, 1994, pp 5-6) the number of users in Britain is estimated to have grown to some 1.5 million (including some 1.3 million households). This estimate appears to have been confirmed in information gathered for Wales, which found 4.8 per cent of households (circa 56,000) with such devices (National Assembly for Wales, 2001, p 131). This would give a pro rata figure for Great Britain of some 1.3 million people without allowing for the higher level of usage that is evident in some parts of Scotland and in several major urban centres in England.

Social alarm services in Great Britain are mostly provided by local authorities. They are used by older people in every district, borough and county. This, and the close association of social alarms with sheltered housing, means that Great Britain probably has relatively more users of social alarms in relation to the total number of its population of older people than is the case for all other countries worldwide. Ireland has relatively few social alarm services, with private sector services predominating in the Republic (see Chapter Seven).

In 1995 it was estimated that there were probably up to 4 million users of social alarm services worldwide (Fisk, 1995, p 145). This number has now probably grown to 7 million. In the United States alone, the leading social alarms company, Lifeline Systems, claimed that, over a period of 20 years to 1999, it had "met the needs of four million frail elderly and disabled individuals" (www://w972.com/ers860/ers864f.htm).

By virtue of the oft-stated role of social alarms in supporting independent living, it might be considered that the main driver underpinning their development and usage would relate to healthcare and social welfare needs.

Arguably, however, this has not been the case. Rather, development in Great Britain, Ireland and elsewhere has owed more to the phenomenon of technology push and to the aggressive marketing techniques of the manufacturers and suppliers. Certainly the advertising messages used to promote social alarms have often reflected such aggression through their negative characterisation of older people and the occasional use of a language of fear that has related both to security and personal health.

Occasionally manufacturers have been censured for such methods. A complaint to the Advertising Standards Authority in Great Britain, for instance, found against Tunstall Telecom for a national press advertisement that featured a teaser that stated "on the 4th December 1984, Olive Bateman had a visitor". The visitor turned out to be an intruder. The Authority considered that the presentation "embodied an unjustifiable appeal to fear and was likely to cause anxiety to some by whom it would be seen".[1] This censure did not, however, stop that company from what appears to be a not dissimilar approach in later advertising (see Plate 1.2).

On account of the extent to which manufacturers have driven the social alarms agenda, it will be argued that social alarm service configurations have often given insufficient consideration to strategic housing, social welfare or healthcare objectives. This is certainly the view of various researchers examining the position in Great Britain (Fisk, 1989, p 1; Thornton and Mountain, 1992, p 5; Riseborough, 1997a, p 1). There have, furthermore, been no known attempts to set out a theoretical framework by which the role and affects of social alarms could be better understood.

The place of social alarms

Social alarms play an increasingly important part within the panoply of equipment known as assistive technologies, defined by Galvin (1997, p 9) as "Any item, piece of equipment, or product system, whether acquired commercially off-the-shelf, modified or customized, that is used to increase, maintain or improve the functional capabilities of an individual with a disability".

In the context of social alarms such a definition might be considered inadequate. The reasons for such inadequacy become apparent in Chapters Eleven to Thirteen where there is discussion of developments affecting social alarm technologies and a consideration of their future configurations.

Insofar as social alarms are assistive technologies, their basic purpose may be seen as having something in common with wheelchairs, stairlifts and walking sticks. All of these artefacts help their users overcome environmental barriers (within and outside of the home) to their participation in normal economic and social activities. In other words, assistive technologies may help support independent living at least in respect of physical mobility.

Plate 1.2 Advertising: the language of fear

Source: Tunstall Telecom advertisement

A broader perspective?

A broader purpose of social alarms is signalled by the way they are linked through communications networks to the means by which help or support can be obtained. There is, therefore, an aspect of the technologies that normally involves communication with service providers. Their typical mode of operation is described below.

However, the role of social alarms is neither clear nor static. To say that they support independent living is insufficient: there are many questions regarding 'how?' and 'in what way?'. More than this, at least some discussion is needed to determine just what is meant by independent living. And it must be recognised that the way that social alarm technologies are developing will result in some new configurations, new uses and the need for new questions.

It can be noted, for instance, that the wider adoption or usage of social alarms will undermine their assistive status. They or their successors might, in other words, join the realms of electric tin openers, remote control garage doors or telephones with memory/automatic dial buttons and become a commonplace feature of our homes. In such a future they would be part of homes that we all might live in and not be viewed as of particular or special benefit to older people or people with disabilities (Mandelstam, 1997, p 7).

It is important, in addition, to note some parallel changes affecting dwelling design. The most notable relate to notions such as universal designs or design for all. These are embodied in the idea of lifetime homes, the objective of which is concerned with the creation of living environments that meet "the broadest range of needs" (Kelly, 2001, p 71). Kelly affirmed that such designs could make it "easier for individuals with different needs to move in and out, and to use the buildings as creatively and individually as they pleased – without their activities being circumscribed by the physical constraints of their house" (p 71). It is within dwellings built according to such principles that independent living can most readily be achieved and support, with or without social alarms and related technologies, given.

A matter of relevance about such dwelling designs, however, is their increasing predisposition to acknowledge the potential of communications technologies therein. This potential relates to the functionality that has been normally associated with social alarms and a wider range of smart technologies (Fisk, 2001, pp 105-6). Smart homes, originally associated with home automation, are discussed in Chapter Eleven. More recently, however, the emphasis has been shifting to include communications technologies and mean that their potential for both supporting and promoting engagement and social inclusion, as well as independent living, is beginning to be recognised.

This broader context is one that has seen the emphatic promotion of communications technologies for older people and people with disabilities by the European Union in successive research programmes. Developments associated with smart homes and social alarms feature strongly within these. The European Telematics research programme, for instance, was concerned to develop new communications technologies and technology applications to assist older and disabled people in maximising their independence (European Commission, 1996). This programme was then developed through certain action lines of the Information Society Technologies (IST) programme (European Commission, 2001). Its importance has been discussed in a number of appraisals (Sixsmith, 1995, p 368; Cowan and Turner-Smith, 1999, p 339ff; Hantrais, 2000, p 144ff).

The criteria for such programmes demanded that products and services be accessible and usable by as large a range of people as possible including older and disabled people. As noted by Tinker (1995, p 30) these programmes, as well as embracing the notion of lifetime homes, had a strong user emphasis that has clear implications for product design and associated service configurations.

Housing and social welfare

In Great Britain it must not go unremarked that although supporting independent living is regularly cited as an objective of social alarms, this objective was, for a period, secondary to that of improving resource management. Indeed, it is suggested that the latter was the primary consideration when some of the earliest social alarm services, particularly in England and Wales, were set up (see Chapter Four). It was not, therefore, the possibility of supporting independent living that initially attracted many local authorities to social alarms, rather it was the ability to save money by reducing, and in some cases removing, on-site sheltered housing warden services.

The notion of extending social alarms beyond sheltered housing, as social alarm systems or services, came later as the technological means of doing this were developed (Oldman, 1989, p 37ff). The context, as noted in Chapters Five and Six, was one where there were frequent tensions between the British housing authorities who had, in most cases, established such services, and their social welfare counterparts for whom the independent living of their service users had been a clear goal over a longer period.

The fact that many social welfare authorities wished to consider the role of social alarm services within broader frameworks of community care counted, it seems, for relatively little among housing practitioners. But the development of services by social welfare authorities would not generally have enabled them to reap financial benefits arising from service rationalisation, since only in Scotland and a small handful of English and Welsh authorities did they fund or manage sheltered housing warden services.

Thornton (1993a, p 20) noted the enmity that existed between housing and social services authorities at that time as having continued in the ensuing period. In her appraisal of social alarm services in England, she concluded that "Some social services departments are suspicious of the way some housing departments have tried to capitalise on spare capacity in a [social alarm] system which in part was set up to meet housing management needs (this suspicion comes to a head when social services departments are asked to contribute financially)".

The tensions between those responsible for administering housing and social welfare functions in Great Britain are noted elsewhere in this book. However, whether or not British housing authorities like it, housing management considerations in relation to social alarm services appear to be of diminishing importance as health and social welfare support needs increase among their users. Regardless, therefore, of the manner by which social alarms evolved in Great Britain, their future development may be most appropriately considered in relation to their potential contribution to meeting health and social welfare rather than housing objectives.

Independent living

Westlake and Pearson (1995, p 8) noted from a survey of 100 older people in the northwest of England that maximising independence was, for them, an "overwhelming concern". Tunstall Telecom (1997, Table 51), in personal interviews with over 200 older people throughout England and Wales, found independence important to 93 per cent of them. English social alarm service users interviewed in a study by Thornton and Mountain (1992, p 19) "were clear that ultimately the benefit of the service lay in enabling them to remain at home".

The notion of independence has multiple dimensions. Abbott and Fisk (1997, p 8) argued that it was "not solely concerned with or determined by an individual's ability to undertake day-to-day living tasks" but also reflected aspects of his or her personality, resources and control over them, opportunity and life circumstances. Clarke et al (1998, p 60) covered similar ground and noted the ways in which individuals redefined "their boundaries of what comprised independence in line with their changing capacities and other circumstances". Westlake and Pearson (1995, p 1) noted that, among older people, independence was "commonly defined with reference to a baseline of living as close as possible to the life they had always led", with (p 10) self-reliant older people taking pride in their ability in "continuing activities which they felt defined their sense of self and their self-worth".

The mention of such things as opportunity and control hints at the importance of social engagement, or at least a sense of being connected with normal aspects of daily living, to independent living. Independence, in other words, means more than being able to get up unaided, wash, eat and go to the toilet. This remains true of those over 85 years of age (the oldest old), with Tinker et al (2000, p 90) suggesting that their view of independence is one that considers it "an enduring personal quality rather than an attribute which depends on their physical, emotional or social state". More than this, they noted for those who had to rely on some support that (p 97) "their continued residence outside an institution allowed them to maintain some sense of independence".

Independent living, therefore, can be considered at two levels. At the basic level it can relate simply to being able to live at home in a suitable and secure environment. At the higher level independent living means not just that but the individual's involvement in the economic, social and family life of the community.

Such differences in meaning are indicated in the outcome of work undertaken by Abbott and Fisk (1997, pp 15-21) from which the following verbatim quotes, from among many, are taken:

> "I'm very independent and always have been. Living in my own home proves it." (Woman aged 88)

> "Independence is very important – at least the ability to feel that you are preserving as much independence as possible in the particular circumstances." (Woman aged 77)

> "What do they mean by independence? Not being ordered about or being told you can't do things." (Man aged 80)

> "Independence is your own way of living. Keep yourself as well as you can without bothering [others]." (Woman aged 96)

> "Independence is very important to me. I am quite happy with the level of independence I have at the moment, as I can lock my door and go out when I like, with no one asking me where I'm going and when I'll be back." (Man aged 78)

Both levels may, it is considered, be assisted by social alarms if, on the basis of available evidence, they can be seen as helping to:

- facilitate speedier interventions and, therefore, the effectiveness of those interventions, in the event of medical or other emergencies;
- improve health, mobility and/or morale through such interventions or through the knowledge that such interventions can be made;
- reduce the number and/or frequency of hospital admissions; and/or
- reduce the length of stay and/or facilitate earlier discharges from hospital than would otherwise have taken place.

The future of social alarms

While the place of social alarms is described in some detail within this book, it should be understood that the standard frameworks within which they operate in Great Britain are idiosyncratic when compared to North America, and to other parts of the European Union. This idiosyncrasy is due to social alarms in

Great Britain being linked to call systems in sheltered housing. The position in Ireland is idiosyncratic for the reasons noted below.

In North America social alarm systems took off with the development of carephones (discussed in Chapter Eight). In contrast to the call systems in Great Britain and Ireland, carephones responded more directly to health, medical and social welfare needs and the services that used them tended to be either run privately or by voluntary/charitable bodies, managed from hospitals or other healthcare facilities.

Compared to less than 300 services in Great Britain and Ireland, there are over 2,000 in the United States and Canada, though generally much smaller in network size – in a recent survey in the United States undertaken by the author, services with as few as 30 users were found (see Chapter Eight).

In the rest of the world, social alarm services generally relate to health and social welfare agendas. Most, therefore, have more in common with the United States than Great Britain. The Republic of Ireland, while echoing the position in Great Britain by the provision of social alarms within sheltered housing, puts particular emphasis on security. This is discussed in Chapter Seven.

Ongoing changes in each of the demographic, political, social and technological contexts suggest, however, that the nature of social alarm services in Great Britain and Ireland will change and will move towards frameworks that reflect service objectives more clearly evident in North America and in continental Europe. The size of services in Great Britain in terms of the number of users will, however, remain high.

Demographic context

In Western countries, the demographic context relating to older people is well known. In all, the number of older people is growing but with particular and, in some countries, spectacular increases in the number of the very old (from 75 to 85) and the oldest old (over 85).

In Great Britain and Northern Ireland the number of people aged over 65 is expected to increase from 9.2 million (1994) to 11.6 million in 2020 and to nearly 15 million in 2040. For those over 80 there is a projected increase from 2.4 million (1995) to 4.4 million in 2040 (see http://www.age2000.org.uk/interim/be/default.htm). In the Republic of Ireland the number of people aged over 65 is projected to increase from 394,700 (1996) to 521,700 in 2011, of whom 227,000 will be over 75 (Ruddle et al, 1998, p 44).

In the United States the number of people aged over 65 is expected to increase from 33.9 million (1996) to 53.2 million in 2020 and nearly 70 million in 2030.[2]

Within the European Union as a whole the number of people aged 60 or more is growing by 0.8 million (1 per cent) each year. This group is forecast to grow from 21 per cent of the 1997 population to 27 per cent in 2020 and possibly up to 40 per cent by 2050, with one third of older people being aged 80 or over.[3]

But the increases in the number of the very old and the oldest old should not be taken to mean that there will necessarily be a burgeoning in healthcare and support needs. The increase in longevity is being accompanied by better health than was formerly the case. Therefore, for any particular age, it can be argued that there will be a lower support need than would otherwise have been anticipated. For governments concerned with holding or reducing the costs of healthcare that fall to the public purse, this means that alarmist predictions about these can, to some extent, be countered.

The goal of compressed morbidity assumes that good healthcare and appropriate lifestyles can enable not just longer but healthier lives in which there is no increased call on health or support services. More people would, in such a context, be able to enjoy independent lives but where the level of support need would be relatively low and/or infrequent. According to this approach any high level of need could, for most, be confined to a short period prior to death (Sidell, 1995, p 162).

At the moment the evidence about compressed morbidity is conflicting. The Organisation for Economic Co-operation and Development (OECD) has, furthermore, pointed out that medical advances cut both ways by overcoming disabilities but at the same time keeping people alive with serious illnesses (1996, p 18). It might be in such a context that healthier lives could be extended but that the need for and extent of healthcare interventions at the end of the life-course could increase. Achieving the goal of compressed morbidity has been called "the greatest challenge for medical science and health education for the twenty first century" (Prophet, 1998, p v).

To claim a role for social alarms in the pursuit of the goal of compressed morbidity should not be seen as pretentious. This book will show that, though some of the claims for social alarms may be little more than marketing hype, there is a core of truth to assertions regarding their successes. Furthermore, the manner of evolution of social alarm systems to embrace activity and lifestyle monitoring (discussed in Chapter Thirteen), promises to offer the means by which preventative and responsive interventions can be made more speedily, be better targeted, and their effects more closely monitored. As will be noted in addition, the few studies that have been undertaken to evaluate the cost–benefits of social alarms, point to substantial financial savings through reductions in hospital admissions, in-patient days, and earlier discharges. The implications of demographic change and the related agendas concerning support and care are, therefore, far-reaching and demand that technologies evolve in ways that respond. However, while social alarm and related technologies might bring cost benefits, it must be recognised that these can only be realised after initial capital investment. Other costs, furthermore, are associated with the development of new patterns of service provision.

For Great Britain and Ireland it is considered that the wider use of social alarms will require new working practices at the interfaces between housing, social welfare and healthcare services. However, the configuration of such working practices is not, in the shorter term, easy to envisage. Much will depend on the extent of commitment to user- or client-focused perspectives and the ease by which tensions and conflicts between services and different professional perspectives can be resolved.

There is some consolation in the fact that concerns about increases in support and care costs, as noted above, may be exaggerated. The main fears that remain, therefore, are that: (a) there may be a predisposition to cling on to established and more institutional forms of housing and care provision such as those that are manifested in some forms of sheltered housing or in care homes; or (b) the financial frameworks necessary to foster new patterns of provision might not be put in place. The incorporation of social alarm technologies within existing frameworks of care could, in other words, help to maintain the status quo and have the effect of fostering dependency rather than supporting independent living, in which case some of the potential benefits associated with social alarms would not be realised.

Political context

The political context is primarily concerned with the minimisation of public expenditure and securing value for money in relation to housing, health and social welfare agendas. Questions arise as to the ways in which service quality is measured and related quality standards are maintained, but the imperative remains to ensure that, in the face of growing needs, public expenditure is restricted.

In Great Britain and Northern Ireland agendas have been addressed for public sector bodies within the Best Value service framework that seeks not only to ensure continuous improvements in service quality but also to encourage exploration of new patterns of service provision. Such objectives are, in part, being achieved by the creation of service frameworks that are more directly accountable to users and/or are delivered, on behalf of local authorities, by private sector agencies or through public–private partnerships. In the Republic of Ireland it is better service coordination and the filling of gaps in service provision that are the main foci, albeit there appears to be some way to go before comprehensive provision for older people is achieved (Ruddle et al, 1998, p 316).

More generally, the Organisation for Economic Co-operation and Development has noted, a growing emphasis in Western countries on alternatives to hospitals and care homes, including home care services and attention to improved housing (1996, p 35). Social alarms were mentioned (p 36) as contributing to this process. Associated with the changing emphases, it was noted, had been attempts to encourage private sector organisations to provide some of the services in question.

Generally speaking, however, most countries have given little attention to social alarms as the shift in emphasis to home-based services has taken place. Finland is an exception having passed national legislation that requires each municipal authority to provide a social alarm service. Complete national coverage on a systematic basis has, as a consequence, been achieved in that country (Cullen and Robinson, 1997, p 11).

While the general lack of municipal provision in many countries may have left the way open for private sector services, there seems little evidence of public sector provision, where it is evident, diminishing. In Great Britain the process of local authorities contracting out social alarm services to the private sector has only taken place to a limited extent, and unlike certain other municipal services there is no statutory requirement for them to do so. Far more commonplace are agreements between local authorities where one provides a monitoring and response service for the benefit of users living in the area of the other. The logic for contracting out is, furthermore, lost if it is assumed that public sector bodies can operate such services with equal or greater efficiency and effectiveness than their private sector counterparts.

The nature of funding frameworks for such services in Great Britain and Northern Ireland are, however, under scrutiny and political judgements are likely to influence the ways in which social alarms are subsidised for those unable to buy in at an economic cost. In Great Britain there are continuing fears among government officials that social alarm services managed by local authorities are being inappropriately subsidised by their housing tenants generally or by their council taxpayers. The extent of such subsidies was signalled in the results of an Audit Commission survey, though clear information on such matters was found to be elusive (1992, pp 6-7).

The issue of subsidies, and the appropriateness of tenants as a whole paying for social alarm services operated by local authorities and housing associations in Great Britain and Northern Ireland, will remain on the political agenda as the need for new service and funding frameworks is explored.

In the Republic of Ireland, as noted above, private sector providers predominate. There are, however, concerns (discussed in Chapter Seven) about the extent of government capital subsidies for carephone provision whereby private sector service providers are able to reap revenue rewards.

Social context

The social context is one that emphasises the importance of delivering care in the community, thereby helping to maintain the integration of older people within family and social networks. Associated with this is a growing consensus about the need to respond to people's rights as consumers and citizens, regardless of age. Acknowledging the place of older people as consumers and citizens means acknowledging their right to exercise housing and other service choices.

In Great Britain and Ireland, the emphasis on care in the community has been associated with the need to foster engagement and social inclusion. Such a philosophy in Great Britain underpinned the 1990 National Health Service and Community Care Act, which aimed to reshape frameworks of service delivery in an attempt to empower service users and facilitate service provision in more flexible ways. Bernard and Phillips (2000, p 38) noted the importance of this legislation for older people. The agenda associated with inclusion and citizenship is one, of course, that is also concerned with supporting independent living. It is a shared agenda with the Republic of Ireland (see Ruddle et al, 1998, p 46).

Any reshaping of service frameworks involves confronting the errors of the past and, where appropriate, removing or reconfiguring the physical manifestations of such errors. The latter are most evident in separate forms of housing provision. It is interesting that despite the plaudits given to sheltered housing such separate provision was not originally favoured by some in the housing profession in Great Britain (Fisk, 1986, p 93). An Institute of Housing report (1958, p 6) stated, for instance, that "We are ... of the opinion that the erection of 32 old person's dwellings in one group is too great a concentration and savours somewhat of colonization", adding (p 7) that "the best solution appears to be the provision of small groups of dwellings for old people interspersed among dwellings built for other age groups".

The fact that things went in a contrary direction, with the provision of sheltered housing around 30 dwellings as the norm, is regrettable. This typical scheme size responded to what was deemed to be the number of older people that a warden could manage, and bore no relation to the support needs of residents (Fisk, 1986, p 135).

In Great Britain and Ireland the issues of care in the community and supporting independent living have become increasingly focal to policy and practice over a period of more than two decades. The question remains, nevertheless, as to the extent to which the aspirations associated with such policies and practices are being met. This question has particular relevance in relation to services for older people at a time when it can be argued that housing and social welfare policies, in promoting separatism and exclusion, have been fundamentally ageist (Fisk, 1999, p 15ff).

Technological context

Among the key technological developments that are likely to have a dramatic affect on social alarms are: (a) the wider availability of interactive cable networks; (b) the use of an increasing range of low-cost sensors that can be used with social alarms to monitor individual well-being and which are concerned with activity and environmental measures; and (c) the parallel development of responsive forms of telemedicine and telecare that facilitate the remote recognition, diagnosis of and response to certain medical conditions.

The wider availability of interactive cable networks points to the possibility of social alarms becoming a part of broad arrays of services. Such networks have an enormous capability for the transmission of visual, audible and digital signals and will be able to accommodate any foreseeable increased data transmission requirements as the technologies associated with social alarms develop.

The linking of different sensors to social alarms has been noted as heralding the movement of social alarms into their 'second generation' and offering the prospect of activity and lifestyle monitoring (see Doughty et al, 1996; and Chapter Thirteen). This is certainly true in terms of the intelligence of such technologies, although it remains to be seen which sensors or combinations of sensors will be found to be most relevant to the needs of users. Sensors such as smoke detectors and intruder alarms are, in any case, becoming more commonplace. Sensors concerned with monitoring users' activity patterns and/or physiology are only beginning to be seriously considered.

The impact of technologies will depend on the outcome of battles between the key actors (health, social welfare and housing professionals) and the extent to which they will take account of user-focused perspectives. It will, furthermore, depend on the happenstance of technological innovation or the discovery of new applications of existing technologies; the marketing strategies of equipment manufacturers; the attitudes of the telecommunications companies to the tariffs that will be levied for network usage; the views and service objectives of private and public sector service providers; and the views and needs of users themselves. In any case there are many unknowns and a tension remains that arises out of the contrary viewpoints espoused by those who pursue commercial or health and social welfare objectives.

Discussion

Each of these contexts point to ongoing or future changes that will continue to influence the shape of social alarm services and the nature of the relationship between service providers and users.

Demographic change, together with the political imperatives concerned with reducing costs to the public purse, will mean that social alarm provision is increasingly focused on those whose assessed needs are greatest or who buy such services privately. This suggests that the influence of those concerned with health and medical care and/or supporting independent living on service configurations will increase.

As to the targeting of social alarm services, this is a positive change especially in countries like Great Britain where, by virtue of the emphasis on housing, targeting has been poor. But there must be provisos that relate to the overall levels of resources, which, in turn, affect eligibility criteria and service accessibility. With resources restricted, those in greatest need are likely to be the main beneficiaries. Others at the margins of need or with modest financial resources are likely to be disadvantaged.

There is a further danger that service frameworks may develop in ways that increasingly respond to narrow medical and health care agendas. Services may, in other words, be provided in ways that reflect doctor to patient relationships, assuming the passive acceptance of social alarms and associated services and compliance with prescribed treatments. In such circumstances the current benefits of some social alarm services, developed within a more holistic context, may be lost.

In Great Britain, at least, a clear trend of social alarms away from their housing origins is apparent. It is a fact that an increasing number of social services authorities use social alarms as part of wider packages of care for older people. This is particularly the case for those with acute medical conditions or who are at greatest risk of falling. A process of medicalisation of social alarm services is under way and has important implications for the location of services, in the sense of who should have responsibility for service management, and the way that the emergencies and other needs that arise are dealt with.

With regard to the technologies themselves, these will respond to changes in needs as determined by the characteristics of service users but may, insofar as the technologies that are available will directly affect their usage, serve to steer the nature of service development. The danger of the latter in the context of social alarms was signalled in the early period of their development when the purchasing decisions of local authorities were deemed to be characterised by a "new toy syndrome" (Butler, 1981, p 20). The phenomenon was still evident nearly a decade later, it being reported that in British local authorities the officers lacked knowledge about the systems and councillors could be too easily impressed by the latest gadgetry.[4] In an international overview of related technologies a similar phenomenon was noted for telemedicine applications. This was described as the gee-whizz factor as in "gee-whizz, we'll have one of those!" (Gott, 1995, p 42). In the same vein, within an appraisal of the role of technologies in supporting care services, Wylde and Valins (1996, p 17) warned of the danger of technologies having a "Boy's Own" fascination.

Herein lies the importance of considering the further development of social alarms in a context where the notion of supporting independent living is underpinned by more than lip service or noble sentiments.

Social alarms in Great Britain and Ireland start at a disadvantage. They, and associated technologies, have been characterised by operational procedures and service frameworks that owe much to notions of ageism and separatism. Users have rarely been properly consulted regarding such frameworks and have acquiesced in the face of so-called professional expertise. There is, as a consequence, a remarkable and widespread ignorance among users about just who is responsible for the management of social alarm services, how they operate and their relationship with other services (Riseborough, 1997a, p 28). Other research has pointed towards a likely growth in the number of users wishing to learn more about their services and the need for services to consider how they can respond, more effectively, to that call (Fisk, 1995, p 151).

It is essential, therefore, for service providers or others who purport to represent the views of social alarm users, including representative organisations, to consider the threats posed and opportunities offered by the technologies in question. This means that greater attention needs to be paid to those aspects of service management or operation of the technologies that serve to disempower or otherwise remove control from the user. Such disempowerment, it is suggested, as well as potentially working against individual rights and freedoms, can work against the objective of supporting independent living.

Objectives

The foregoing discussion provides an overview of the place of social alarms and the context in which they operate. A number of concerns and issues have been touched upon which were instrumental in shaping the objectives of the book and determining its key hypothesis. That hypothesis affirms that social alarms and the services associated with them help to support independent living. Recognition of this, it is suggested, is reflected in the move away from perceptions of such services as narrowly concerned with responding in emergencies.

The objectives of this book are as follows:

- To establish the position regarding social alarms in Great Britain and Ireland; to explore their evolution and the services provided; and to consider their place within social policy frameworks.
- To establish, in broad terms, the position regarding social alarms in other parts of the world; the services provided; and to make comparisons, where possible, between them and with Great Britain and Ireland.
- To consider the role and effectiveness of social alarms in supporting independent living.
- To explore the implications for social alarm services of current technological developments associated with smart homes, certain aspects of telemedicine, telecare, activity and lifestyle monitoring.

An outline of the chapters

This chapter has sought to lay the foundation of the book by which the reader will be better equipped to understand the context within which social alarm services operate, together with the importance of social alarm systems to patterns of housing, social welfare and health services in Great Britain, Ireland and beyond. Given the lack of familiarity of most people, including most older people, with such services and technologies such a foundation is especially important.

Chapters Two to Four explore the relevance of different social theories, review the literature and describe the origins of social alarms. Chapter Two addresses the relevance of established and emerging theories of ageing to social alarms. In so doing it brings a fresh perspective to social alarms, which hitherto have been seen simply as adjuncts of other services for older people. However, this book is disadvantaged by the failure of academics, to date, to consider closely social alarms from any social theoretical perspective.

Chapter Three explores the literature on social alarms, much of it from Great Britain and the United States, as social alarms are widespread in these countries. Academic journal articles and a small number of cost–benefit studies and some broader service reviews are included. The chapter examines the literature from technical, management and user perspectives.

A historical overview of social alarms and their evolution in Great Britain is provided in Chapter Four. This provides an insight into early technological developments and the passing of a crucial milestone when the capability of alarm devices to communicate via radio or telephone networks was established. The chapter plots the course of some of the battles regarding alternative technologies and service frameworks. Importantly, however, the chapter enables an understanding to be obtained as to why, in England and Wales, social alarm services developed as essentially housing rather than social welfare services.

Chapter Five profiles the current position of social alarms in England and Wales, and Chapter Six covers the position in Scotland. Both chapters offer some service profiles drawn from the local authority, housing association, charitable and private sectors. Evidence is drawn from case studies, published and unpublished sources. The more emphatically social welfare perspective of Scottish services and their operation in more rural contexts is noted as having helped to underpin their different perspective to that of England and Wales.

Chapter Seven examines the position Northern Ireland and the Republic, which have distinctly different perspectives from those in Scotland, England and Wales. These differences bear testimony to the nature of needs and the particular social, administrative and security context of Northern Ireland and the wholly different framework and administrative context for the Republic.

The evolution and present position of services in the United States is documented in Chapter Eight. This mines a reasonably rich vein of published material and, among other things, offers the outcome of a nationwide survey of 20 services. The position in Canada is also discussed. Chapter Nine takes a more cursory look at other Western countries and the distinctive characteristics that underpin their social alarm service frameworks. This includes a number of European countries together with Australia, Israel and Japan. It reveals that social alarms have now extended eastwards in Europe and are to be found in emerging countries like the Czech Republic, Hungary and Slovenia, and to a number of countries in South East Asia.

Chapter Ten compares and contrasts the position of social alarms in different parts of the world and attempts to foster a clearer understanding of their current role and the way in which their potential is being developed. In so doing it reaffirms the fact of social alarm services in Great Britain, notably England and Wales, being somewhat idiosyncratic. It notes, however, that there is evidence of some convergence. This reflects the changes taking place in Great Britain rather than elsewhere.

Chapter Eleven explores the development of smart homes and the implications of the technologies employed in such contexts for social alarms. The origins of smart homes within the context of building automation is noted and is then contrasted, in Chapter Twelve, by a further range of technological innovations associated with telemedicine and telecare.

Chapter Thirteen takes the discussion further in examining the extent to which social alarms and related technologies are, or will be, able to deliver in the context of three challenges. The first relates to falls and, therefore, to a long recognised agenda for social alarms. The other two, however, relate to activity and lifestyle monitoring and the ways in which technologies relating to social alarms can help to meet the needs of older people with dementia. These are more recent challenges for which the role of social alarm technologies is only beginning to be considered.

Finally, Chapter Fourteen draws together the different themes and issues; summarises the lessons to be learned from other countries; and discusses the implications of technological changes including those associated with smart homes and telecare. Importantly it finds that the evidence presented finds in favour of the hypothesis that social alarms and the services associated with them help to support independent living. It also offers some pointers to the future and, thereby, signals a substantial potential for their wider use.

Notes

[1] Advertising Standards Authority case report 124 (1985).

[2] American Association of Retired Persons leaflet (1997) 'A Profile of Older Americans'.

[3] From Eurostat Datashop Rm 1.015, Office for National Statistics, Cardiff Road, Newport, South Wales NP10 8XG.

[4] Murray, B. (1994) in paper to international workshop on the potential of information technology for solving housing problems, Building Research Institute, Tsukuba.

TWO

Social theory and social alarms

Moving on from old certainties

Social theories relating to older age are changing and developing. The old certainties about older people and their place in the social order are being swept aside as new agendas are followed in Great Britain and other Western countries. The readily adopted perspective that saw older people as neatly fitting within a particular stage of the life-course, defined by retirement at one end and death at the other is being questioned and theorising now increasingly starts from a perspective that sees older age as a meaningful period of life that warrants more considered attention. This means that some questions about older people and their place in wider society are being addressed for the first time.

The questioning and theorising is, in part, being driven by the demographic changes that are resulting in growing numbers of older people. They also result from agendas concerned with social inclusion, individual rights and freedoms and the questioning of traditional, often institutional, frameworks that have been the locus of care and support for older people in the past.

The paucity of social theories relating to older age has been pointed to by such analysts as Phillipson (1998) and Estes et al (1996). With regard to gerontology, that is the study of older age, Estes et al (p 350) referred to its "broad and fragmented theory". And, as becomes clear in this chapter, such fragmentation remains. But given that gerontology is itself interdisciplinary, the fact that it may draw on social theories that are extant in different disciplines should come as no surprise. The attempt to include social alarms within such theories possibly adds to the fragmentation.

Wilson (2000, p 12), after reviewing the array of social theories pertaining to older age, lamented that "the idea that any one theory is going to be a useful guide to understanding the immense variety of later life begins to look optimistic". She did, however, argue the need for any theory to take a life-course perspective that acknowledged that "men and women are not just old, they are ageing people with pasts and futures" (p 12). There are, in other words, certain things about the life-course that may warrant the development or adoption of social theoretical approaches specifically focusing on older age, albeit that elements may be borrowed from elsewhere.

Estes (1991, p 21), in adopting a theoretical approach that drew from the field of political economy, claimed that our understanding of the position of older people had generally been as a "social product of the market and the social relations it produces", noting (p 25) that "in capitalist society, the relation of class and age is profoundly influenced by the fact that being old is characterised by dis-attachment from the productive process".

Phillipson (1998, p 2) noted that "up until the late 1970s at least, social theory tended to play a marginal role in studies of ageing" and argued that in the ensuing years we entered a "period of crisis in respect of the identity of older people" where there was an urgent need for new perspectives. This was reflected in the 1980s, according to Bernard and Phillips (2000, p 38), in the fact that "social policy was increasingly vacillating between seeing older people as dependent social casualties, and seeing them as individuals capable of exercising choice". In Great Britain in this period the vacillation was reflected, for housing and social welfare policy frameworks, in growing uncertainty as to the appropriateness of the traditional separate or, in a word of Estes (1991, p 25), the "dis-attached" forms of accommodation manifested in sheltered housing and care homes.

Bernard and Phillips (2000, p 38) pointed to the 1990 NHS and Community Care Act as being the key turning point in Great Britain, albeit that its effect in moving social policy away from frameworks which fostered stereotypical views of older people to more targeted approaches was seen as slow. With that legislation they noted the emergence of a new language, which included terms such as empowerment, user involvement and consumerism. The word empowerment is important here in that it has resonance with broader social theories, such as those espoused by the social theorist Foucault, which see social (and political) relationships as being concerned with power. According to such views power relationships are integral parts of the frameworks within which we all live. Power, Foucault asserted, acts on people and "allocates them to their position within the social body" (Callinicos, 1999, p 278).

The reference to empowerment suggests a possibility that policy frameworks might be developed that permit or encourage the emergence of older people from positions in which they are disempowered. The empowerment that has, to some extent, been encouraged and facilitated for older people, more specifically in the context of housing and related services, has been noted by Riseborough (1998, p 27ff) and Fisk (1999, pp 19-20).

Riseborough considered the implications for housing policy and practice frameworks arising from the recognition of older people first of all as consumers and then as citizens. While supporting a more consumerist perspective she noted (p 18) the difficulties encountered by some older service users when access to those services was "restricted by their purchasing power and knowledge". Her work drew, in particular, on the experience of older service users and service provision in other parts of Europe, most notably the Netherlands.

Fisk followed a similar agenda although one which, in part, specifically addressed the role of communications technologies. He also reported on research that sought to examine the consumer or customer perspectives for older people with the highest levels of support need (see Abbott and Fisk, 1997, p 44ff;

Wigley et al, 1998). Such perspectives were concerned to extend the notion of independent living to the frailest and most vulnerable of older people and, in so doing, to help to counter the notions of dependency associated with the inability to exercise consumer choices or to fulfil some of the responsibilities of citizenship. As noted in Chapter One, he also explored some of the meanings of independence (Abbott and Fisk, 1997).

The emergence of the agendas addressed by Riseborough and Fisk points to the importance of social theories to the social policy frameworks that underpin housing and social welfare policies and practices. They signal that policies and practices have tended to reflect approaches that have been too closely focused on political economy approaches (and, therefore, emphasising the effects of structures and institutions) and gave insufficient consideration to the needs and rights, views and understandings of older people as consumers and citizens.

Regarding the 1970s (the main period of social alarms development) it can be noted that Phillipson (1982, p 7) suggested that a distorted view of older people had developed. This saw them as the target of government and social policy objectives but in ways that reflected a focus on the needs of the minority who had support needs. Media images that tended to focus on the frailest older people, sometimes as the victims of crime and apparently deserving of greater sympathy than younger people, helped to sustain such perspectives. In Foucault's view of power relationships, older people were assuredly disempowered and arguably the 'victims' of power structures reflected in the service frameworks (see Mann, 2001, p 111).

The fact of older people being immensely varied in their needs, aspirations and expectations was, as a consequence, often overlooked, and the way was open for policy makers and practitioners to promote and nurture separatist and ageist forms of service provision.

The emergence of a critical gerontology

It is in the 1990s that a critical gerontology had emerged sufficiently to begin to challenge the old perspectives. It must be said, however, that critical gerontology, while sometimes taking cognisance of social welfare issues, generally failed to touch on issues relating to housing policies and practices. Social alarms never featured.

Phillipson (1982) was particularly influential in promoting the critical gerontology agenda. The theoretical frameworks extant at the time (and which supported the status quo) were, therefore, increasingly countered. Heywood et al (2002, p 25) noted that critical gerontology "appears to acknowledge the importance of social and economic processes in marginalizing older people but, at the same time, to listen to and understand how individuals cope with, counteract or respond to these wider societal processes".

Internationally, most notable among earlier theories relating to older age was that put forward by American gerontologists, Cumming and Henry (1961). Their disengagement theory pointed to the withdrawal of people from social and economic life as they became older. It also postulated that society, in a sense, withdrew from older people. This took place most particularly through the enforcement of retirement and thereby precluded, for most, the opportunity for continuing paid work. It also meant that older people generally experienced a loss of income. This perspective is, of course, compatible with that of Foucault by reference to power relationships that would evolve as people reaching retirement age are required to relate to new and disempowering institutional frameworks.

According to disengagement theory, passing retirement age meant crossing a threshold into another status and was accompanied by the need for older people to assume a new identity associated with being non-productive, potentially dependent and often living in new, distinct and identifiable types of accommodation. In Great Britain that status can be seen as reflected in the public sector policy emphasis on provision of separate forms of accommodation for older people.

When notions of disengagement are considered together with the broad-brush policies framed by reference to notions of care and dependency, the extent to which there has been special and separate provision of housing services for older people in Great Britain is unsurprising. The continued existence of such separate provision, together with somewhat rigid frameworks of associated care and support provision, however, militates against the development of more flexible forms of support that might reflect the adoption of different theoretical viewpoints. The link between social alarms and those separate forms of housing provision has served to ensure the association of the former with the negative social construction of old age even though, through dispersed alarms, they also had and retain the capacity to operate in different contexts.

Housing and Christian care

We can note, in addition, that the provision of special forms of accommodation in Great Britain reflects the need of service providers to be seen as caring. To give care in what was, and remains in terms of its ethos, a largely Christian society, is seen as fundamentally virtuous. It was perhaps natural, in this context that local authorities would seek to frame policies and practices that created forms of housing within which they considered that care could be given. To give such care, whether or not motivated by Christian love, could of course be seen as offering recompense for those subject to institutional and service frameworks that might disempower and marginalise. The desire to claim public credit for such care was noted by Fisk (1986, p 93) and influenced both the form of sheltered housing schemes and their names.

Arguably there is an association between some of the social theories that are now being questioned and Christian beliefs that have helped to foster separate forms of accommodation for older people. In the public sector the problem is that through adopting housing and social welfare policies and practices that reflected Christian virtues, there was a sell-out to social constructions of old age. In housing terms it resulted in, at best, separation and, at worst, helped to nurture discrimination against and the disempowerment and exclusion of older people.

From a different critical perspective, however, it is interesting to note that Lyon (1999, pp 52, 107) suggested a reinvocation of Christian values as offering hope in a world where communications technologies "help to propel us into uncertain terrain" (p 59). Lyon's reference point was one that recognised the importance of power (and the relevance, therefore, of Foucault's theories) in helping us to understand the dynamics of what some term our 'postmodern' society, but also is one that is concerned about the rapidity of change and our ability to adjust to it. In reference to the break-up of the traditional (modern) institutions and service frameworks, Lyon (p 15) suggested that "Like ice floes on a river during spring break-up, the world of meaning fractures and fragments, making it hard even to speak of meaning as traditionally conceived".

And while the analogy provides us with a perhaps unsettling perspective on contemporary social change, there may be some reassurance in the consistency of the direction of flow!

Adjusting to changing circumstances

Criticism of Cumming and Henry's disengagement theories continues. The power of the theory remains, however, and perhaps lends itself to easy acceptance because of the evidence that shows many older people as withdrawing and taking on new identities associated with different, marginal and arguably lower social status.

But the notion that older people have to adjust to changing circumstances is a key element within other theories. It was noted in Chapter One as important to maintaining independence and self-worth. It is, of course, entirely appropriate that such adjustment should take place in relation to both some aspects of biological ageing and the changing social and economic situations experienced by older people. Old age, after all, brings with it greater risks relating to ill-health or disability, of bereavement and the certainty of a nearing death. Personal goals, social relationships and self-identity are inevitably affected by such things. The activity theory offered as the main alternative to disengagement theory, however, argues about these adjustments in a more positive light.

The activity theory was originally put forward by Cavan et al (1949) and therefore predates disengagement theory. Its central postulate is that the outlooks of older people remain fairly stable throughout life and that, given the changes in circumstances that occur with older age, individuals will sustain or substitute the activities that reflect such outlooks. This, at least, it shares with disengagement theory, although the envisaged outcomes are different. The tendency of older people to substitute activities that they were no longer able to undertake because of disability, the expense of travelling or other reasons was noted.

Phillipson (1998, p 16ff) pointed to the emergence of an array of theories that relate to the theme of adjustment, these having, he suggested, helped to further undermine the notion of disengagement and to help nurture broader debates about ageing. It was to political economy, however, that he turned in order to attempt to loosen the bonds that held social studies of older age so firmly within structures set out by the state and which, in turn, had their manifestation in established service frameworks and the belief systems that underpinned them. Through political economy approaches he affirmed that health and social service frameworks within Great Britain at least reinforced "the dependency created through the wider economic and social system" (1998, p 19).

Estes et al (1996, p 347) also explored the range of political economy approaches that pertained, these falling within what they saw as either consensus or conflict perspectives. Whichever of these applied depended on the extent to which service frameworks were underpinned by common values supporting universalist approaches or by notions relating to the assignment of resources to competing groups supporting particularist approaches. Traditional housing and social policy perspectives in Great Britain can be seen as particularistic insofar as separate provision was provided in accordance with a view that ascribed certain needs to a segment of the population. A universalistic element, however, was also present by virtue of access being available to a wide range of older people.

Questioning the British framework for social alarm provision

In such a context traditional services frameworks in Great Britain and other countries where separatist forms of accommodation predominate can be seen to be out of step with policies and practices that respond to the notion of supporting independent living, at least when the latter is considered in the broader sense that includes older people's engagement and social inclusion. There is, furthermore, no ready recourse to traditional Christian values since the Christian view may fail to give sufficient attention to the way in which older people develop strategies to cope with or compensate for difficulties or challenges that many will have encountered. This much was acknowledged in the report of the Board for Social Responsibility (1990) which noted (p 63) that:

> With increasing age the possibilities for risk taking become limited. Physical frailty may be an inhibiting factor, as may poverty, but boundaries are often set by others. People become protective of their elderly relatives or friends. They urge them to wrap up warmly in cold winds, to be careful of uneven pavements, to think twice about taking that holiday abroad, not to go out at night, not to dig the garden or paint the house. This may demonstrate care and responsibility for a person but may also undermine their autonomy.

The traditional ethos of Christian caring was also called into question by Parsloe (1995, p 9) when she stated "there is a tendency amongst some Christian organisations and social service staff to deny or ignore the question of power and to see only Christian love as the moving force in the provision and acceptance of social care. This ... is unrealistic and unhelpful", adding (p 15) that "a better way may be to strive for reciprocity".

A balance, in other words, is called for, acknowledging that it is fine for an older person with support needs to accept care but that their views regarding the same should be properly taken into account. Growing older, the Board for Social Responsibility (1990, p 51) suggested, "involves getting the balance right between retaining independence and an active initiatory style of life on the one hand and accepting increasing dependence which rejoices in the help and companionship that others want to give".

The activity theory as put forward by Cavan et al (1949) has been noted as offering an alternative perspective and is less inclined to be constrained according to the ties associated with negative social constructions of older age or, for that matter, the somewhat rigid frameworks that characterise housing and related services in Great Britain. It avoids negative or 'special needs' perspectives on older people. Instead there is a more flexible approach that recognises that growing older is a very different process from person to person.

An in-depth discussion of these theories of ageing is not appropriate here. Rather consideration is given to some of the implications for housing and related social policy frameworks as new and less disempowering social theories of older age emerge. This, in turn, has important implications for social alarms. With regard to such matters Bernard and Phillips (2000, p 34) have been prominent in calling for a new integrated social policy framework that could potentially facilitate greater social inclusion and redress errors of the past that have served to separate, exclude and disempower. Echoing the view of Phillipson, Bernard and Phillips lamented (p 37) the lack of vision among social policy analysts concerned with older people on account of their continuing support for separatist forms of accommodation and housing provision.

Notable, given the focus of this book, is that Bernard and Phillips (p 48) argued that technology should be "at the heart of social policy", reflecting their appreciation that technologies, in a sense, know no boundaries. They recognised, in other words, that technologies could be of benefit to all people, regardless of age. Importantly, they saw that technologies could support truly universalist policy frameworks. "The technological revolution", they claimed (p 49), "has altered the relationship between the individual and the spaces and places within which we live our lives".

Related perspectives

Social theories relating to the context in which social alarms operate and the potential for supporting independent living for those with such technologies are very relevant. They provide a clear pointer to the inappropriateness of separatist forms of accommodation for older people. A much broader context exists that includes a wider variety of forms of housing within which the role of social alarms can be considered. Bernard and Phillips argued (2000, p 49) that:

> It is about facilitating communication which can enable people, of whatever race, age or gender, to participate as citizens in decision-making and can empower people as they shop, vote and seek expert help on line in all areas of policy. Technology can assist us to overcome some of the barriers ... between conventional policy areas such as housing, health and social services, education and work.

For social alarms, as noted earlier, specific and applicable social theories are absent. Theories of ageing have been framed without consideration of technologies. Theories that might have some applicability, however, are those concerned with social emergency, liberation, risk and surveillance.

Social emergency

Social emergency is, in the words of Soulet (1999, p 407), an idea that has gradually "acquired credentials", at least for social or medical events. It offers a theoretical framework in which intervention in what might be deemed to be emergencies can be legitimised and relates, therefore, to at least one aspect of social alarms. Soulet, however, did not consider his theory in this context. Rather, it was concerned with the needs of people who found themselves homeless.

Soulet's theory is associated with a number of difficulties. Not least is the fact that emergencies are, as he noted (1999, p 417), to some extent imagined. Intervention, in other words, is often justified on the basis of an assumed potential for adverse consequences arising out of non-intervention. The urgency by which acts of intervention take place means, furthermore, that they are reflexive and that detailed preplanning may not be possible. And, finally, the legitimacy of intervention often depends on the person intervening having what Soulet termed an "empathetic proximity" to the sufferer, that is having had appropriate training or being employed by an appropriate agency (1999, p 416).

Liberation theory

Also of potential applicability is what is termed a liberation theory. This has been developed by the author and responds to the concern that existing theories could not be seen to explain or underpin the service frameworks and the position of older people in the context of social alarms and related technologies (see Fisk, 1999, pp 26-7). It hypothesised that the living environment and the social world of older people might be transformed in a beneficial way through the use of such technologies.

The technologies in question and their use can be covered by the term telecare. This includes both social alarms and responsive forms of telemedicine

(Fisk, 1997a, p 1057; and Chapter Twelve). It includes services that, in some part, utilise communications networks in order to help achieve objectives concerned with supporting independent living. This means ipso facto that the physical distance between service users and persons involved in service provision may be greater that would otherwise be the case.

The potential for social alarms to facilitate a breaking away from old and to some extent discredited frameworks of service provision is a recurring theme within this book. The liberation theory outlined below, furthermore, enables the placing of new frameworks of service delivery within a broader context of service provision that discards what would otherwise be a special needs perspective.

Underpinning the liberation theory is the notion that new communications technologies can now extend beyond the role traditionally associated with social alarms and could help support independent living in its broader sense. This is facilitated by the development of interactive communications networks by virtue of which new ranges of services operating in new kinds of ways can now be explored. Such networks could permit people's involvement and engagement in areas of social, educational and economic opportunities; and could foster the formation of virtual communities. Such outcomes are not, of course, features of today's social alarm services, but they are increasingly realisable and facilitated by the greater availability of interactive cable networks. Indications of the range of these services including teleshopping, chat forums and video-telephony, have been offered in a number of studies (Cullen and Robinson, 1997, p 39; Mills, 1999, p 37).

Importantly, such technologies, properly configured, would permit users to exercise more control over their interactions with their environment, services and other people. In so doing they could liberate users from restrictive, disempowering, patronising and sometimes ageist regimes of care and service provision. As noted by Thornton (1993a, p 18) the technologies could, at the same time, liberate carers and others by relieving them of worry and reducing some of the stress and restrictions of caring.

The development of interactive technologies and the raft of services that will develop thereon is, therefore, of immense importance to older people and those for whom some social, educational and economic activities may be restricted or precluded. They can give meaning to notions about individual rights and can potentially afford the means by which people, previously excluded, could more effectively exercise their rights as customers and meet their responsibilities as citizens.

Communications technologies incorporating the second generation of social alarms will, it is considered, have the potential to bring about a shift in the balance of power from service provider to service users and to help support independent living in ways that are more meaningful than appears currently to be the case. As such they may undermine, in the housing and social welfare arenas, any professional predisposition to develop or maintain separate or special forms of accommodation provision. They may also undermine any predisposition of professionals and other service providers to determine and implement service frameworks without adequate consultation with, or consideration regarding the choices, opinions and tastes of, service users. Established power relationships could, therefore, be countered.

In summary, it is suggested that new technologies, including new configurations of social alarms, can (with suitable development) liberate their users through:

- permitting and being compatible with the development of forms of accommodation that, while incorporating design features that may help support independent living, are not segregated from people of other ages;
- helping older people and others to stay put and potentially playing a more prominent role within mixed age and more spatially balanced communities, facilitating cross-generation contacts and the breaking down of the kind of ageist views that can be nurtured in other contexts;
- facilitating individual involvement via interactive networks in virtual communities of people, regardless of age, who may have shared or contrasting interests and views;
- enabling individuals to take on new roles and/or become involved in the virtual communities in ways that could facilitate relationships characterised by partnerships and reciprocation as opposed to professional provider and passive recipient;
- giving access to independent advice and information on all matters of concern, including finance, health, transport, support service availability and so on, as well as to a wide array of other services;
- offering a means by which direct support or care packages may be obtained or bought in as determined in accordance with the individual's wishes, that is by using social alarm and related technologies configured according to parameters determined and changed by users;
- permitting an escape from forms of care based on personal contact and which may be characterised by ageist and patronising attitudes on the part of carers or service providers and unequal or oppressive power relationships; and
- giving people a much greater degree of control in all aspects of their lives plus access to relevant knowledge and expertise, thereby promoting a sense of self-worth and, in so doing, helping to support independent living.

Gerontechnology

While not a recognisable social theory, mention must be made of the notion of gerontechnology. It is a term that was put forward by Graafmans (Bouma, 1992, p 1; Graafmans and Taipale, 1998, p 3) to define "the study of technology and aging for the improvement of the daily functioning of the elderly".

Importantly, in making the case for gerontechnology, its interdisciplinary nature was recognised, as was the need for technologies to respond to different life situations (Bouma, 1992, p 2). Its place within theoretical frameworks concerned for empowerment rather than simply compensation for frailty or disability was, furthermore, made clear by Graafmans and Taipale (1998, p 5) whose vision sought to place gerontechnology in the future and to offer the means by which technologies could "let people not only hold the line but often become better than they were before as they explore their new horizons". Peeters (1997, pp 10-11) specifically noted the role that social alarms could play in gerontechnology.

Risk

Technological change and the freedoms offered by technologies can, according to Nettleton et al (2000, p 49), invoke feelings of stress and isolation as well as providing "one of the means by which new forms of social connection and support will emerge".

Nettleton et al's work formed part of a broader appraisal of the potential for what was termed e-social policy (social policy that embraces the use and understands the potential of interactive communications networks). Included within their appraisal was a consideration of the theory of reflexive modernisation as put forward in the early 1990s by Beck and Giddens (see Beck et al, 1994). This saw the emergence of a risk culture within which individuals were able to enjoy certain freedoms and exercise various lifestyle choices. Technologies were seen as a key element in this, offering the prospect of the "emergence from below ... of the sorts of systems of virtual self-help and social support" (Burrows and Nettleton, 2000, p 15).

What the theory of reflexive modernisation does, according to Beck (1994, p 5), is create a society that "makes decisions according to the pattern of old industrial society", but where "the interest organisations, the judicial system and politics are clouded over by debates and conflicts that stem from the dynamics of risk society". He warned (p 6) that "with risks, avoidance imperatives dominate", these being manifested in attempts to control the risks but where, paradoxically, opposite effects may be produced. That modernity has, four 'institutional' dimensions (and can, therefore, be related to some of the ideas of Foucault) was asserted by Giddens (1990, p 55ff). One of these was surveillance (see below).

The issues of risk in the context of healthcare services have been discussed elsewhere (Alaszewski, 1995; Alaszewski et al, 1997). Alaszewski (1995, p 13) pointed to a "tension between the dominant ideology of individualism in modern society and the provision of long-term care and support for vulnerable individuals", with a shift being evident from "autonomy to more protection" (p 15). Such ideas relate both to the risk culture noted above and to Soulet's ideas concerning social emergency. Regarding the former Alaszewski (p 20) noted the growth of "technology induced risks" and their consequence in terms of the increased vulnerability of those for whom the technologies are intended. Placed in the context of services delivered in the community

Alaszewski et al (1997, p 21) noted that risks became more difficult to control and manage than is the case within institutions. As a consequence they noted that "surveillance within a limited and clearly defined space has to be replaced by generalised surveillance".

The use of social alarms can be considered in this context and the notion of lifestyle monitoring (see Chapter Thirteen) even more so. Consideration, therefore, needs to be given to the extent to which reflexivity and the desire to reduce risks may, through the application of technologies, have adverse and disempowering effects. Conversely, the question can be asked as to whether awareness of the potentially adverse effects can result in appropriate safeguards being put in place as those technologies are employed. Regardless of the answer, reflexivity may be difficult for some older people. As pointed out by Mann (2001, p 167), "No amount of reflexivity can prevent the decline of the body ... How much reflexivity does it take to know that death awaits us all?"

Surveillance

As indicated above, some consideration must be given to the relevance of social theories in relation to surveillance. Surveillance has been noted by both Giddens (1990) and Lyon (1999) as a consequence of modernity. It has for a long time been focal to many services associated with the needs of older people, is important to the role of sheltered housing and ipso facto to social alarms. The surveillance involved is rarely, however, referred to as such with job descriptions of wardens. Instead the issue is sidestepped through references to being a good neighbour, keeping an eye, ensuring well-being and the like.

But developments in communications technologies bring with them a potential for surveillance that may herald a shift from what might be described as benign and acceptable forms in the way that most of us 'look out' for our neighbours and friends to the more sinister forms where it becomes more intrusive, voyeuristic, a tool for social control and a continuing means of effecting disempowerment. With regard to the kind of surveillance exercised in sheltered housing, for instance, Henwood (1998, p 8) stated that electronic surveillance systems were likely to be "highly impersonal and potentially more intrusive than monitoring that might be carried out by a warden". The nature of the distinction, if any, between monitoring and surveillance was not explained.

With regard to such technologies and in recognition of the threat that they posed, Lenk (1982, pp 288-9) noted surveillance as the starting point for social control and a potential area for discrimination by those with the information and knowledge that such technologies can provide. In the context of systems that gathered information he lamented (p 289) that "it is astonishing that so few efforts have been made clearly to identify the benefits and dangers of changed patterns of information flow, of information control and of surveillance". Glastonbury and LaMendola (1992, p 8) similarly observed that new technologies were something of a two-edged sword.

Dilemmas and different perspectives on surveillance were summarised by

Lyon (2001). He noted (p3) that it "both enables and constrains, involves care and control". He warned (p 4), however, that the net effect of surveillance is to "strengthen the regimes behind their design and programming, whether for good or ill", this arising from the fact that "technological artefacts and systems effectively guide, constrain, enable and limit social activities" (p 24).

With regard to surveillance in the context of social theories, however, Lyon had some difficulty. The question he posed (2001, p 109) as to "what social theory is adequate to the present information-saturated social environment" went unanswered. He did, however, note a number of what he called strands or themes, one of which was concerned with organisational efficiency, which saw surveillance as "magnifying the power of the institution" (p 118), this having resonance with the theories of Giddens (1990, 1991) and Foucault (see Callinicos, 1999) and relating to the frameworks of care within which social alarms are used.

As social alarms develop to include lifestyle monitoring (see Chapter Thirteen) the matter of surveillance becomes even more problematic since the operation of second generation social alarm systems becomes increasingly dependent on information, much of which, by virtue of relating to personal health, is, as noted by Glastonbury and LaMendola (1992, p 36), of high sensitivity. British Telecom (1996), one of the pioneers of such systems, recognised (p 145) that there was a 'Big Brother' aspect that would result in some loss of privacy. Wilson (2000, p 148) opined that "many people will not be happy with this level of surveillance".

Taking matters a little further, some thought must be given to video-surveillance. Such capacity for video communication is now appearing in an increasing number of initiatives that have similar objectives to those characterised by established social alarm technologies and services (see, for instance, Robinson, 1992, p 307ff; Gott, 1995, p 94ff; Erkert, 1998, p 185; Schoone et al, 1998; Burrows and Nettleton, 2000). The indications are that such technologies may be acceptable to older people but only within a context where users have substantial control over them.

Discussion

As this chapter demonstrates, placing social alarms within a context of social theory requires a number of difficulties to be addressed. In the first instance the place of social alarms within housing and social welfare contexts has not, to date, been properly considered, though this book attempts to do this. Secondly, issues relating to social policy specifically concerned with older people, their accommodation and support needs have been insufficiently considered within broader frameworks of social theory. Thirdly, social theories are themselves in a state of flux with the appropriate reference points changing. And fourthly, the very nature of technologies is such that they are developing rapidly, can transcend boundaries, and can be considered in different contexts to which different social theories might, and service frameworks do, apply.

The challenge is one, therefore, which will have to be addressed further as social alarm and their successor technologies are developed and as the context within which they may be harnessed to support the independent living of older people becomes clearer.

What is clear now, and is the tenet of this book, is that being concerned with supporting independent living in a wide sense (that is not being narrowly construed in relation to special needs, medical or disablist models of older age), is in keeping with the direction of change demonstrated by relevant social theories. In Great Britain, the arguments lodged by the author both in this book and elsewhere (notably in Fisk, 1999), about social alarms and the separate accommodation contexts to which they often relate, seem to be substantiated by the thrust of social theory belonging to the school of critical gerontology. In other words, we have moved on from what Estes et al (1996, p 356) noted as the separatist policies that served to constitute what might be described as the "aging enterprise" in which "the service system promotes a dangerous dichotomy between the aged and non-aged that institutionalizes and re-inforces the marginality of the aged".

This chapter helps to develop an understanding of that "aging enterprise" in the context of social alarms but, at the same time, points to broader issues relating to risks and surveillance and to the means by which technologies might liberate older people from their adverse effects. The pointer to technologies as having a place within social theories that underpin more universalist housing and social policies (as indicated by Bernard and Phillips, 2000, p 48) is, therefore, endorsed.

THREE

A critical review of the literature

Introduction

Little of authority has been written about social alarms. This reflects the manner of their evolution and the fact of their perceived marginality to mainstream housing and social policy. In Great Britain it also reflects a widespread and unquestioning acceptance among housing service providers that they were and are a good thing.

Justification for this view of social alarms in Great Britain was readily made, as noted in Chapter One, by reference to the management efficiencies and cost savings that they permitted. In addition, in every service, it was possible to point to real events where the use of a social alarm had enabled help to be obtained in necessitous circumstances with, in many cases, lives being saved and a contribution made, therefore, to supporting independent living at least in its most fundamental of senses.

The glow of satisfaction felt by housing service providers about such benefits militated against any deep sense of enquiry about the technologies. As a consequence, caution before making purchasing decisions was often thrown to the wind, with the benefits that were anticipated being taken for granted. Searching questions about the effects of social alarms, their role and their wider potential were generally not asked and were, as noted in Chapter Two, not prompted by any attention within relevant debates about social theory. Much of what was written, therefore, tended to be descriptive accounts of services that were intended to give, and succeeded in giving, positive publicity to local service providers and equipment manufacturers.

Examples, from many, in Great Britain include one published in a national newspaper in 1983 (*Daily Telegraph*, 15 January). This described the service in North Wales launched by the then Alyn and Deeside Council. It claimed that "local councils are turning to modern technology to overcome the fears of thousands of old people who live alone … many have a real fear of being unable to summon help in the event of a fall or an accident in the home". The system provided cover when resident wardens were off-duty, with responses to calls being made by mobile wardens. Mrs Phoebe Catherall, aged 81, was quoted as saying, "I've never used the alarm but I feel so much happier knowing that I could. I feel safer, I sleep better and I know there is always someone there if I pull the cord". This kind of article also featured regularly in local newspapers.

Outside Great Britain social alarms received similar publicity at national and local levels. In 1987 a local paper in Halifax, Canada, described a service based at an older people's housing development (*Chronicle Herald*, 23 September). Mrs Dorothy Stewart 76, a service user, was quoted as stating, "I have angina and lately I've been having chest pains. I wouldn't be without this Lifeline for all the money in the world". A local paper in Arkansas, United States, was able to report in 1988 that Lynn Reese's life may have been saved by her dog Goldie who activated the alarm button on her carephone when she had an epileptic seizure (*Ketchikan Daily News*, 20 February).

Such positive publicity and the acceptance of their message meant that few studies were undertaken that attempted to examine key questions such as those posed over a decade ago by the author of this book (Fisk, 1989, p 1). These were:

• what role should social alarms have in relation to domiciliary social welfare and health services?
• which client groups stand to benefit most from social alarm devices?
• to what extent do social alarm services represent a means of reassurance rather than a means of obtaining help in the event of an emergency?
• can social alarms result in a reduction of support from family, friends and others, and contribute to an increase in social isolation?
• what effect do social alarms have on the self-esteem of users?

Different perspectives

Published work on social alarms can be seen as coming from three main perspectives – technical, management and user. The categorisation is not totally definitive since several studies include more than one perspective. Most studies, however, can be categorised and the way in which interest in social alarms has developed separately within different disciplines and professions is thereby indicated.

The technical perspective has been evident throughout the period of social alarm development but was emphasised more in some earlier studies. This, it might be considered, reflects the extent to which agendas (as noted in Chapter One) were in the earliest period of development, largely technology led. It is a perspective that more recently has regained prominence as social alarms move into their second generation and are more closely involved in meeting healthcare needs.

However, it is the management perspective that tended to dominate during the main period of development of social alarms and which largely determined the path that social alarms have taken. This is at its clearest in British work that examined the role of social alarms in the context of sheltered housing and which attempted to grapple with issues surrounding the role of the warden and her/his part in fulfilling duties that involve monitoring or surveillance.

The management perspective has also been evident in studies that have noted the tensions between housing and social welfare authorities.

The user perspective has been evident in fewer studies. These have tended to be those more recently undertaken and which have responded to both the consumer and user agendas that have been increasingly emphasised in policy frameworks.

Early studies in Great Britain

The earliest studies of social alarms in Great Britain came mainly from a technical perspective. The first of these, undertaken by Feeney et al (1974), was within a broader framework that also examined light, bell and buzzer systems. This study was concerned with both ergonomic aspects of alarm devices and their technical efficiency. In their preliminary statement (p 2) sentiments were expressed that were beginning to be evident elsewhere concerning the importance of social alarms in contexts where older people were unable to obtain help in an emergency. Of older and disabled people they stated that "there is the possibility of an emergency occurring in which they may be unable to draw attention to their predicament. Some have been known to wait for hours or even days before being discovered".

The study was also concerned with user perspectives and included personal interviews with 210 clients of social services authorities, 120 of whom had alarm devices. The study's findings, therefore, while focusing on technical issues, did make some important observations relating to users. Regarding the former, substantial technical shortcomings were found in the devices tested. All but two were considered "unsafe, unreliable or unsuitable" (Feeney et al, 1974, p 7).

From the user perspective Feeney et al found that most (77 per cent) older people with alarms did not use them when they experienced emergencies, with it being stated (p 8) that "they preferred to rely on the more traditional methods for summoning help, such as banging on an adjacent wall with a walking stick". Notable, given ensuing debates about such technologies and their role in supporting independent living, was that the authors raised a key question about alarm acceptance and use when observing (p 8) that non-users may have been those who felt that to be given an alarm "was an indication that they were becoming elderly, infirm and therefore likely to be involved in an emergency".

Following the work of Feeney et al, a close examination of call systems within sheltered housing schemes of 12 English housing authorities was made by Attenburrow (1976). Attenburrow was essentially concerned with management considerations, in this case relating to the experience of housing rather than (in contrast to Feeney et al, 1974) social welfare authorities. Attenburrow (1976, p 6ff) discussed the relative merits of speech and non-speech systems and identified a move away from bell alarms from about 1968. He claimed that, in sheltered housing schemes, it was impossible to consider call systems without, at the same time, considering the role of the warden stating that "the parts each play are so intertwined that it is difficult to discuss one without the other" (1976, p 20). With regard to the growing popularity of speech systems, he observed that "the addition of speech communication to a system lifts it out of the category of an emergency alarm system into an extension of the warden service" (p 9).

Like Feeney et al (1974), Attenburrow noted the use by some housing providers of activity monitoring. The devices, he explained (p 9) comprised:

> small mats at the bedside of each tenant, electrically connected to a console in the warden's dwelling. A light is displayed on the console for each mat; once the mat is trodden on the light goes out. Usually the whole system is switched on overnight. By checking the lights at, say, 10 in the morning the warden can identify those tenants who have not got out of bed since she last monitored the console.

The study signalled the impending obsolescence of non-speech alarms and indicated need for social alarm technologies to be developed to reach "dwellings scattered among the community" (p 1) for which Attenburrow considered responsibility would normally rest with social welfare authorities.

In the 1970s, therefore, social alarms were beginning to emerge as a distinctive technology for the support of older people in sheltered housing. Their emergence was noted and applauded in articles within the professional journals (see, for instance, Davis, 1979; and Lewis, 1979) but little in the way of authoritative research regarding them had been undertaken. The work of Attenburrow (1976) and, to some extent Feeney et al (1974), were the exceptions.

The 1980s

It was a long-term study of sheltered housing undertaken by Butler et al (1983) that led to the next important publication on social alarms. This followed a workshop (in Leeds) specifically on their role (Butler and Oldman, 1981). The report of that workshop re-emphasised the fact that social alarms or, specifically, call systems had become one of the defining features of sheltered housing but that little was known about their usage or usefulness (Butler and Oldman, 1981, p 1). Also noted was the growing interest in the idea of dispersed alarm systems. One matter agreed within the workshop was the need for service providers and others interested in the housing and support needs of older people to adopt approaches that would counterbalance the kind of discussions initiated by equipment manufacturers, whose primary objective was seen, not unnaturally, as selling their wares. A perspective was being adopted, therefore, which was concerned to include management and user rather than technical perspectives.

The workshop was unable to do justice to all the issues arising in what was probably the first forum of its kind. A persistent theme was the concern that alarm systems were "yet another sign of society's obsession with risk at the expense of the old person's own concern for their circumstances" (Butler and Oldman, 1981, p 4).

Butler accused local authorities of a tendency to ask "what make of alarm system should we buy?" rather than "why do we need an alarm system?" or "what do we want it to do?" (Butler, 1981, p 18). This was, he considered, a major concern in the light of limited evidence as to the efficacy of alarm systems and their non-usage by many people who had them (p 25). Other contributions to the workshop reported on pioneering social alarm initiatives, two using radio and one using the telephone network. These were respectively at Stockport (Epps, 1981), in the Central Region of Scotland (Cameron, 1981) and in the London Borough of Hammersmith (Thompson, 1981). In relation to these, a particularly useful debate took place regarding the nature of calls on the systems and the way that responses were made. The services in question are profiled in Chapters Four and Six.

A subsequent conference in Glasgow was reported on by McGarry (1983 and 1985). This testified to some of the concerns about social alarms that had begun to be considered at the workshop in Leeds and echoed their management-cum-user perspective. The relevance of the shared concerns was heightened by virtue of three new social alarm services having been newly established in Scotland, all by social work authorities. These included the Highland Helpcall service, which, in serving a massive and mostly rural area, ensured that the potential role of social alarms in supporting independent living for older people in isolated areas was a primary consideration (Sewel and Wybrow, 1985). The Highland Helpcall service is profiled in Chapter Six. Part of the motivation for developing social alarms in Scotland, it was made clear, resulted from a perceived shortage of sheltered housing at a time when financial restrictions on public spending were beginning to be felt.

A study of the Scottish Central Region service was also offered by McWhirter (1984 and 1987). From a healthcare management perspective this sought to remedy what was seen as a lack of research into the effectiveness of such services. Its objective was served in that comprehensive data were gathered regarding service usage. Notable was the presentation of clear evidence regarding the merits of the technologies for users who fell, were stuck or who had urgent medical needs (McWhirter, 1984, p 59). This service is also profiled in Chapter Six.

Few other publications around this time were giving attention to social alarms. Occasionally social alarms did warrant some discussion within larger volumes and Tinker (1984) afforded them a whole chapter, albeit also including light, bell and buzzer systems, in her thorough review of staying-put options for older people living at home in England. Her report took an essentially management perspective and indicated the kind of experimentation that was taking place as the new technologies were becoming available (Tinker, 1984, p 10ff).

Tinker found that over a third of housing and social services authorities in England had a small number of social alarm devices either linked to a monitoring and response centre or linked older people for mutual support. In doubting the efficacy of alarms, she placed greater emphasis on the need for older people to have a telephone link to good neighbours (Tinker, 1984, p 12). A similar concern had also been expressed elsewhere and cast doubt on the usefulness of social alarms when compared to such other options (Hunt, 1985, p 59). Tinker (1984, p 18) described what was believed to have been the first dispersed alarm service in the United Kingdom, established in 1975 by Christchurch District Council (profiled in Chapter Four).

In this period, a report in the Republic of Ireland offered a chapter on social alarms (National Council for the Aged, 1985). This documented, from a management perspective, the position in the Republic and served to signal what has proved to be an ongoing emphasis on their role in promoting security. The report called for further research into social alarms.

In the following year a chapter on alarms was included in a volume written by the author of this book (Fisk, 1986). This explored, mainly from a management perspective, a wide range of services for older people at the interface of housing and social welfare. It brought together a number of local studies of social alarm usage and began to debate their potential impact on future service frameworks.

In considering the commercial context, Fisk offered an examination of the approaches of manufacturers to the marketing of their products (Fisk, 1986, p 60ff). He was severely critical of monopolistic practices of manufacturers that rendered local authority service providers their hostages. Concerns regarding the manner of development of such services, as expressed in earlier publications, were reaffirmed, Fisk stating (p 63) that:

> The essential need is for the development of community alarm systems to be viewed as a service to the community and for appropriate objectives and response services to be worked out, not according to the specific short term needs of housing and social work authorities (e.g. dispensing with relief wardens of sheltered housing schemes) but according to the needs of the elderly or other vulnerable clients who stand to benefit from provision of the same.

Fisk argued (p 62) that there was a clear social welfare remit for social alarms and suggested that their funding would be more appropriately vested in social welfare and health rather than housing authorities.

In the Republic of Ireland an important study was undertaken by O'Connor et al (1986). This was commissioned by the Department of Health and responded to the call for such work that had been made by the National Council for the Aged in the previous year. The study drew heavily on secondary sources from Great Britain and echoed their mainly management perspectives. The context was one where there were growing concerns about the numbers of older people living alone and the decline in neighbourliness. The report, written after consultations including older people, echoed the work of the National Council for the Aged (1985) in finding a primary concern with security rather than healthcare.

The 1986 report of the Research Institute for Consumer Affairs

Laudable though these early reports and appraisals were, by far the most important contribution to the emerging debates on social alarms at this time was that of the Research Institute for Consumer Affairs (RICA, 1986). This report can be seen as primarily technical in its perspective. The technical content was complemented, however, by a substantial dialogue that helped to open up a wider debate including both management and user perspectives.

The report followed the testing of 19 brands of dispersed alarm units. It offered a recommendation regarding those devices that were regarded as value for money and identified those that were considered not to comply with British Standard electrical safety tests. It found an overall improvement on the position found in 1974 by Feeney et al (1974, p 7).

The RICA report had a dramatic effect. It became the immediate reference point for those interested in the potential role of social alarms. The recommendations that it made regarding the best products provided a fillip to the favoured manufacturers, one of which was Tunstall Telecom, and there was a shakeout among the others. Some products were quickly withdrawn and new products were launched to emulate the functions incorporated in the two best buys.

From a management perspective the RICA report concluded (p 10) that social alarms were most effective when "given to clients who are selected because they are particularly at risk". The report was concerned to find (p 81) a general lack of collaboration between housing authorities, the main providers, and their social welfare colleagues.

Pellow's anomalous contribution

Finally, comment must be made regarding an uncompromisingly patronising book by Pellow (1987). Its focus was on management but from a perspective that can arguably be regarded as obsolete. It marked the end of the early period of social alarms and represented something of a throwback to views and ideas that belong to the poor house.

Pellow (1987, p 9) stated that the context of his book was one where "pressures on care for the elderly have never been greater". He suggested that "cracks are appearing in the system leading to acute suffering for individual frail elderly people, strain on relatives and a growing realisation by Government and local authorities that there can never be enough money to improve drastically a rapidly deteriorating situation".

The experimental service on which he reported was based in the London

Borough of Tower Hamlets and was largely funded by that authority. It commenced in November 1984 and had expanded to provide a free service to 3,500 users by the end of its first year. However, Pellow's work appears to have owed more to his views as to how older people should be cared for and less to responding to user views and needs. His view, it seems, was that older people were lonely, powerless and had a need for TLC, that is tender loving care, a shorthand he used regularly in his book. He stated, for instance, in a bleak generalisation that (Pellow, 1987, p 106), "the young have moments to spend when they are the centre of attraction. They can become engaged, buy their first car, get a job, have children, exercise authority. The old can die and that is the horror of loneliness". Given such sentiments, attention to his book might seem inappropriate. But it remains very relevant by virtue of the very nature of those sentiments.

A minor saving grace is the documentation that Pellow provided regarding emergency calls to the monitoring and response centre. This gave further evidence of the role of social alarms in relation to both medical and social welfare needs, the latter including falls, illness, incontinence and domestic violence – this in addition to property- or security-related matters such as blocked sinks, a mouse in the house, break-ins and vandalism.

The action taken by the service in response to calls clearly varied according to circumstances. It included, where appropriate, a visit by a mobile warden. But TLC, Pellow stated, was offered as standard (1987, p 47). Pellow recorded comprehensive information, but plaudits cannot be offered since he was sometimes opinionated or judgmental. For instance, Mrs L (p 47) was referred to as "an amiable but deeply potty old lady"; and Mrs W (p 52) was "an extremely intelligent lady who is out for all she can get".

A maturing debate

The shock of the RICA report was followed by a more mature debate about social alarms in Great Britain. In Scotland, the Housing Corporation regional office commissioned a review. And while this focused on the relevance of social alarms to housing associations in Scotland there was much in the report of wider importance.

The report (Duncan and Thwaites, 1987) covered both management and user perspectives and provided a useful overview of social alarms in Scotland at that time. The social welfare orientation of Scottish services was, as with the McGarry reports (1983 and 1985), clearly apparent and was noted as underpinning most of the social alarm initiatives (Duncan and Thwaites, 1987, p 3). Notable was the finding regarding the lack of importance attributed to alarms by tenants when making decisions to move to accommodation. Perhaps associated with this was the finding that a very low proportion of tenants wore the pendant transmitter devices supplied with their alarms (Duncan and Thwaites, 1987, p 48).

In taking cognisance of the user perspective, Duncan and Thwaites (p 127) argued that "users must want to have an alarm and accept the service which accompanies the package" and drew attention to the fact that "it is easy for users to hide a pendant away in a drawer and psychologically to turn away from the alarm service and the feeling of dependency that it may convey to some".

This Scottish report was followed by what was the most wide-ranging discussion of social alarms that had, to that point, been undertaken in Great Britain. The volume, edited by the author of this book (Fisk, 1989), was the first to draw together case studies of social alarm services, five in all, and to debate many of the dilemmas associated with their development. It offered management, user and technical perspectives. In relation to the first of these Fisk (p 1) noted a "natural and understandable" bias towards housing and the perspectives of housing authorities in the material published up to that time and remarked, with concern, about the consequence that "objectives for [social alarm] system development often had little to do with social welfare" (pp 1-2). In signalling the need for services to become more person-focused Fisk (p 3) put forward what he described as the property–person continuum (see Table 3.1). This served to point to the property orientation of most services that then operated in Great Britain and to contrast this with the opposite, person orientation, of many services elsewhere. The need to explore the greater potential role of social alarms in social welfare arenas was strongly reinforced within the volume by Oldman (1989) who considered the position of different agencies of housing and care service provision. The book also explored the affect of social alarms on the role of the warden in sheltered housing (Butler, 1989).

In addition, Fisk (pp 116-17) explored the notion of stigma from a user perspective in relation to older people's predisposition to accept or not social alarms and to wear pendant transmitters. Echoing the early concern of Feeney et al (1974, p 8) and Duncan and Thwaites (1987, p 127) he raised broader questions regarding the psychological effects of such devices.

Finally, of importance in this volume was Fisk's exploration of potential technological developments, notably with regard to activity monitoring (Fisk, 1989, pp 119-22). This pre-empted more recent discussions that herald the movement of social alarms into their second generation and the advent not just of activity, but also lifestyle monitoring (discussed in Chapter Thirteen).

Table 3.1: Social alarms: the property–person continuum

Property based				Person based
Sheltered housing	Grouped dwellings for elderly people	Elderly people in other suitable housing	Needy elderly people in non-institutional accommodation	Vulnerable elderly people with special needs

Source: Fisk (1989, p 3)

Fisk furthered this debate in his later report (1990) which, as well as documenting the number and range of services then extant in Great Britain and Northern Ireland, addressed some of the social and psychological issues (p 6ff) and gave consideration to the wider range of people who might benefit from social alarms.

In the Republic of Ireland, meanwhile, social alarms had found a place within an important strategy document that remains a reference point for social welfare service development. This document took an emphatically management perspective and, while acknowledging the security role of social alarms, also saw their potential in relation to social welfare and healthcare agendas (Working Party on Services for the Elderly, 1988, pp 100-1).

Social alarms 'come of age'

In the ensuing years, maturation of the debate continued with a report of a conference held in London (Walker, 1991); through important research supported respectively by the Joseph Rowntree Foundation (Thornton and Mountain, 1992) and the Anchor Trust (Riseborough, 1997a); and in a monograph by Harding (1993). All these covered both management and user perspectives. The Walker report, in addition, considered some technical issues.

The context of the Walker report was one in which it was considered that social alarms had come of age. There was a critical mass of operational services which, on the whole, had begun to move away from the narrower perspectives associated with sheltered housing. There was also a growing realisation that such services could be important components of packages of care proffered by those more concerned with social welfare.

Associated with these was a growing sense among service providers that they might be able to exercise their collective muscle to influence the manufacturers and, therefore, the design and functionality of products. This was clearly pointed to in one paper (Corp, 1991, p 21) and was implicit in the formation of the Calling for Help Group, which had supported the conference from which the report emerged. The Calling for Help Group comprised the Anchor Trust, Help the Aged, the National Housing and Town Planning Council and the Research Institute for Consumer Affairs. It led to the establishment of the Association of Social and Community Alarms Providers in 1994 (the Association of Social Alarms Providers, ASAP, since 2002).

Some things, however, had changed little and there were further calls to service providers not to continue purchasing social alarms on the assumption, yet to be properly established, that they were a 'good thing' (Walker, 1991, p 11). Ceely and Loughlin (1991, p 6) called for more account to be taken of user perspectives. They noted (p 6), for instance, the extent to which respondents to a survey said that the alarm was most wanted by others (56 per cent) rather than themselves (37 per cent).[1]

A broadening view

The narrow perspective of many social alarm services in Great Britain was a central theme of the next important publication on social alarms. This report, by Thornton and Mountain (1992, p 5) lamented that social alarm services were too often "designed and delivered on the basis of broad assumptions about need and in ignorance of the impact on their proposed users". Their call for a broader view added to the many which had sought a clarification of the role of social alarm services and for them to be reconfigured to meet a wider range of support needs (see, for instance, Fisk, 1989 and 1990).

While recognising the role of social alarms in relation to medical emergencies, Thornton and Mountain (1992, pp 8-9) pointed out and echoed the findings of McWhirter (1984, p 59) regarding the benefits of social alarms, for example, where users became stuck, anxious or confused. They also noted their role in giving reassurance and helping to maintain social contact.

The Thornton and Mountain report pointed to the need for greater involvement of social welfare and health practitioners but noted that, where this was the case, proper procedures for service monitoring and review were often not in place. The provision of a social alarm was too often seen as meeting an assessed need, as a result of which a case could be closed. Thornton and Mountain (p 43) were clear in their response. Resolution of these difficulties required the development of effective partnerships involving health and social welfare practitioners. They fell short of echoing Fisk's view (1989, p 62) that social alarm services should be transferred from housing authorities, but did suggest that health and social services authorities might go it alone in developing services, seeing this as giving users more choice about how their support needs would be met (p 45). Although the report took an essentially management perspective it was very sensitive to user issues. Notable was the observation (p 24ff) about the uncertainty of users as to the purpose of social alarms and as to what calls were deemed by users to be acceptable to service providers.

Endorsement of the importance of social alarms in the context of social welfare then came with a monograph by Harding in 1993. This reported on an evaluation of an intensive support scheme for frail older people living at home in two areas of southwest Wales. It offered a management perspective but was similarly sensitive to the position of users.

Importantly, emphasis in the monograph was placed on the way in which human resources were deployed, reflecting a definition of social alarm systems as "socio-technical systems in which technological communication devices and human resources together allow service users to summon assistance in an emergency" (Harding, 1993, p 3). Of note is that users in one area appeared to use the alarm system "to actively re-arrange the home care aspect of their package of services, in that they use the alarm to request a home care assistant to call" (p 21).

A particularly intensive use of the service was found to take place outside normal working hours, particularly for assistance in going to the toilet. Users, in other words, took more control in relation to services they required in order to respond to their care needs. The extent to which this was directly encouraged or endorsed by care managers was not stated. Nonetheless, in establishing the value of the service to people with high support needs, Harding assisted the debate regarding the social welfare role of social alarms.

Passing mention should be made of a survey in England by Ernst and Young (1994) and a study in Scotland by Dick and Pomfret (1996). Both reflected essentially management perspectives. The Ernst and Young survey was reported on in a supplement to a major Department of the Environment study that explored the range of housing needs of older people. The wider study considered, as is explicit in its title, *Living Independently*, ways in which older people could be supported independently at home (McCafferty, 1994). Interestingly, this report established that, aside from handrails, alarm devices were, by that time, the most frequent addition to the homes of older people (p 95). Ernst and Young (p 41) established that four fifths of specialised accommodation for older people included social alarm provision. Most such provision by local authorities included links to a monitoring and response centre.

Dick and Pomfret (1996) offered a comprehensive picture of social alarm services in Scotland and noted their consolidation in a social welfare context. They concluded from a survey of service providers that for a majority of respondents to their survey (p 6) "assessments for community alarms and allocation decisions are now carried out as part of the community care assessment process". While giving credit to the initiatives of some service providers, the report signalled the need for an extension of social alarm services to more emphatically reach those potential beneficiaries from ethnic minorities and a range of non-elderly people with support needs (Dick and Pomfret, 1996, pp 7-8).

Of note was the 'spectrum' Dick and Pomfret offered (p 11) about the social welfare credentials of social alarm services (see Table 3.2). This contrasted crisis services with welfare services. The trend within Scotland, they saw as increasingly emphasising the latter.

Finally, Riseborough (1997a), in gathering information from providers and users of four social alarm services in England, took an approach that balanced management and user perspectives. Three of the services were operated by local authorities, with the fourth operated nationally by a housing association. The objective was to give "an informed analysis on future directions" for services in the social housing sector (Riseborough, 1997a, p v).

Table 3.2: Social alarm service spectrum

Crisis services	Welfare services
Straightforward and technically efficient, essentially responsive services	Services involving a more all-round approach including preventative care

Source: Based on Dick and Pomfret (1996)

Substantial emphasis in Riseborough's work was placed on discovering the views and expectations of users. Having established these she was able to endorse the broader perspective concerned with the role of social alarms in social welfare and gave clear pointers to some of the additional responsibilities, often substantial, being placed on response staff. Social alarm services were seen as having to deal with increasing numbers of calls involving stressful circumstances, requiring operators at the monitoring and response centres to demonstrate a high level of interpersonal skills (pp 15-16).

Crucially Riseborough found (pp 22-3) a lack of knowledge about social alarm services not just among users but also among housing and other staff who were often in positions to advise and inform users or potential users about them. Such a finding is relevant to both management and user perspectives. Confusion was noted in the understanding by users and staff as to when it was appropriate to use social alarms and how services related to emergency services. Riseborough noted with concern (p 38) the potential for social alarms to not be used when they might have offered the means of obtaining help.

Other issues included the lack of information about and the growing potential need for social alarms among ethnic minorities and the growing role of social alarms in meeting the needs of a wider range of users other than older people (p 14). Riseborough also noted (p 9) the way in which mobile wardens who responded to emergency calls in localised areas were seen as increasingly engaged in plugging the gaps left by other social welfare services, sometimes on a routine basis. Crucial questions arose, therefore, as to how such services, when managed by housing authorities, should work with their social welfare counterparts. The need for at least an equal partnership was implied.

Riseborough noted that security issues featured among the primary reasons why users would use their social alarms, though this was not generally recognised by service staff (pp 25-6). Finally, she offered some interesting insights (p 57) into the ways in which users decided to have an alarm, those choosing to have them having a much more positive view of their role. Acceptance of such technologies was seen, in other words, as not just relating to their functionality but also to the way they were presented and perceived by others.

The studies by Thornton and Mountain (1992) and Harding (1993) and, more especially, Riseborough (1997a), are considered to have heralded a moving on from that more mature debate relating to social alarms insofar as they were consistent in their affirmations of the need for further development of their social welfare role and in their recognition of the importance of user perspectives.

International perspectives

The literature emanating from countries other than Great Britain and Ireland is relatively sparse, with the main exceptions of the United States and Canada where various research studies have been undertaken, particularly (and as was the case in Great Britain) during the early period of development of social alarms. The sparsity can be seen as reflecting the fact that social alarms in other countries are used by smaller populations than in Great Britain and Ireland (both in absolute and relative terms). It is clear, furthermore, that attention to social alarms has been greatest in those countries where the spread of social alarms has been in part funded by central or local government. That there should be a reasonable range of literature in Great Britain, Ireland, Australia, Canada, the Netherlands and Sweden is, therefore, to some extent explained.

It is interesting that it is outside Great Britain and Ireland that the most in-depth studies concerned with the cost benefits of social alarms have been undertaken. This, in most cases, appears to be a response to the orientation of social alarm services in several of those countries towards healthcare. This means that the potential for cost benefits was explored through examining social alarms as a means of reducing the need for relatively expensive hospital or nursing home care.

In relation to technical, management and user perspectives most studies outside Great Britain and Ireland can be seen as management oriented. The main early study, however, also took account of user perspectives. This study, by Sherwood and Morris (1981), is examined in more detail in Chapter Eight. It was the first to ask probing questions about social alarms at a time when such technologies were in their infancy. It remains one of the largest studies of social alarms ever undertaken anywhere in the world examining, over a period of three years, samples of more than 150 older people with carephones and a further matched sample (or control group) without. More than this, Sherwood and Morris attempted to examine different outcomes for older people with different levels of support need. In so doing they gave a clear indication that the greatest benefits of social alarms, when measured in terms of increasing the likelihood of maintaining independent living, accrued to those people with functional impairments but who were not socially isolated (Sherwood and Morris, 1981, p 11). Importantly, however, the potential for people with functional impairments, but who were socially isolated, to be psychologically harmed, was also signalled (p 14).

While it can be argued that the samples used by Sherwood and Morris were relatively small, the study must be afforded credit for its robust methodological framework and for providing indicative information about the potential benefits of services that just a decade before had been completely unknown.

The general conclusion they drew about the benefits of social alarms to service users were endorsed in a number of subsequent studies in both the United States and Canada. These include works by Koch (1984), Cain (1987), Dixon (1987) and Gatz and Pearson (1988). And though less thorough in their methodologies, they helped to provide a critical mass of literature that was used to promote further service developments. These studies were generally management oriented in that their conclusions regarding cost savings to service providers (through, for example, avoiding hospital admissions) were generally assumed to also reflect user aspirations. With the exception of Gatz and Pearson (1988) user views were not sought.

Of subsequent studies in North America the most noteworthy are those by

Roush and Teesdale (1997) and Chumbler et al (1997 and 1998). Each of these combined management and user perspectives and endorsed the general conclusions made by earlier studies. The work by Chumbler et al examined the position of social alarm service users in Arkansas. It was particularly useful in providing insights into issues relating to public subsidies through the Medicaid programme and to service targeting (Chumbler et al, 1997, pp 124-5; 1998, pp 209, 224). Complementing the above are a few studies that reflect a technical perspective, these listing products and comparing their functionality (American Association of Retired Persons, 1987, 1992; ECRI, 1998).

Of note elsewhere is a very comprehensive analysis of the cost benefits of social alarms for a service in the Veneto province of Italy. This study was undertaken by Tamborini et al (1996) and was positive in its endorsement of social alarms in terms of enabling people to stay living in their own homes. They called (p 13) for public investment to facilitate this. The study was strongly user oriented and drew on the outcomes of a personal interview survey with nearly 700 service users. Although, in contrast to Sherwood and Morris it lacked a longitudinal element and a control group, in terms of the number of users it represents the largest known study of social alarms from this perspective.

In Australia studies by Farquhar et al (1992) and the Department of Human Services (1998) are the most noteworthy. The former was user oriented, had a longitudinal element and had direct contact with nearly 80 service users through telephone surveys. It endorsed the findings of other research in expressing a positive view of the benefits of social alarms. The latter was essentially management oriented and provided a thorough overview of a service in Victoria, the users of which enjoyed substantial state funding. This report was important in illustrating the way in which social alarms were becoming more closely integrated within support frameworks for large numbers of older people.

Finally, note must be taken of volumes edited by Dibner (1992) and Wild and Kirschner (1994). The general picture offered by the first of these, and which was reflected in discussions and debates at the symposium to which it related, was one that recognised social alarms as being poorly developed and with there being substantial variation between countries. There were, however, repeated pointers to the benefits of social alarms, albeit in very different contexts (see, for instance, Prass, 1992; Rodriguez, 1992; and Schantz, 1992). The same is true of those sections of the Wild and Kirschner volume that examined social alarms (see, for instance, Östlund, 1994; Zoche, 1994).

Current agendas

Published material relating to what might be termed current agendas is, of necessity, sparse. This sparsity is regrettable in view of social alarms being now more established and being on the threshold of major change.

The published material relating to current agendas follows earlier work in that it has adopted predominantly management perspectives. Unsurprisingly, however, given the pace of technological change, a technical perspective is sometimes offered.

Two publications demand special attention, both relating to work in Great Britain. The first was that of Gann et al (1999). This publication offered a technical perspective but was important, not because it linked especially to social alarms, but rather because it recognised the central role that smart homes that incorporated communications technologies could play in supporting independent living. It was stated in the Foreword (p xi) that "in creating smart homes the aim is not to automate for the sake of it, but to build up a specification that responds to real needs which people may have". Among four groups who might especially benefit they cited "people with physical disabilities and older people".

The second publication was that of Porteus and Brownsell (2000). This included both management and user perspectives. It focused on a lifestyle monitoring initiative undertaken by British Telecom in collaboration with Anchor Trust and was specifically concerned with the use of technologies to help older and disabled people to live independently. The importance of the Porteus and Brownsell study in relation to this book is substantial in view of its focus on technologies that represent an evolution in the role and operation of social alarms.

Having said this the Porteus and Brownsell study, as is noted in Chapter Thirteen, loses a little credibility when some aspects of the methodology are scrutinised. Their conclusions that reflected positively on outcomes, for instance, must be taken with a pinch of salt in view of the difficulties that they encountered in recruiting participants; the relatively short period of monitoring; and the fact that evident high expectations of service users were, at least for some, unfulfilled (Porteus and Brownsell, 2000, p 36; Sixsmith and Sixsmith, 2000, p 191). Nonetheless, important issues were aired.

Summary note and conclusion

This chapter has critically examined the contents of the main publications concerned with social alarms and has noted the others that relate to current agendas. It has considered them according to their technical, management or user perspectives.

What is clear from this is that while the range of publications is somewhat limited, it has at least evolved to some extent to address what might be regarded as many of the key issues concerning the role of social alarms. This means that there is now an altogether more critical and conceptually broader approach being taken, which contrasts with earlier perspectives that either assumed the worth of social alarms or were narrowly focused on their potential for realising savings in service costs.

Studies that adopted emphatically technical or management perspectives have increasingly been added to by other work, which recognises the need for a user perspective. That there might be a cyclical element to this is apparent in that more studies with technical perspectives would be expected at times of rapid technological change. This would apply now as new technologies are expected to transform social alarms and the role that they can play. Key points are as follows.

In the early period of social alarms development in Great Britain and Ireland there was little debate, with the possible exception of Attenburrow (1976), about the implications of speech-based social alarm systems. This was despite their being instrumental in transforming social alarm services from ones solely concerned with emergencies. What discussion there was in the literature tended to be concerned with the impact on the warden within sheltered housing schemes and the convenience for her/him of not having to make visits in response to every call. The studies generally had, therefore, emphatic management perspectives.

Psychological issues were, in the earlier period, hardly touched upon and have only begun to be addressed following Fisk's work (1989) and subsequent studies that examined user perspectives (eg Thornton and Mountain, 1992; Fisk, 1995; and Riseborough, 1997a). This book makes a further contribution to this debate.

Few, apart from Fisk (1990), Thornton (1993b) and Riseborough (1997a) noted the merits of social alarms for users other than older people and only as stronger user-oriented and more all-embracing approaches have developed has their potentially focal position within community care strategies begun to be considered. This is despite the fact that community care issues are fundamental to the use of social alarms and that they have been particularly strongly promoted by some Scottish social welfare authorities with responsibility for rural areas and island communities (see Chapter Six).

Also notable is the parochial nature of most of the research into social alarms in Great Britain. Most has focused on evaluations of services that developed according to a somewhat narrow view of the needs of older people. Little note was taken of practice abroad despite, or perhaps because of, the generally very different patterns of service provision. The exceptions, where the context of social alarms in Great Britain was set alongside those of other countries, are in Fisk (1989, 1990 and 1995) and the edited volume by Dibner (1992).

In other countries the literature has been meagre. Two of the exceptions are the United States and Canada where there is a reasonable range of research, albeit that much of it is preoccupied with management perspectives concerned with potential cost savings. The early work of Sherwood and Morris (1981) has been mentioned as important and as taking account of user views. That there was a maturation of the debate about social alarms in the United States became evident, however, especially in the work of Chumbler et al (1997 and 1998). Elsewhere studies have, in the main, taken management perspectives, the main exception being the study in Italy by Tamborini et al (1996) where a strong user perspective was also evident.

Overall it can be stated that, despite the limitations in its quantity, the extent of research regarding social alarms has gradually increased in the countries where such technologies are used. Social alarms are, as a consequence, being seen less as a peripheral and more as a future tool by which supported independent living, among other objectives, can be achieved.

Distorted views arising from unfamiliarity with the technology are becoming a thing of the past. Likewise, the patronising views epitomised in the work of Pellow (1987) have been marginalised. As a consequence there is less likelihood that social alarms will be viewed as necessarily a good thing without further thought being given to their role and to understanding user perspectives regarding them. Such changes in perspectives are timely insofar as the debate in all countries must move on to address the many questions that arise as a result of technological change and the potential that is being explored for new applications as social alarms enter their second generation.

Note

[1] Research undertaken by the Harris Research Centre for Help the Aged (1990).

FOUR

The origins of social alarms

Introduction

This chapter documents the evolution of social alarms and discusses their emerging role within the context of housing and social welfare service provision for older people in Great Britain and, to some extent, Ireland. Evident from this discussion are a number of dilemmas and choices that had to be addressed by service providers as social alarm technologies developed and were marketed. At the same time social policy and, notably, housing policy frameworks relating to older people were changing.

The key to the latter lay in sheltered housing and the then emerging role of the warden. Associated with this were a number of questions about the relationship between wardens and the services they provided to the older people living in sheltered housing schemes. The technologies and their use clearly had an impact on this by providing a means and a medium of communication that was previously unavailable.

That housing policy for older people took this course can be partly explained by long-standing concerns at that time about the inadequacy of residential care. Such concerns were particularly highlighted in the work of Townsend (1962). An irony, however, is that in seeking to develop sheltered housing as an alternative, key features of residential care were reintroduced as the sheltered housing model became more clearly defined. Call systems can be seen as having helped to consolidate such definition.

Bells and buzzers

The broad definition of social alarms adopted in this book, that is including call systems, makes it impossible to point to their origin with any precision. In Great Britain, however, and as noted in Chapter One, the widespread use of such technologies followed the development of sheltered housing and the adoption of what were to become known as social alarms as a standard feature to link individual residents to a responder living elsewhere in the scheme. In the earliest period of sheltered housing this responder would have been as likely to be an active older resident as a warden.

Originally the alarms used in Great Britain were simply bells and buzzers activated by switches or push buttons and individually wired to a panel in the responder's dwelling. The context was one in which wardens, sometimes known as housekeepers, may have been employed by the landlord or managing organisation but where the term sheltered housing had not been coined to describe such provision. Developments in Ireland followed those in Great Britain.

Some idea of this early provision was provided in a report, *Housing for Special Purposes*, of the Central Housing Advisory Committee (published in 1951 and quoted in Institute of Housing, 1958, p 8-9). This gave guidance on the design and facilities within hostels for old people. As well as pointing to the appropriateness of bed-sitting rooms, this report argued for provision of a "self-contained flat for the warden". Notable is that the report suggested that tenants should have electric bells near the bed and the bath.

Parry and Thompson (1993, p 6) noted reports of a housing scheme for older people in rural Devon that was built in 1948 where "residents were linked to their resident warden by a bell that they could activate to let the warden know when they needed assistance". This scheme, they affirmed, was one of the models on which Townsend (1962) based his ideas regarding the need for an appropriate alternative to residential homes. Parry and Thompson (p 12) observed of the bell systems that:

> Clumsy and primitive though these systems were, they did have the advantage of encouraging neighbours to take responsibility for each other, especially in the warden's absence, for at this time there were few organised relief warden systems.

The context, it must be recognised, was one where residents in such schemes did not, generally speaking, have high levels of support need or acute medical conditions – hence the fact that many residents acted as responders and later as wardens or deputy wardens. Older people with greater support needs were generally not resident in sheltered housing but were often accommodated in residential or nursing homes. Although not always explicit, the objectives of such alarm devices and the associated means of response related to providing a means of getting help in an emergency.

One precursor of systems that linked to a warden was the flashing lights provided by some local authorities outside dwellings occupied by older people. Like bell and buzzer systems, these were activated by switches or push buttons. Their efficacy was, however, always uncertain and their continued role was brought unequivocally into question by Tinker (1984, p 11ff). She was unable to find information regarding their usage or evidence of their effectiveness. Parry and Thompson (1993, p 12) also noted a disadvantage of these flashing lights because they labelled the tenant as vulnerable and advertised their presence to "unscrupulous burglars".

As the notion of sheltered housing began to take shape in the 1960s alarm systems were given more consideration. They were specifically mentioned in work by the National Old People's Welfare Council, which later became Age Concern. The organisation noted that "bells or intercommunication systems" were fitted in a majority of schemes for older people, especially those provided by local authorities (National Old People's Welfare Council, 1966, p 7). Also signalled was the role of such systems not just in enabling older people to obtain help in an emergency but also in providing reassurance.

Important was a 1968 Ministry of Housing and Local Government study that considered the effectiveness of special housing provision for older people in grouped flatlets. This helped to determine the standard configuration of sheltered housing that was integral to the Circular (82/69) issued in the following year. The Circular designated categories of sheltered housing within which alarm systems could play a part. Alarms were optional for what were termed Category 1 schemes deemed appropriate for more active older people; and were mandatory for Category 2 schemes deemed appropriate for older people with higher levels of support need.

The study (Ministry of Housing and Local Government, 1968, p 3) remarked on the unsatisfactory configuration of some alarm bells and pointed out that "in some cases it is not possible to tell which bell has been ringing after it has stopped". It suggested that indicator lights should be fitted in corridors so that the warden might be alerted to alarm calls when not in her own home. A powerful rationale for alarms was offered in the study by reference to the fact (p 3) that in a flat without such a device, "an old lady of 80 had had a serious fall ... and had lain there all night before being found".

From a more social welfare perspective a report by Harris (1968) looked at the use of bell systems in sheltered housing in different parts of England. For Rutland she observed (p 28) that "every bungalow is fitted with a bell system of communication" and that in Kidderminster (p 31) flashing lights were installed for bungalows without a warden. Grants made by Hampshire County Council towards sheltered housing schemes in Gosport she noted as being contingent on there being (p 27) a "system of communication from each unit to the warden's accommodation".

In the 1970s, alarms were increasingly seen as "an integral part of the support network" and had, therefore, to operate efficiently with the warden able to identify the origin of any call (Butler et al, 1979, p 106). Although alarm systems with two-way speech were beginning to dominate, some bell and buzzer systems were still being installed in 1975 (Attenburrow, 1976, p 3). In 1978 it was estimated that 6 per cent of older people at home in England had a bell, buzzer or bleeper device by which they could "signal for help" (Hunt, 1978, p 54).

In the United States, as noted by Parker (1984, p 62) and Dibner (1990, p 505), similar bell and buzzer systems were used in certain forms of accommodation; but, in the absence of an equivalent to sheltered housing, call systems with speech were not, it appears, utilised at this time. Certainly the possibility for such speech-based systems was overlooked in a 1984 design guide for retirement communities and grouped dwellings for older people. This guide, instead, suggested that older people should have the option of phone lines "for an emergency button which can activate individual warning lights in the administrative office or in the local police station" and saw such devices as integral to typical grouped dwellings (Parker, 1984, pp 62, 90).

The reason for such a focus on phone lines probably reflected growing awareness of the role and potential of carephones that were becoming more widespread in the United States at that time. Such carephone devices had been developed by Andrew Dibner (see Chapter Eight) who had invented the concept of social alarm equipment in that country in 1973. It was then the subject of demonstration projects and an evaluation programme funded by the United States Department of Health, Education and Welfare (Stafford and Dibner, 1984, p 1).

Lifeline Systems, the company that Dibner founded, went on to exploit the technologies and dominate the social alarms (PRS) market throughout North America. The company was set up in 1974 with product sales starting in 1979 (Devins, 1984, p 3). The carephones, in contrast to early call systems in Great Britain, offered full two-way speech and were marketed directly to healthcare providers. The adoption of carephones as the standard form of social alarm technology in the United States meant that much of the debate that took place in Great Britain about the merits of such technologies and the implications of two-way speech (see later in this chapter) were bypassed.

Taking account of the respective positions relating to social alarms in Great Britain and the United States it can be stated that it is in these two countries that their origins lie, albeit that their respective foci were different. Hence, while Andrew Dibner was the originator of carephones, technologists in Great Britain can at least claim the accolade that relates to call systems.

Speech or non-speech systems?

The debate in Great Britain about the merits of call systems that offered two-way speech gives some insights into the dilemmas that faced local authorities who were making decisions about their use. The arguments for sticking with the simpler non-speech systems were, essentially, threefold. First, it was considered that speech systems could be liable to abuse by users and, as a consequence, increase the pressures on resident wardens. Second, in obviating the need in many instances for a personal visit by a responder, speech systems would, it was considered, result in less social contact, with the monitoring role of service providers being undermined. And third, it was considered that there was a risk with systems that incorporated a speech facility that some tenants might feel themselves under observation. The National Old People's Welfare Council (1966, p 8) affirmed, at least for scattered dwellings, that "it is not desirable to suggest that, for fear of an emergency, tenants are in need of continuous supervision, and generally the simple bell-system is, therefore, to be preferred".

The notion of abuse or the inappropriate use of alarms and the issue of surveillance are matters that hinge, almost needless to say, on questions about the overall purpose of social alarms. It is interesting to note an example of abuse given in the Ministry of Housing and Local Government study (1968, p

3). Here, after an elderly tenant had activated his buzzer in the early hours of the morning, a male warden responded. The tenant, the report stated, "was found fully dressed, nodding in front of a dead fire, oblivious of the time and greeted the warden with:'Ee, lad, m'pipe's gone out. Ast a match?'". No other examples of abuse were unearthed in this study even though it had involved interviews with the wardens of six grouped dwelling schemes.

Despite the fears of abuse that might occur with speech-based systems, Attenburrow (1976), in studying schemes managed by 12 English housing authorities, found only one person among service providers who favoured non-speech systems. The officer in question had stated (p 10) that "We have always installed bell alarms. We know of no emergency when the bell has not been effective. Over the years the only modification we have made is to substitute cord pulls for bell pushes".

Butler (1981, p 17) observed that some service providers feared that two-way speech could lead to systems being "reduced to a medium for gossip and casual chat so that the alarm function is undermined" and might replace face-to-face contact between wardens and their tenants. One study (Heumann and Boldy, 1982, p 141) had, in fact, found a reduction in the proportion of what were deemed genuine emergencies for sheltered housing schemes in Devon over the period 1973-77 after two-way speech systems were installed. However, the context of that study was one where the average number of alarm calls made to wardens per week had risen steeply from 0.7 to 3.5.

On the matter of speech in the context of dispersed alarm services (discussed below) it was claimed by Epps (1981, p37) that:

> Speech systems are, at best, irrelevant to the needs of old people compared with a simple (non-speech) alarm; at worst they can frustrate the roles played by the rest of the support network because a) support ... relies largely on face to face contact, not communication devices; b) an alarm call is an alarm call – it doesn't need someone to say it. This causes delays and maybe some confusion; and c) most importantly, it allows only half the intelligence function to be carried out – that is the hearing not the seeing.

For sheltered housing, however, the consensus was, as noted by Attenburrow (1976, p 9), that speech systems were better. A representative service provider view was quoted as affirming:

> A two-way speech system provides an immediate verbal response to a call from a tenant. An old person, distressed and alone, knows immediately that her call has been received, has the assurance of her warden that something is being done about it, and knows that she is no longer isolated. The warden can establish the nature of the emergency before leaving for the tenant's flat and can summon help that may be required. With a simple bell alarm system, the tenant does not know that her call has been received until the warden appears at the flat door. The warden cannot establish the nature of

the emergency without visiting the tenants. Should outside help be required the warden has to return to her office or dwelling to summon it by telephone. Valuable time may be lost in doing this.

Views of the labour-saving value of speech-based systems were noted elsewhere (Scottish Local Authorities Special Housing Group, 1980, p 2; Wirz, 1982, p 94). The above extract clearly points to the reasons why speech alarms were favoured and why the report in question was able to point to the eventual demise of bell alarms (Attenburrow, 1976, p 1). The extract is valuable because it points very clearly to the perceived rationale for social alarms at that time, focusing on notions of emergency, distress and isolation.

Others reasons for favouring speech systems were cited elsewhere. Davis (1979, p 133), albeit with a vested interest as managing director of a manufacturer of such systems, stressed their usefulness in enabling "accidental calls" to be "sifted out and minor matters ... settled quickly". This was in the context of linking calls, via the telephone network, to deputising sheltered housing wardens and heralding the arrival of carephones (discussed below).

Wardens interviewed by Attenburrow (1976, p 10) expressed similar sentiments and were able to point to occasions where the speech facility had enabled them to give appropriate reassurance and avoid what were deemed as unnecessary visits. One, however, alluded to the speech facility enabling her to monitor the well-being of a tenant who was ill, stating that:

> I listened in to her breathing to make sure it was regular and steady – then I knew she was asleep. When I heard her moving around in bed and coughing I could ask her if she wanted anything without disturbing her by sounding the buzzer or going to her flat.

It is not clear whether the tenant consented to this eavesdropping and while Epps (1981, p 37) supported the notion of surveillance it is doubtful that he would have approved of it being done in this manner. Another report, however, suggested that eavesdropping might be positively endorsed by tenants, McLuckie (1984, p 375) stating, of installations within sheltered housing schemes in Edinburgh, that:

> A privacy switch position to prevent eavesdropping is provided as well as a standby position to allow the warden to listen in from time to time for activity if the person is happy to allow this. In practice this is both popular with tenants and wardens, enabling them to open the speech channel and listen for movement.

Relevant, perhaps, is the lack of attention by Attenburrow (1976) to the matter of personal privacy except to note the ability of tenants to switch off at the dwelling unit. Such matters were addressed in guidance later issued by the British Standards Institution (BSI). This precluded such invasions.[1]

Worth noting at this point, and following swiftly on the heels of speech-based systems with wired links from every dwelling, was a further innovation seen as giving greater flexibility to the warden – the portable receiver or handset. This innovation is discussed below. But before moving on it is worth emphasising that while most people favoured speech-based systems, some argued that the benefits for residents could be equally readily achieved by use of the telephone. The telephone, it was argued, could suffice as a means of obtaining help in an emergency and was, in any case, an important tool for maintaining social contact.

Hunt (1985, pp 59-62), for instance, suggested that alarms might be reassuring but could also have an adverse affect on the extent of contact with family and friends. He recommended that "the alarm systems in sheltered housing should be phased out gradually and replaced by telephones for individuals as required". Dowling and Enevoldson (1988, p 29) found in a survey of older housing association tenants in Liverpool, a lack of knowledge of social alarms and concluded that "most tenants would prefer a telephone to any kind of alarm system".

Others, as noted earlier in this chapter, argued that there was the potential for speech-based alarms to reduce social contact. This, however, was in response to the possible combined effect of an alarm and a warden presence, with Middleton (1982, p 29) suggesting that these may also have served to "engender a self-image of vulnerability that is neither necessary nor desirable".

The arguments that favoured telephones in place of alarms were succinctly countered by the Research Institute for Consumer Affairs (1986, p 36). They found in a survey of 401 alarm users that "in 46 per cent of emergencies, accident victims were unable to get to the phone or unable to dial", and concluded that "for people at risk the telephone is not a substitute for an alarm". No evidence was found of reduced social contact.

Passive alarms and activity monitoring

Before exploring the main components of social alarms, call systems and carephones, note must be made of the key distinction between active and passive alarms. Active alarms, as noted by Robinson et al (1995, p 48), "involve the party in need of help triggering the alarm themselves". In other words users must pull a cord or push a button. Passive alarms, by contrast, are those where the 'user' need do nothing in order for calls to be triggered.

A simple passive alarm feature, the timer, was and remains commonplace with carephones in North America (but absent in Great Britain). This feature can be set by users, resulting in a call being sent to a third party if not cancelled or reset before a specified period (perhaps 12 or 24 hours). Part of the rationale for the incorporation of timers was the need to be able to determine when someone died (Fisk, 1989, p 121).

The notion of active alarms should not be confused with 'activity' monitoring. Activity monitoring utilises passive alarm features. It requires the usage of features or sensors that pass information about the system user to a responder in 'real time' (as the event takes place). Activity monitoring according to this definition has, therefore, been a feature of some social alarms since the early period.

The presence of a warden in most locations where social alarms were used in Great Britain meant that many considered that there was no need for passive or activity monitoring facilities. However, that wardens cannot necessarily be seen as such a safeguard has been made clear in occasional reports of sheltered housing tenants being found dead several days or even weeks after death. One such report related to a sheltered housing scheme in Looe, Cornwall. Here, Thomas Batten lay dead in his sheltered flat for two weeks when the warden was on holiday. No call had been made to the monitoring and response centre to which his social alarm was linked (*Cornish Times*, 31 October, 1997).

In the earliest period of social alarm development passive or activity monitoring was the subject of some conjecture in Great Britain. It was seen as potentially providing for circumstances where older people were unable to activate their alarm because of, for instance, immobility or unconsciousness. The prospect of someone lying or being stuck and unable to get help might, therefore, be avoided. The fact that such facilities were under consideration reflects, in part, the initial interest in social alarms by some social welfare authorities at a time when the now standard functional capabilities of social alarms had not been established.

Fennell (1989, p 21) described a typical way in which activity monitoring was incorporated. He encountered this facility in Scotland within sheltered housing schemes managed by Bield, Kirk Care and Hanover (Scotland) housing associations. Some of the alarms, he described as:

> equipped with a 'pressure mat' system whereby the warden can verify for herself that the tenants have been moving about within the recent past and take whatever action she thinks appropriate. The warden's office is fitted with an electrical array, a bulb lighting up for each flat as the tenant passes through his or her hallway on the way to the front room. At the touch of a button, the warden can 'clear the board'. All the indicator lights go out, only to come on again as tenants progressively move about. Wardens generally keep a record of when they last 'cleared the board' and can tell at a glance if there is any cause for concern.

In the same volume, Butler (p 16) noted the potential for such systems to use a selection of sensors to monitor the opening of fridge doors or the flushing of toilets, with any failure to activate the system "in any given time cycle" serving to trigger an alarm and alert the warden. Automatic signalling, in other words, could replace the need for wardens to monitor arrays of lights.

Butler noted (p 17), however, the requirement associated with activity monitoring for wardens to know the comings and goings of tenants if such systems were to operate effectively. This begs the question as to the extent to which issues relating to the privacy of users were considered and as to the limits of surveillance that were considered appropriate in these contexts. The National Old People's Welfare Council (1966, p 8) was noted as having some concerns about user privacy but seemed to indicate that where there are higher levels of support need that rights of older people relating to the same might be compromised.

Fisk (1986, p 120) described an activity monitoring system devised in the 1970s by Clark. The context in which it was developed was one where the designers considered that the ideal device should (Clark, 1979, p 214):

> be reliable, detect a range of emergencies, require no positive action on the part of the user, not need the user to remember to activate it, to detect a variety of hazards, have low running and installation costs and not be so intrusive that it causes anxiety in its user.

Such ideals feature later in this book as activity and lifestyle monitoring are more actively promoted (see, for instance, Porteus and Brownsell, 2000; and Chapter Thirteen).

Clark's device was called EMMA (Environmental Monitor/Movement Alarm). It utilised pressure mats under carpets and a vibration detector on the bed. The monitoring of each would result in an alert being signalled unless the user reset a clock device. Other sensors monitored room temperature. In addition to these passive facilities the system offered ceiling-mounted pull cords and touch strips on the skirting boards whereby an alarm could be activated.

The Research Institute for Consumer Affairs (1986, p 12) found some interest among social alarm providers in activity monitoring and, more particularly, in the potential to incorporate temperature sensors. Edinburgh District Council, one of few authorities with experience of activity monitoring, utilised both pressure pads and infrared sensors in their sheltered housing schemes (McLuckie, 1984, p 377). Their use of these devices allegedly followed years of testing out different methods of monitoring including the use of live microphones, making it possible to listen in to the user's home, and switches that were automatically reset when the toilet was flushed. Such monitoring, it was noted by the Scottish Local Authorities Special Housing Group (1980, p 2), was intended to "save some of the warden's time and effort".

As the new technology of call systems associated with increasingly standardised forms of sheltered housing developed, activity monitoring was, however, omitted. Fears about the non-activation of alarms, by which the arguments in favour of activity monitoring might have been strengthened, were overcome by ensuring the provision of ceiling-mounted pull switches in most rooms within dwellings, and through attention being given to selecting positions in which they could be deemed to be within reach for most circumstances. Accompanying this was the sanctioning of closer monitoring involving personal visits by wardens or, where the call systems offered two-way speech, daily calls via these. The locus of call systems within sheltered housing schemes with on-site staff obviated the need for activity monitoring.

With the advent of carephones (discussed later) it might have been expected that there would have been renewed interest in activity monitoring, but such interest did not materialise at that time. The experience of Great Britain in this respect is different from the United States and Canada where the passive alarm function through timing devices was and remains, commonplace.

Speech-based warden call systems

The early speech-based warden call systems encountered by Attenburrow (1976) evolved quickly to take the form generally found in sheltered housing throughout Great Britain today. Such systems normally comprise a wall unit with integral pull cord in every dwelling. Ceiling mounted pull cords in other rooms are linked to these. The pull cords are such that they terminate an inch or two above floor level. The wall units are wired back to a central receiver unit controlling the system. Where schemes have communal areas, laundry and/or guest rooms, additional room units and ceiling-mounted pull cords are provided.

The warden of such schemes can receive or make calls via a portable handset and sometimes, in addition, from a fixed console. The handset in such systems, plugged into room units so that if the warden was visiting a tenant she/he could still make calls to and receive calls from other locations. With such systems, calls made by tenants when the warden's handset is not plugged in, is out of range or switched off, are stored in the system memory so that the warden is alerted at the earliest opportunity.

The importance of two-way speech within such systems has been noted, having had substantial implications for the warden and the manner in which her/his pattern of work has evolved. Butler (1989, p 11) summarised some of the consequences of two-way speech:

> The warden could provide regular calls to check upon occupants, receive incoming requests, and relay messages. Many wardens began to institute a regular 'morning round' calling all their occupants in turn. Others gathered up requests for shopping or repeat prescriptions. In some cases the alarm became the medium for conversation and gossip thereby arousing the ire of the 'puritans'. In their eyes the alarm was in danger of replacing daily face-to-face contact, and was on those grounds to be deplored.

It is interesting, with the benefit of hindsight, to consider the hostility with which two-way speech, or rather its consequences, was greeted by some. In keeping with the notion that technologies might liberate older people (as noted in Chapter Two) it is arguable that a more arm's length relationship with wardens was, and is, preferable. Morning calls, however, are still clearly written into the job descriptions of most sheltered housing wardens. It is arguable, furthermore, that the use of alarms for social purposes may promote other forms of more personal social interaction. Conversely, as technologies were progressively seen as assisting the warden in her/his tasks, there may have been a diminution in mutual support among sheltered housing residents.

The freedom for wardens to roam, however, was not initially achieved without some inconvenience. By modern standards, many plug-in portable receivers were at first far from being 'handsets'. They were cumbersome and somewhat bigger than today's laptop computers. Only later did they reduce in size to little larger than a packet of cigarettes. Now, most handsets do not require to be plugged in and appear little different to mobile (cell) phones.

No studies are known to have examined the extent of mutual support between tenants in sheltered housing schemes, although this was a routine theme used to justify such provision. It is impossible to verify, therefore, the suggestion made by Parry and Thompson (1993, p 13) that:

> A somewhat subtle, but nevertheless significant disadvantage of [portable receivers] ... was the idea that the more easily the warden could be contacted, the less motivation there tended to be for tenants to take responsibility for each other's well-being.

Since the 1980s, the advent of microprocessors has resulted in the development and installation of call systems with more intelligence. These are able to convey to the warden a wider array of information about calls that she/he receives. This includes not just the origins (and type) of calls but also the manner of their activation. This, in part, has been facilitated by room units allowing for linked devices such as temperature sensors and smoke detectors to be added. This book gives further consideration (in Chapters Eleven to Thirteen) to sensors and their role in operating with call systems. Initially, however, it is appropriate to give some consideration to the debate that took place, and is still relevant in the context of today's sheltered housing, regarding the relative merits of pull cords and pendant transmitters as the principal means of activating social alarms.

Pull cords and pendants

The debate about pull cords and portable pendant transmitters arose in the early 1980s when dispersed alarms first appeared on the British market. The primary means of their activation, aside from directly pressing a button on the unit, was through use of the radio pendant. The benefits of the latter were seen to be that they could be used anywhere within the dwelling. They potentially overcome, therefore, the problem that people might fall out of reach of a pull cord and be unable, as a consequence, to obtain help. Pendant transmitters were by this time reasonably well established as standard accessories to carephones in the United States. In Great Britain the debate, as was the case for all developments in social alarms, had to consider the position in relation to call systems and ipso facto their operation within sheltered housing schemes as well as with dispersed alarms.

The disadvantages of pull cords were summarised by Butler (1989, pp 14-15). He argued that:

> First, they might easily be confused with light switches, particularly in the bathroom and/or lavatory.... Secondly, pieces of furniture may be placed against the wall in such a way that the alarm-pull is concealed and thereby rendered inoperable.... Thirdly, following a fall, the occupant may still be unable to reach the pull cord. Finally, a few older people have failed to have the alarm system explained to them ... and, as a consequence, have not disentangled the cord from its packaging.

The last of these can be discounted as an anomaly that, perhaps, reflected a particular encounter of Butler's. But to these problems can be added the predisposition of tenants to tie up pull cords out of the way. Fennell (1989, pp 23, 25) noted in his survey of Anchor Housing Association sheltered housing tenants that 60 per cent of households had at least one pull cord disabled in this manner and in research that he had undertaken in Scotland, 46 per cent. Other studies of sheltered housing schemes in Liverpool (Middleton, 1982, p 27) and Birmingham (Birmingham City Council, 1986, p 7) echoed this finding with 57 per cent and 71 per cent of households respectively.

Pull cords are, however, permanent fittings and are always potentially available for users wishing to raise an alarm. The manner of their operation is simple and the nature of the device is familiar and understandable to the user. But to be effective they need to be located strategically (not easy given the natural predisposition for people to arrange their furnishings in different ways) and it must be recognised that wherever they are located there will always be circumstances in which they cannot be reached.

Remarkably, pendant transmitter devices have been the focus of only limited study. This follows from their being seen as simply part of the package associated with carephones and for which there are no ready alternatives. Initially, however, the arrival of pendant transmitters was accompanied by a belief that they would also be appropriate for use in sheltered housing schemes, either replacing or working alongside pull cords.

The possibility of pendant transmitters replacing pull cords was not, in the event, realised. This followed the recognition that many, and possibly a majority, of older people did not like wearing pendant devices. As a consequence it was considered that there might be an increase in the number of occasions where a resident, in experiencing an emergency, might not be able to raise the alarm because the transmitter device had been left in another room, put in a drawer, forgotten or lost. Instead, pendant transmitters where present were and remain, generally speaking, only linked to call systems in addition to pull cords.

Where they are used it is often the case that sheltered housing wardens keep a small number of pendant transmitters that can be used by residents who might be particularly at risk and may wish to have this additional means of calling for help. The variant of the pendant transmitter, the device worn on the wrist like a watch, has generally not been pursued in the context of call systems even though this kind of device appears more acceptable to social alarm users (see, for instance, Fisk, 1995, p 150).

Different systems

Dispersed alarms, including both carephones and radio devices, offer links between older people who live in non-sheltered dwellings and a remote responder. They can meet the needs of people with support needs but for whom sheltered housing might be inappropriate, unavailable or unwanted.

Awareness of the need for carephones in Great Britain arose from an appreciation that call systems were only available to the relatively small proportion of older people who lived in sheltered housing. The enthusiasm of local authorities for the newer social alarm technologies was in many cases, however, fuelled by the 'new toy syndrome' noted earlier (Butler, 1981, p 18) and reinforced by the widespread and often patronising wish to do good for older people. The latter perspective was particularly conspicuous among local authority officers and also by councillors who saw the expenditure on social alarms as proof of their social welfare credentials and worth a few extra votes in the ballot box at local elections. But that such views were not confined to local authorities was borne out in the work of Pellow (1987) whose review of a service in East London was noted in Chapter Three.

Butler (1981, p 18) described the new toy syndrome thus:

> A certain intoxication with the 'new toy' element in this gadgetry is evident in some local authorities' enthusiasm for the systems. On visiting some [local authority] departments one is reminded of a father playing with his son's new trainset at Christmas. The seductive way in which such systems are sold adds to this enthusiasm as does their undoubted attraction for councillors and the local press. New schemes are frequently opened with widespread publicity and a ring of civic pride.

Butler added (p 19) that "the rhetoric of dependency, degeneracy and crisis leads to the conviction that an alarm system is the appropriate response we as a society must make in order to protect our ageing members". As far as manufacturers of such technologies were concerned, therefore, local authorities were ripe for the taking and, with their seductive sales pitches, did not let the opportunity slip.

Radio systems

Despite the commonplace adoption of call systems in sheltered housing and the early indications that speech communication would be extended through the telephone network, the first social alarm systems that linked to a remote monitoring and response centre used radio. The focus of early radio-based services was not the residents of sheltered housing schemes and had nothing to do with improving the terms and conditions of wardens. Instead, radio-based social alarm services were generally set up by social welfare authorities and were seen as helping them in their endeavours to support older people in their own homes.

Telephone-based systems

Support for telephone-based social alarm systems grew rapidly. They, rather than radio-based systems, were increasingly recognised as the best way to respond to the pressures on sheltered housing wardens. Such pressures and the need for change arose for a number of reasons including:

- the growing support needs of a minority of tenants in sheltered housing;
- the increasing predisposition for scheme residents to use speech-based call alarms for a wider range of purposes and not just in the event of an emergency;
- the inappropriateness of older people who were active residents acting as deputy wardens;
- the inclination of wardens to stay on call even when off duty for fear that a resident could have an emergency that might not be responded to, with attendant adverse consequences; and
- the growing dependence on the part of some residents on the support and, therefore, time of the resident warden.

The last of these, it must be stated, was a problem that many housing authorities and wardens made for themselves. The National Old People's Welfare Council (1966, p 6) and Fisk (1986, p 138), for instance, noted the enthusiasm of housing authorities to recruit wardens with experience of caring for older people in institutional contexts. It is not unsurprising if they carried forward into their new posts some of the ethos of their former roles. The difficulty was, and still is to some extent, compounded by a failure to properly define the boundaries of the warden's role and to insufficiently emphasise the limits to her/his responsibilities.

CHRISTCHURCH DISTRICT COUNCIL

The first social alarm system in Great Britain is believed to be the local scheme set up in 1975 by Christchurch District Council (Tinker, 1984, p 18). This followed that authority's wish to extend the benefit of resident warden services in sheltered housing schemes to older people living in nearby properties and who wished to stay put. They saw this initiative as potentially reducing the level of need for sheltered housing.

By 1981/2, 155 older people in non-sheltered council accommodation had been linked, each having a non-speech radio device that could be activated by pushing a button. No charge was levied. Responses to calls on the system were made by the sheltered housing warden or one of a team of relief wardens.

STOCKPORT METROPOLITAN BOROUGH COUNCIL

The first authority-wide radio-based social alarm service was established early in 1979 in the Metropolitan Borough of Stockport. It is particularly commendable as it emerged from a comprehensive review of services for older people that was conducted in 1975. The service involved social services, housing and health authorities (Lewis, 1979, p 27ff). Reformist zeal was apparent, this following the authority's establishment as a unitary authority after local government reorganisation in 1974.

The focus of the Stockport social alarm service was not on sheltered housing. Indeed, the authority decided as a result of a service review not to build any more sheltered housing but rather to put resources into enabling older people to stay put in their own homes. The new service was, therefore, focused on supporting a wider range of people in the borough. This, in some cases, was achieved with the help of a social alarm device. The strategy followed their estimate that some 8,000 older people in the borough could benefit from the support of a warden whereas sheltered housing and other designated dwellings could only accommodate 1,200 (Day, 1979, p 12).

As the new service was developed, sheltered housing wardens were redeployed and a team of 16 mobile wardens was established. This did not take place without some resistance (Day, 1979, p 14ff). Sheltered housing schemes and residential homes were, however, regarded as important parts of overall service provision for older people and suitable for those with a higher level of support need. The service, jointly funded by social services and housing, benefited from additional funding from the area health authority. The approach, according to Epps (1981, p 36) exemplified corporate management at all levels.

Adoption of a radio-based system in Stockport followed consideration of the telephone-based alternative. The latter was rejected on the grounds that the telephone links, where needed could not be quickly installed or removed and that carephones would be less easily operated by people who were ill or possibly confused (Day, 1979, p 13). Day (p 14) described the equipment in the home thus:

> The transmitter is roughly the size of a large transistor radio set and may be plugged into the mains; alternatively, if no power is available, the set may be operated by batteries. The alarm may be activated by a push button on the set ...

He noted that the equipment had options to link pull cords, had pressure pads for activity monitoring, temperature sensors and smoke alarms.

As an experiment, some dwellings were fitted with thermostats to monitor for low temperatures (Lewis, 1979, p 30). Also linked were the borough's sheltered housing schemes, each of these being provided with a single radio transmitter device and an indicator panel by which the household that activated the alarm could be identified by a responding mobile warden.

By 1981/2 the Stockport service covered 1,640 households on a full-time basis. This included 1,360 in grouped dwellings, some of which it is presumed had been sheltered. A further 500 households, resident in sheltered housing schemes, were covered when the resident warden was off duty (Tinker, 1984, p 16).

Tinker noted (p 16) a number of problems encountered by the Stockport service. These perhaps take the gloss off some of the more glowing reports quoted above but reflect, in several instances, the inevitable consequence of organisational change associated with new service provision. These were:

- the amount of staff time involved in setting up the service;
- the retirement and deployment of resident wardens;
- the recruitment and training of mobile wardens;
- the establishment of an appropriate records system;
- difficulties over electricity supplies and the placing of necessary equipment especially for grouped dwellings linking to a single radio device;
- the lack of housing subsidy to help cover scheme costs in the private sector; and
- the unsuitability of the scheme for confused older people.

Tinker's analysis also reported on the generally positive views of the service among housing services staff. This was despite a view that primary responsibility for it might have been more appropriately vested in the social services rather than the housing department. To a number of management advantages cited by the housing department she added (p 16):

- the feelings of confidence given to older people through availability of the 24-hour service and the flexible working arrangements of the mobile wardens;
- the speed by which the radio alarms could be installed; and
- the contribution made to users being able to stay put in familiar surroundings.

The radio technologies have since been replaced by a telephone-based system and the social alarm service has been widened to include private sector users and monitoring services for housing associations and an adjoining authority.[2] By 2003 6,150 households had been linked.[3]

The number of similar radio–based systems installed by other authorities indicates the general success of the Stockport initiative. These tended to be in authorities where there was a strong social welfare interest that were concerned with the ability of social alarms to reach out to and support older people in the wider community and be part of wider packages of care, at least part of which were to do with supporting independent living.

Radio versus telephone

The debate about the relative advantages of radio- and telephone-based systems in Great Britain was one that was fiercely fought by the manufacturers of social alarms anxious to extol the virtues of their chosen medium. In truth, both had advantages and disadvantages. These were summarised by Baker and Parry (1984, p 27; see Table 4.1).

However, with the drive to develop social alarms coming mainly from housing authorities for essentially management reasons, telephone-based systems would be generally favoured – sheltered housing schemes were normally in accessible locations and the cost of telephone line installations and calls thereon could be met from the housing revenue account. This was often not the case for older people in private accommodation spread across local authority areas and for whom the housing authorities did not, in any case, have a specific duty of care.

Social welfare authorities, meanwhile, were wary of placing themselves in a position of having to pay for installations on behalf of eligible clients at a time (in 1980) when just 61 per cent of households with one or more older people had a telephone (Goddard and Savage, 1994, p 16). Furthermore, the alternative approach of establishing radio-based systems in parallel with telephone-based systems would have required substantial additional capital expenditure and, because of the lack of two-way speech for at least the former, would have necessitated the establishment of response frameworks that extended beyond sheltered housing schemes and, for some authorities, into less accessible rural areas.

The advent of two-way speech radio systems in the mid-1980s came, perhaps, too late. The momentum, except in Scotland (see Chapter Six), was by this time with housing authorities and the course, at least for the ensuing 15 years, of social alarms in Great Britain as essentially housing services had been established.

Table 4.1: The advantages and disadvantages of radio- and telephone-based social alarm systems

Telephone-based systems	Radio-based systems
• No limit on distance	• Limited range
• Requires telephone line	• Possible interference
• Dependent on British Telecom engineers	• Unsuitable in some areas
• Subject to faults	• Greater flexibility in installation
• High running costs if used for communication	• Higher capital costs
	• Lower running costs

LONDON BOROUGH OF HAMMERSMITH AND FULHAM

The first authority-wide telephone-based social alarm service, established like the Stockport radio service in 1979, was in the London Borough of Hammersmith and Fulham. Its primary purpose was to give out of hours cover to that authority's sheltered housing schemes (Thompson, 1981, p 40). Thompson affirmed the benefits as being:

- resident wardens being able to take proper time off, secure in the knowledge that any calls would be dealt with;
- tenants knowing that their calls would be answered at all times; and
- the authority not having to employ relief or deputy wardens for each sheltered housing scheme.

The Hammersmith and Fulham service arose partly for management reasons and was led by the housing department. A very important feature, in contrast to the radio-based initiatives at Christchurch and Stockport, was that it was speech based. Being speech based a receptionist, on receipt of a call, could in most cases ascertain the nature of any problem before giving instructions, via a paging system, to the duty mobile warden who would then go to the caller's home (Thompson, 1981, p 41). Calls were dealt with, in this initial period, by a call answering service in central London.

Problems encountered included (p 42ff):

- the need for specific training of the staff handling calls, particularly regarding ways of communicating with people at times of stress; and
- the lack of accountability in relation to decisions made as to what kinds of calls constituted emergencies and required, therefore, attendance by a mobile warden.

The early experience at Hammersmith and Fulham led to a review of the service and to the authority establishing its own monitoring and response centre. This was located at a sheltered housing scheme in the centre of the borough and also provided a base of operation for the mobile wardens.

Most important from this early initiative was the realisation by the local authority of the need for professionalism, a clear management structure and staff roles for all aspects of the social alarm service. This resulted in, among other things, the establishment of effective joint working practices involving sheltered housing wardens, relief wardens, call receiving staff and mobile wardens.

At September 2000, the Hammersmith and Fulham service had some 2,025 households linked of which two thirds were within sheltered housing schemes.[4] Most of these were owned and managed by the council. Some 650 carephones were also linked, most of which had been provided for older people and others, following needs assessments. Particular needs being addressed by Hammersmith and Fulham included those of people with AIDS/HIV and monitoring for bogus callers.

Like that of Stockport, the success of Hammersmith and Fulham's initiative was reflected in the large number of authorities taking similar paths. A recognition was growing fast that such systems, in the words of Parry and Thompson (1993, p 16):

> created freedom previously undreamed of for resident wardens. They could work a 5 day week with evenings and nights off; they could attend training courses and wardens meetings; they could go away on holiday without feeling guilty.

Conspicuously, these new services were mostly established by housing rather than social welfare authorities. Management as opposed to social welfare reasons were, therefore, to the fore.

Carephones

In the vast majority of cases social alarm systems operate via the telephone. The carephones associated with them generally offer a push button means of activation on the device itself complemented by a radio trigger, which is normally a pendant. A typical carephone is illustrated in Plate 4.1. Pendant transmitters are discussed below.

Carephones come in two types. This was and remains true for Great Britain, Ireland, North America and other parts of the world. First are those that work alongside the conventional telephone; second are those that incorporate a telephone, effectively replacing any prior provision. Each on activation seizes control of the telephone line and sends a call to a responder. In most cases a responder means a monitoring and response centre, but some devices can dial directly to numbers, often of a relative or friend, where they leave a recorded message that help is needed. The former, linking to a monitoring and response centre, predominate. Both types have been actively marketed from the earliest period of social alarm development.

The first study to examine dispersed alarms and their role in any detail was that undertaken by the Research Institute for Consumer Affairs (RICA, 1986). The importance and the substantial impact of this publication were discussed in Chapter Three. Of the 17 carephones that they tested, 13 operated alongside the user's ordinary telephone. Most offered the portable radio trigger as standard. While pendant transmitters were the norm, RICA examined (p 159) alternative wrist-worn and hand-held devices. The report described their modus operandi thus, noting that:

> a portable trigger is the most useful activating device for an alarm system. It is a small, easy to carry alarm button which when activated sends a radio signal to a receiver in the home unit [the dispersed alarm unit] to initiate the alarm.

Plate 4.1 *Typical carephone device*

Source: Tunstall Telecom Lifeline carephone (photo from press release)

Their tests showed substantial variability in the performance of such transmitters, these having ranges of up to 100 metres (pp 170-1). Such variability was determined by battery power and the configuration of the aerials. In most pendant transmitters the aerial was in the neck cord, adequate performance being predicated on a belief that the device would be worn as intended, that is hanging from the neck (p 160ff).

RICA's tests also included the functionality of the carephones themselves and their modus operandi after activation, whether or not this involved use of a pendant transmitter. Various features and facilities were noted including whether there was the ability to operate if the telephone handset had been displaced; the extent of back-up power to facilitate operation after mains failure; the number of repeat dialling attempts to get through to the responder; and the incorporation of warnings for such things as a faulty telephone line. Design features and ergonomic considerations were tested for both the carephones and pendant transmitters. The latter considered, in particular, the difficulties in operation that might be encountered by persons who may have fallen, had poor sight or might lack dexterity (p 163ff).

That the RICA report resulted in a new benchmark for carephones was discussed in Chapter Three. What RICA regarded as key features were almost all incorporated in the two devices that they recommended as good value (p xxiv). RICA's continued interest in carephones resulted in further studies and regular product testing, the results of which are evidenced in various publications and notably the consumer magazine *Which?* (Calling for Help Group, 1993; Research Institute for Consumer Affairs, 1987 and 1997; Ricability, 2000).

In the United States such rigorous testing of social alarm products does not appear to have been undertaken though such devices were, and remain, subject to the Underwriters' Laboratory regulatory frameworks that ensure their electrical safety and proper operation over the telephone network. What have been available, however, are a number of product guides. These included a detailed documentation of the functionality of different carephone devices by ECRI (1998), one of a series of reports comparing healthcare products, and successive reports by the American Association of Retired Persons (AARP, 1987 and 1992).

Conclusion

The origins of social alarms lie on both sides of the Atlantic. These relate to a more narrowly focused approach associated with sheltered housing in Great Britain and a more expansive approach seeking to develop devices via the public telephone network in the United States.

The subsequent paths of product development can also be contrasted, with that of the United States being remarkably straight. This is borne testimony to in Chapter Eight. But for Great Britain progress took a winding path and was hampered by technological dilemmas relating to speech or non-speech systems, radio or telephone media, and to debates that reflected uncertainty about the role of social alarms in sheltered housing. It was only after such issues had been largely resolved that the position regarding both social alarm systems and services became clearer.

Other countries simply followed the leads given by Great Britain and the United States, depending on the context. Call systems, for instance, became a commonplace feature of sheltered housing or grouped schemes for older people in such countries as Ireland and the Netherlands while the carephone was more widely adopted and has become the mainstay of social alarm services throughout most Western countries.

For Great Britain, however, the difficulties of reconciling the role of such technologies within sheltered housing were very apparent. The debate is fascinating in the extent to which it revealed concerns relating to the impact on the role of the warden and the potential for abuse of the call system. It appears that the technologies in this context were considered, at least by housing authorities, subordinate to the role of the warden and could not be permitted to affect it.

The high regard with which sheltered housing was held meant, furthermore, that the broader potential of social alarms in Great Britain was at least to some extent overlooked. Social welfare authorities who, in some cases, had a broader vision, often lacked the resources or the political muscle to harness such technologies for wider benefit. As a consequence, social alarms were, and remain, poorly targeted in relation to the support needs of many older people and the social alarm services that developed are generally at odds with their counterparts in other countries.

On the positive side it must be said that social alarm services in Great Britain, by virtue of the emphasis on sheltered housing, expanded rapidly to support relatively large numbers of older people living in social rented housing and who on the whole had relatively limited financial resources. The poor targeting has, therefore, been compensated for in the larger number of recipients. Social alarms have, furthermore, played a part in enabling older people in sheltered housing at least, to stay put. The potential losers were those older people in the wider community whose needs were only later attended to.

By contrast, the framework of development for social alarms in the United States is one that was and remains firmly within the private sector. Poorer people and those without state-funded assistance have consistently lost out. So although the United States can be said to have been the cradle of social alarms, a better reference point in relation to their effective use within broader care and support service frameworks might be found elsewhere – in Australia or the Netherlands perhaps. The position in such countries is documented in Chapter Nine.

Notes

[1] See British Standard BS6804:1986 'British Standard Code of Practice for Social Alarm Systems', British Standards Institution.

[2] Short, M. (1991) in paper to seminar on social alarms, The Planning Exchange, Glasgow.

[3] Correspondence with Peter Wilson (Stockport Metropolitan Borough Council).

[4] Per correspondence with Jane Endersby (London Borough of Hammersmith and Fulham).

FIVE

Social alarms in England and Wales

Introduction

Of the 300 public sector services in Great Britain identified by Fisk in 1990, 280 were managed by English and Welsh local authorities (Fisk, 1990, p 3). These included many of the largest and smallest services, in terms of the number of their service users.

The establishment of the early schemes in Stockport and the London Borough of Hammersmith and Fulham have been described in Chapter Four and some of the debates concerning the technology options and ways of configuring social alarm services have been initiated. Notable, however, is the extent to which the social welfare perspective, exemplified by the Stockport scheme, was set aside as housing authorities developed services that primarily responded to their management requirements for sheltered housing. To put it bluntly, older people with high levels of support needs, whether or not living in sheltered housing, were not their responsibility and they, generally speaking, saw their social welfare objectives in terms of responding in emergencies rather than supporting independent living. But social alarms were attractive to housing authorities because of their perceived ability to improve the efficiency of sheltered housing services, make revenue savings and, in the words of Parry and Thompson (1993, p 16) make a "major contribution towards improving the working conditions of many wardens".

It is small wonder that social services authorities had to stand on the sidelines while their housing colleagues were almost indecent in their haste to acquire the new technologies and garner the associated kudos. In some instances the social welfare practitioners may have appeared suspicious and/or hostile towards such developments and that, perhaps, was entirely predictable.

The technology rush among housing practitioners was borne testimony to in articles within the professional housing journals over a considerable period (see, for instance, MacCreath, 1980; Sand, 1986). By contrast and with few exceptions (see Fisk, 1985) social welfare journals were virtually silent on the issue.

As noted in Chapter One, the whole business of developing social alarm services was technology led. The local authority, mainly housing sector purchasers, were wooed and seduced. Articles in housing journals were, in many cases, adulatory and often appeared little more than a means of marketing the wares of a particular manufacturer. Some were written by service providers, others by the manufacturers themselves. An example of the former is Shepherd

(1985, p 17), then the Assistant Director of Housing, regarding Rotherham's service in which he articulated the authority's pride at being "the country's first operator of the [Tunstall] Piper Network Controller". His article went on (pp 17-18) to describe the full range of Tunstall equipment, which his authority purchased as part of their £1.3 million investment. An example of the latter is Johnson (1987) then Marketing Director of Tunstall Telecom. He pushed the argument about the cost savings of social alarms hard and documented what he considered to be essential features of the technologies utilised (p 8). The sales pitch used language that has typified the literature that Tunstall Telecom and other companies employed. Johnson stated that:

> ... new telecommunications technology has meant that many lives are saved which might otherwise have been lost and the limited resources ... of our communities are not unduly stretched by having to cope with more and more elderly people going into care. In the future many will be able to continue to live in their own homes simply because they know that help and reassurance is no further away than the press of a button.

The context was one where Fisk (1984, p 22) argued that the development of social alarms had been "characterised by failure on the part of most authorities to work out their objectives". He lamented that "in a rush to take advantage of the new technology available, many authorities have failed to consider whether the interests of the elderly might be better met in other ways or by alarm systems with greater versatility". He went on to point out (p 23) the potential of extending, through the use of social alarms, the concept of sheltered housing to "others in the community" but identified two problems. These were:

- the need to maintain a comprehensive approach towards the development of systems that transcended the boundaries of the interested statutory services; and
- the failure of the manufacturers to develop systems that were able to interface economically with even a small part of the range of call systems installed in sheltered housing schemes.

He called (p 23) for authorities to stand firm in their demand for compatible equipment in order to avoid local monopolies in social alarm equipment in order to "fulfil the needs of the elderly" rather than "fill the pockets of the company shareholders".

The theme of interfacing infused subsequent articles by Fisk. He alleged (1985, p 84) that the problem of incompatibility had arisen as a result of hastily made purchasing decisions and the fact of some housing authorities being "overawed by the pace of technological change [with] their judgement, as a consequence, impaired". The result he noted was that social welfare and health authorities were, in effect, excluded and the possibility of social alarms meeting broader community benefits was constrained.

The debates, partly stimulated by such articles, did have some positive outcomes and helped the development of more cautious approaches. This was reflected in the configuration of more rigorous specifications for social alarm equipment supply. In 2003, most equipment at monitoring and response centres in England and Wales is compatible with a wide range of social alarm equipment.

Local authority perspectives

A good example of an authority, which, in its early stages of development, sought to avoid a manufacturer monopoly, is Barnsley Metropolitan Borough Council (Borgia, 1989). This authority had installed the receiving equipment of three manufacturers and was one of just 12 authorities throughout Great Britain (10 in England, 2 in Scotland) with a similar capability (Fisk, 1989, pp 56-7).

The preoccupation of some English authorities with such alarm technologies was, of course, justified in relation to their obligation to ensure good value for their public expenditure. The perceived potential of social alarms was, however, often too narrowly considered. Butler (1981, pp 21-2) and Oldman (1989, p 47ff) were other voices arguing the need for greater awareness and greater caution on the part of local authorities.

Despite the calls, however, in only a very small number of English authorities was responsibility for social alarm services vested in a social services department. In only one instance, Avon County Council, was this in a shire county, that is at a different tier of local government than the housing authority (Fisk, 1989, p 13). In unitary authorities, however, management by social services was, and remained, more usual. Stockport is an example of this (see Chapter Four). And while a clear majority of social alarm services within the shire counties were operated by housing authorities, there are indications that, where it was not previously the case, social services authorities did become more involved and in some cases are increasingly playing a part in service development and management.

Such changes have come about through a greater awareness of the potential social welfare role of social alarm services for a wide range of older people and others with support needs. Other user groups include, for instance, younger people with physical disabilities, women at risk of violence in the home, people newly discharged from hospital, households at risk of racial harassment, and people who are chronically sick and terminally ill (Fisk, 1989, p 8; Riseborough, 1997a, p 8).

The more recent changes in approach are, furthermore, a product of the increasing though limited amount of published research. Greater attention to social alarms in reports that have been influential in government policy frameworks (eg the Audit Commission, 1998); numerous reviews by housing provider agencies of sheltered housing services; and the simple recognition that warden services as usually configured can only be provided for a relatively small proportion of older people with support needs. But the greater involvement of social services authorities has not been readily achieved. In 1990 the Department of the Environment (1990, p 10) found just three local authorities in England where housing departments were not responsible for the management of sheltered housing or warden services.

The dilemma faced by housing authorities arose from the increased support needs of older people in sheltered housing and of other people in the remainder of their housing stock. These needs, it had to be acknowledged, increasingly had to be met by packages of care determined by those who had the requisite assessment skills, that is within social services authorities, and who had to take into account both formal and informal support needs and the role of wardens.

This, and changing funding frameworks (see Fisk and Phillips, 2001), means that the role of housing authorities as direct social alarm service providers will diminish. Instead, social alarm services are increasingly likely to be operated corporately or directly by social services authorities as an integral part of wider care and support frameworks.

OLDHAM METROPOLITAN BOROUGH COUNCIL

Illustrative of the dilemmas associated with a repositioning of social alarm services is the experience of Oldham Metropolitan Borough Council. Like other authorities, Oldham followed the example of nearby Stockport in setting up a non-speech radio system. The need to replace this equipment and warden call systems in some of its sheltered housing schemes was the trigger for a major service review and the subsequent launch of a new service.

In 1980 Oldham announced its decision to establish a mobile warden service. Its focus was to be on the needs of tenants of its sheltered housing schemes and it would act as a back-up for resident wardens. The mobile wardens were to be provided with vans, linked by radio to a monitoring and response centre, and would carry keys to facilitate access to the dwellings of service users. The service commenced the following year.

By 1985 the Oldham service had developed to cover some 2,900 households. Most of these were within sheltered housing schemes. In addition, some radio units for individuals, most of whom were elderly, were provided for those not living in sheltered housing. A subsequent (internal) review reported the particular usefulness of the service in providing routine assistance with personal tasks as well as facilitating responses in an emergency. This followed a decision to use mobile wardens for domiciliary care when they were not responding to calls. The potential of the social alarm service was, in other words, being seen from the social welfare as well as a housing perspective.

By 1990 the number of dwellings linked to the Oldham service had risen to 3,335. At this time an increase in demand from frail elderly clients was noted as putting greater pressures on the mobile wardens. Management of these was transferred to social services and became the responsibility of homecare team leaders.

Required changes to radio frequencies and awareness of the shortcomings of the service in relation to growing needs led to further change. Its outcome resulted in responsibility for the new social alarm service being vested with social services, though subject to service specifications that would safeguard the interests of the housing department (see Fisk, 1995, p 148). A new monitoring and response centre was established in a former residential home owned by the authority, which commenced operation with a new management structure and substantially increased staffing levels. The new facility also provided a base for emergency social work staff. An integrated framework, with staff working both as at the monitoring and response centre and as mobile wardens, was adopted.

That customer satisfaction levels with the service were high was evident from a subsequent survey of its carephone users. This was part of a comparative study with a service in Ottawa, Canada (see Chapter Eight). Though the sample size was small (just 18) this found that 17 were satisfied or very satisfied with the service. All regarded having a carephone as enabling them to live at home for longer and, the survey established, this meant more than just coping or surviving, since most had social networks that involved visits to and from family and friends, with eight often or sometimes going on day trips or holidays (Fisk, 1995, p 150).

Nine of the respondents had used the service in an emergency. In four cases this was a result of a fall and in two because of medical problems. Three hospital visits ensued. The three other emergencies were attributable to non-medical events – the intercom to the door having been switched off; a light bulb having blown; and a home carer not having arrived (Fisk, 1995, p 151).

By November 2000 the service had developed to serve 4,500 households, most of which were within the council's own sheltered housing schemes. The biggest growth area was in carephones where, in keeping with the service's use of social alarms to complement and underpin social welfare services, some 600 households were supported.

As a consequence of the growth of the service the mobile wardens were more involved in care tasks including putting people to bed, getting them up and helping them to the toilet. Where, however, the care tasks were particularly onerous, others undertook them.

Other perspectives

In local authorities in England and Wales where social alarm services are more firmly anchored within housing departments, the developing social welfare role, insofar as it had taken place, usually involved agreements being made with social services departments in respect of users they might wish to link to the services in question. Such agreements have not necessarily been simple with social services authorities still, in some cases, smarting at their lack of involvement at the earlier stages of service development and demanding growing roles in relation to, for instance, staff recruitment and training.

The debates run in parallel with those that are concerned with greater social services involvement in sheltered housing schemes. Here, there is ample evidence of wardens, like social alarm service managers and operators being required to change their working practices and develop new skills in order to respond to the increasingly complex needs of service users. The process of professionalisation that affects wardens is, therefore, of equal relevance to social alarm services and the operators associated with them. Changes in funding frameworks will, it is considered, help to ensure that the warden's role is better targeted towards older people in need of their assistance; less tied to individual schemes; and, therefore, may promote the usage of carephones.

A picture of local authority services in England emerged from an Audit Commission survey in 1998.[1] This found:

- a tendency to fewer, larger services;
- increased cooperation between agencies (notably housing and social services authorities);
- a wider range of service users including more vulnerable people and hospital dischargees;
- increasing evidence of the establishment and operation of community warden services who were less tied to sheltered housing schemes;
- increasing attention being given to the provision of support for carers; and
- greater recognition of the de facto role of social alarm services in filtering calls for emergency services.

The conclusion drawn was that local authority social alarm services were, when managed by housing departments, in the wrong place with poor service targeting arising as a consequence. It was also noted the extent to which services were subsidised by local authorities, with just 30 per cent stating that their service charges covered their costs.

TELFORD AND WREKIN COUNCIL

In the mainstream of social alarm services managed by local authorities is Wrekin Link. This service was established in 1983 by Wrekin Council (now Telford and Wrekin) in Shropshire. Its initial remit was concerned with providing a social alarm service to tenants living in the authority's sheltered housing and grouped dwellings for older people. The origins of Wrekin Link are, therefore, entirely in keeping with those of most other services in England and Wales. It is an example of a service, however, that has been actively developed and marketed both within and outside the local authority area both in relation to its focal social alarm service remit and other services including out of hours repairs reporting, the monitoring of security alarms and some CCTV installations and, more recently, lone worker monitoring.

A survey of 28 randomly selected users of the social alarm service who lived in the Telford and Wrekin or adjoining areas was undertaken in January and February 2000. Households were selected from user listings and were confined to those with carephones. This found that three quarters (21) of respondents lived alone and over half (16) were aged 80 or over.

Over half of the respondents (16) received some kind of formal help at home. All but four were women. Two thirds (18) lived in houses or two-storey cottages and over a quarter (5) lived in rural areas. Over half (16) had lived in their present home for more than 20 years, the longest period of residence being 64 years and the average 25. All but one (27) were owner occupiers.

For all respondents this was their first experience of having a social alarm. Most (20) had been linked to Wrekin Link for five years or less, though the average was four years. One had been linked for 12 years. Most (23) considered that having a social alarm had enabled them or would enable them to stay put in their present home for longer than would otherwise be the case. Only one respondent, however, had been considering moving home before having a social alarm.

By far and away the main advantage of having a social alarm was seen as peace of mind. This was cited by nearly three quarters (20) of respondents, with security (4) and reassurance of the family (3) being others. Respondents had difficulty in indicating any problems with their social alarm, although four suggested that it was too expensive, three disliked the pendant transmitter, two were concerned that it would not work in a power cut, and one referred to slow responses from the monitoring and response centre.

All were confident that, if the need arose, they would be able to use their social alarm; and most (24) felt confident or very confident that they would receive a prompt and efficient response. For five respondents, this view was in part based on their direct experience of using the service. The nine circumstances in which they sought such help were varied and were typical of those dealt with by Wrekin Link on a day-to-day basis. They had:

- fallen or were stuck (6);
- experienced a mains power failure (2); or
- left their social alarm unplugged (1).

The five respondents were unanimous in stating that they received a satisfactory response from Wrekin Link on these occasions.

Ten respondents testified to not using Wrekin Link at some time even though they had needed urgent help or assistance. While this was potentially a matter for concern it should be noted that in most instances the respondents took alternative courses of action that were arguably more appropriate and potentially speedier ways of getting help. In any case, the option of calling Wrekin Link was, in relation to some of these events, unavailable by virtue of respondents not wearing the pendant trigger device.

The circumstances were, again, typical. Interestingly they all related to falls. Two of these resulted in cuts, two in broken limbs (toe and wrist) and another in bruising. In three of the cases the pendant transmitter was elsewhere, and in four cases help was obtained by using an ordinary telephone. In one of the cases a lady who had fallen and cut her head, waited through part of the night before ringing a nurse at 9am. This resulted in a visit to hospital for treatment. In other cases rescue came via visiting neighbours or relatives or respondents themselves managing.

Housing association perspectives

As with local authorities, social alarm services managed by housing associations in England and Wales were for the most part established essentially for housing reasons. The number of such services has been small and has tended to relate to the largest associations or those who have had a particular remit or specialism in sheltered housing and the accommodation and support needs of older people. The number of housing association services has, however, been increasing on account of stock transfers from local authorities. Probably a majority of older residents in housing association dwellings, where they have the benefit of a social alarm device, are linked to services operated by other service providers.

There was an initial interest among housing associations, regarding social alarms at the same time as these were being considered and debated by local authorities. However, the housing investment programmes of housing associations were generally small and it would have been difficult for many to make the case for service development.

Their interest was manifested in a number of ways. In 1980, for instance, Co-operative Development Services, a registered housing association in Liverpool, took over 49 properties owned by a private landlord. Three quarters of the tenants were pensioners and it was decided to provide carephones for them (Darroch, 1987, p 19). These were linked to a monitoring and response centre on the Wirral. Unusually for such a scheme, by virtue of it being within an ordinary terraced street, capital funding for the equipment and telephone line installations was paid for by the Housing Corporation.

In 1984 a daytime social alarm service was launched by Hyde Housing Association in the Progress Estate, Eltham southeast London, later to be joined by similar initiatives for their tenants in Lewisham (also southeast London) and in Southampton (McTavish, 1989, pp 103-4). The services are of particular interest because of their being firmly rooted in the local communities in question. This is apparent from the fact that wardens' duties, though similar to those conventionally encountered (that is involving visiting and/or regular contact with residents) were extended to cover wider areas (see Wertheimer, 1991, p 43). The tailoring of the services to met local needs in Southampton was evident through the efforts made to embrace members of the Asian community within that scheme. The warden's role included, at least in this context, that of translator/interpreter and sometimes escort to out-patient clinics, benefits agencies and so on (McTavish, 1989, pp 105-6).

A review of the Southampton service in 1991, after four years of operation, reported that there were over 50 older people within the scheme. Almost half came from ethnic minorities, some of whom were not able to communicate easily in English. All but one were of Asian origin (11 Punjabi, 6 Gujerati, 8 Pakistani and 2 Bengali) with a mix of religions (mostly Hindu or Moslem) and first languages. Close cooperation was noted with the social services authority, this helping to ensure that individualised care plans were in place with the social alarm service playing an important part. By 1993 the scheme had expanded to cover 69 users (Wertheimer, 1993, p 7).[2]

By 1990, in England and Wales there were 11 social alarm services operated by housing associations (Fisk, 1990, pp 3, 24). In 2003 there are more than double that figure.

PLACES FOR PEOPLE (FORMERLY NORTH BRITISH HOUSING ASSOCIATION)

One of the earliest housing association social alarm services to be established was that of North British Housing Association. This was set up in Bolton in 1984 and initially linked some 1,100 households. Its development was associated, according to Wertheimer (1993, p 23), with "the association's wish to improve the working conditions of its wardens in sheltered housing schemes". Housing management considerations, in other words, were at the forefront.

Ten years later the North British Housing Association service was receiving some 250 calls daily from sheltered housing wardens or from among the more than 5,000 elderly and disabled people who were linked (Wertheimer, 1993, p 23). Many of the latter were in the association's sheltered housing or grouped dwelling schemes, although 1,750 others were residents in leasehold or private properties. Just 60 had carephones. As with other services run by larger housing associations and where users were dispersed nationally or throughout a region, responses were through resident wardens in sheltered housing schemes and/or nominated contacts. Wertheimer (1993, p 25) considered the strengths of the service to be:

* providing a sense of security for older people;
* allowing wardens greater flexibility and improving working conditions;
* enabling the inclusion of tenants in 'dispersed' housing or otherwise without a warden;
* providing cover when wardens are on sick leave or posts are vacant; and
* enabling older people to take more risks, knowing that they can summon help if necessary.

The above hold few surprises except for the last, an aspect of social alarms that is not often suggested but which ties in with the possibility that they might support independent living in a broader sense, including the motivation of service users. The challenges Wertheimer reported (p 26) were the need:

- for a proper assessment of needs in order to avoid "offering a service of this kind to people who do not need it" and "create unnecessary dependence";
- to keep abreast of technological change and to avoid incompatibility of equipment; and
- to consider how the technologies might incorporate other functions such as remote door release mechanisms.

After Wertheimer's appraisal the North British Housing Association social alarm service grew, by 1998, to link some 6,800 households, but with virtually no change in the number of households with carephones. There was little indication that the association was adjusting its service in order to target those with the greatest need, regardless of the type of housing in which they lived, except insofar as allocations procedures for sheltered housing gave some priority to those with support needs. There appeared, however, to have been an increase in the number of emergency calls in the 1993-98 period.

A personal interview survey of users of the North British Housing Association service was undertaken in May 1998. In all, 33 people, randomly selected from among sheltered housing tenants (including some leaseholders) in Macclesfield, Nottingham, Hull and Bolton, were interviewed.

There were predictable findings about the reasons why tenants and residents sought the accommodation in which they were living. The largest number (15) cited health factors and 13 stated that the social alarm was important in their decision. All were reasonably clear as to the purpose of the social alarm, this being generally stated as for use in medical and other emergencies. Those who had used the social alarm in an emergency were most positive about its merits.

Twenty of the tenants and residents had used the call system in an emergency or urgent circumstances. The reasons were largely typical of such services including:

- felt ill (7);
- experienced angina or heart attack (6);
- had fallen (4);
- was dying (1);
- a break-in was taking place (1); or
- an urgent repair was needed (1).

Fourteen of the 20 calls were dealt with at the monitoring and response centre. In common with one of the findings in research by Riseborough (1997a, p 28) there was some uncertainty as to how the service operated and the nature of its links with the emergency services.

ANCHOR TRUST

England's largest provider of sheltered housing, Anchor Housing Association (now Anchor Trust), established a social alarm service, AnchorCall, in 1993. The monitoring and response centre was set up in Altrincham, near Manchester. The size of the service, in terms of the number of users, and geographical spread (reflecting the association's long-standing national remit), was and remains unmatched in Great Britain.

The setting up of the service followed a regional initiative in the northwest of England. Riseborough (1997b, p 6) reported that "there is little doubt that AnchorCall was a top down initiative", this being pointed to in negative comments made by some staff respondents to her survey about the service as being imposed (see below).

Seen as central among the initial benefits of AnchorCall was the improvement in terms and conditions for sheltered housing wardens. Riseborough noted (p 6), for instance, that "AnchorCall made it possible for wardens to have a more reasonable working day" and "provided wardens with some reassurance" that calls would be answered in their absence.

The service was developed rapidly and by 1996, 22,000 households were linked (Riseborough, 1997b, p 8). No other service in England and Wales, whether or not developed by a housing association, is believed to have exhibited such a speed of development. The size and distribution of the sheltered housing schemes linked clearly militated against any notion of providing a mobile warden service, responses instead being made through nominated contacts.

The service objectives were summarised as follows (Riseborough, 1997b, p 9):

* providing reassurance to consumers and relatives;
* obtaining assistance for users in emergencies;
* facilitating communication to services including housing management;
* providing these services by trained operators 24 hours a day; and
* responding to calls within two minutes.

AnchorCall was one of the four social alarm services that Riseborough studied (1997a) and it stands out from the others, all local authority services, for several reasons. Some of these relate to the fact that most respondents to Riseborough's postal survey were either residents or wardens of sheltered housing schemes, a quite natural consequence of the housing characteristics of those older people benefiting from the AnchorCall service. Also notable was the typical characteristics of the schemes within which they lived. To use somewhat dated jargon, these were mostly Category 2 schemes – generally enclosed schemes with a good range of facilities, often characterised by internal corridors, foyers and door entry systems. This meant that hard-wired smoke detectors and door-entry facilities could be and were installed in most schemes. Also provided were key safes, that is safes holding master keys or keys for individual dwellings that could be released remotely in the event of emergency access being required (Riseborough, 1997a, p 8).

All told, 2,000 older users were surveyed together with 600 officers, most of whom were wardens. The surveys elicited remarkably high response rates of 60 per cent and 71 per cent respectively (Riseborough, 1997a, pp 5-6). This, she suggested (p 6), may have reflected Anchor Trust's previous good research experience that had been characterised by, among other things, a feedback of information to respondents. Riseborough's work also involved focus group interviews with 110 older people who were AnchorCall users.

Findings included that a disproportionately high number of users garnered information about the social alarm service from their sheltered housing warden, though this was not, of course, possible for the small minority (150 in 1996, see Riseborough, 1997b, p 8) of users of carephones who were linked to the service.

A relatively high ranking ascribed to calls received at the monitoring and response centre because of concerns about security (Riseborough, 1997b, p 33) seems, however, rather odd given the more protective environment that typifies Anchor Trusts schemes. This may reflect the disproportionate presence of such schemes in urban areas. Interestingly, given the nature of the response service, via nominated contacts, 21 per cent of respondents expressed an interest in the idea of having mobile wardens (Riseborough, 1997b, p 41). No check was made as to the extent to which this interest would have been maintained in light of any increased services charges.

The AnchorCall service is now part of a range of care and support functions that operate within Anchor Trust. These include the provision of domiciliary care and staying put services. The Anchor Trust directorate stated their "commitment to offering flexible choices to those people throughout England who are no longer able to manage entirely independently" (*The Guardian*, 29 October 1997). In this context Riseborough noted (1997b, p 22) a changing relationship with users, with AnchorCall "moving closer to being a community care service" (p 15) and monitoring and response centre staff being in more frequent contact with carers and social welfare organisations.

Private and voluntary sector perspectives

Probably less than 20 private social alarm services operate in England and Wales. These vary in their character and distribution some being largely reliant on service users with carephones. A few owe their existence to local authorities having chosen to contract out their social alarm services and are providing a service, therefore, to both individuals and older people living in sheltered housing.

Notable is that some private sector services offer more than just a response service via nominated contacts, at least within designated geographical areas.

This reflects the fact that social alarms, for at least some private sector providers, are essentially social welfare services and are an important element within a broader range of care services by which users can call for assistance with going to the toilet, dressing and other routine tasks. In so doing, private sector social alarm services in Great Britain are in an important respect, developing in ways that echo some practice in North America (see Chapter Eight).

The experience of private sector social alarm service providers is very different from that of local authorities or housing associations because of the general absence of any public subsidy either to help with set-up or operational costs. Several services have been set up but subsequently closed as a consequence of being unable to generate sufficient revenue income within a short time. The fact that many local authority services are subsidised was noted earlier in this chapter.

Those private social alarm companies set up more recently as a consequence of successfully bidding to manage services contracted out by local authorities, especially where this includes management of an existing response centre, are likely to fare better by virtue of having, almost instantaneously, a critical mass of users and a guaranteed income.

AGE CONCERN (AID-CALL)[3]

There is one major voluntary sector social alarm service in Great Britain. It is provided by Age Concern England and took over from the pre-existing private Aid-Call service. It now operates as a not-for-profit trading company alongside the national charity.

Aid-Call was, for a considerable period, the largest of the private sector social alarm services. It regularly advertised in the national press, notably in the colour supplements of Sunday newspapers. In the late 1990s the company employed sales staff on a commission-only basis. This helped to generate sales of about 1,200 carephones each year.

The manner in which the Aid-Call service marketed itself was open to criticism. It relied heavily on the portrayal of older people in a very negative way. Their literature and advertisements, aimed both at potential users themselves and at their carers and relatives, regularly featured an older woman lying on the floor after some kind of accident, fall or seizure (see Plate 1.1, p 2). Some 60 per cent of responses to advertisements came from younger relatives of older people, but such enquiries were only responsible for about a third of sales.

Expansion of the Aid-Call service was assisted by the provision of services to local authority and housing association clients and by service acquisition. By the time of it being bought out by Age Concern England in the mid-1990s, Aid-Call had expanded to serve some 25,000 households including tenants of several councils. Some 2,000 new service users were linked when Age Concern arranged for their customers to be transferred from over 30 other monitoring and response centres. By 1997 it had grown to 27,000 and the annual number of new users had increased to 5,000.

SURECARE[4]

SureCare is an example of a smaller private service provider. Established in the early 1990s, this service buys in the support of the Merseyside NHS Trust to operate its monitoring and response centre in Chester, thereby obviating the need, associated with many such monitoring and response centres, for separate provision of a facility with staff dedicated to the social alarm service.

This, it may be considered, has the disadvantage that the staff who respond to calls have been trained in a somewhat different context and not unnaturally, tend to regard the purpose of the social alarm service as facilitating a response to medical emergencies. They may be less inclined to develop the kind of social relationships that are often a hallmark of other services. As a consequence, there is the management advantage to the service provider that users, conscious of the service's particular focus, are less likely to use it for social reasons and may even be disinclined to use it in circumstances such as getting stuck or fear of break-ins. Both may be stressful but may be perceived as outside the remit of the service.

On the other hand, the location of the monitoring and response centre anchors the service within a medical context and has the benefit of ensuring the immediate availability of medical help through ambulance staff and/or paramedics and, where appropriate, on-line qualified medical advice. The user, in other words, gets the benefit of a direct link to an important service, whose role is central to the purpose and operation of every social alarm service, without having to go through an intermediary.

The medical orientation of the service is clear from SureCare's literature, which also bears the ambulance service logo. Like Age Concern/Aid-Call, the marketing has in part been aimed at sons and daughters and the service can be criticised for having used somewhat negative images of older people. The message from their literature is:

> If you live alone, are retired, need specialist medical supervision, or have elderly parents, the SureCare home monitoring system will bring you complete peace of mind....The SureCare system provides a vital communication link between the home, your family and neighbours, and the medical services.

And, it points out, that the response centre is "run by the Ambulance Service and manned by trained ambulance staff".

SureCare has a relatively small customer base but steadily expanded by virtue of winning modestly sized contracts to monitor individual users and households in grouped dwellings for a number of social services authorities. The company has, furthermore, widened its remit through also managing domiciliary care services.

Thanks to its regular advertising and the link with Age Concern, no other private sector social alarm service was as well known as Aid-Call, although now a few have comparable customer bases. Peverel Careline, for instance, is a service that operates from Hampshire and has specialised on providing out of hours cover for housing association sheltered housing schemes. Like Aid-Call, their customer base increased through service acquisition.

Discussion

The development of most social alarm services in England and Wales followed the housing route. The sometimes heated discussions and debates that had taken place in the 1980s about the role of social alarms are now over. Social alarms may not have established a focal place within frameworks of social welfare services but they certainly had proved their worth in terms of providing cover for sheltered housing wardens and bringing about commensurate cost savings. Some, like Oldham, established mobile warden services to provide cover when resident wardens were off duty. Others went so far as to dispense with resident wardens altogether.

Some social alarm services established within local authority housing departments have become more entrenched, with the authorities in question extending the role of their services to monitor for various out of hours functions. Most notable among these have been repairs reporting for council tenants. Several authorities, furthermore, have provided such services for other authorities and for housing associations, especially where the latter were locally based.

The typical social alarm service has become one, therefore, which while largely true to its housing roots, manifests a wide variety in the roles played. Despite any arguments that might have been put in favour of a transition to a more social welfare orientation, diversification has enabled most housing-based services to argue their value more widely than simply providing cover for wardens. They have become multi-purpose services within which social alarms are just one, albeit important, part. A question that arises now is the extent to which such diversification may have jeopardised, at least in some places, the social alarm function in thwarting development of a more social welfare oriented service; creating conflicts regarding service priorities; and placing unreasonable demands on staff responsible for service operation.

Contrasting positions are, for instance, clearly evident between the service at Oldham and that at Telford and Wrekin. The Oldham Helpline service is continuing to develop a social welfare role with the authority seeing the service as integral to packages of care and support responding to the assessed needs of older people and others. This was and remains assisted by Oldham being a unitary authority. Wrekin Link, by contrast, remains a multifaceted service within which the social alarm function may be less able to develop. The AnchorCall and Places for People services stand outside such frameworks and enjoy greater freedoms to develop. Both, however, have remained fairly focused on their own sheltered housing.

More interesting, perhaps, are the private sector services and those linked to voluntary organisations. Here it is clear that the intention is to continue developing a strongly social welfare orientation that responds to assessed needs as well as the demands of the market among older people who rent or purchase social alarms privately. The growth of private sector services has, however, been slow. This has largely been because of the difficulties that they have had in competing with local authority services.

The position is unlikely to change dramatically in the shorter term. The service operated by Age Concern, however, has a strong brand name by which it is able to market its wares. More than this, the charity is able to utilise volunteers to visit, install and remove carephones over extensive areas of Great Britain. The expansion of this service is, therefore, assured.

Notes

[1] Green, J. (1998) in paper to AGM of the Association of Social and Community Alarms Providers (ASAP).

[2] Correspondence with Paul Rushton and Vijay Oliver (Hyde Housing Association).

[3] Correspondence and meeting with Hugh Risebrow (BUPA Dental).

[4] Correspondence and meetings with John Ford (Surecare).

SIX

Social alarms in Scotland

Overview

As noted in Chapter Four, many social alarm services managed by Scottish local authorities are distinguished by the extent to which social work departments were instrumental in their establishment. This is despite social alarms in Scotland sharing, with the rest of Great Britain, their provenance in sheltered housing. The fact, however, that resident wardens in sheltered housing schemes were generally paid for or subsidised by the social work authorities meant that those authorities had greater influence.

The earliest social alarm services in Scotland were those of East Lothian and Central Regional Councils, both social work authorities. Both used non-speech radio equipment. They were, therefore, part of that early raft of pioneers that included Stockport and Oldham south of the border.

EAST LOTHIAN COUNCIL

The East Lothian service commenced in 1979, served the City of Edinburgh and was supported by funding from the Lothian Health Board (Duncan, 1988, s 7.1). Like that in Stockport, it was not intended to give cover to sheltered housing schemes managed by the council, but rather was to be focused on the needs of others, essentially older people in the wider community.

While it had a remit to serve both older and younger people with support needs, the Lothian service grew only slowly. Just 300 users were linked in 1988. Keys were in most cases held by mobile wardens who, together with a coordinator and clerical assistant, managed the service. Management was later vested in a monitoring and response centre facility operated jointly with Midlothian Council. By 1996 this had grown to serve the needs of 2,150 users with carephones and to provide an out of hours service to 350 sheltered housing tenants (Dick and Pomfret, 1996, Appendix).

(FORMER) CENTRAL REGIONAL COUNCIL

Better documented and evaluated than the East Lothian service is the Mobile Emergency Care Service (MECS), set up by the then Central Regional Council in 1980. This service had been particularly influenced by the English experience at Stockport (McWhirter, 1984, p 11).

From the outset, the challenge facing Central Region in setting up a service was substantial. The authority had responsibility for services to older people over a huge geographical area and experienced difficulties with regard to radio signal reception in some rural areas. But by the end of the first year of operation the social alarm service had linked 243 individual users (40 of whom benefited only over short periods, having subsequently died or moved). As well as individual users, 24 sheltered housing and four local housing association schemes within the region were linked (Cameron, 1979, p 8).

Important features of the scheme were its use of mobile wardens who, when not responding to alarm calls, were responsible for routine visits to users. As a consequence users became familiar with the staff that might attend in the event of the service being used. McWhirter (1987, p 244) pointed to the visits as serving to "establish rapport and to maintain and check their equipment". Cameron (1981, p 63) expanded on this theme, stating that:

> It is the social contact which the [mobile] warden can make with users that is the most important aspect of a service such as this. Someone who can spend more than the two minutes available to the Meals on Wheels driver will be of great benefit in reducing the social isolation of many 'at risk' elderly people.

Cameron noted (p 63) a "great overall improvement in the condition of many ... elderly users simply from the security that comes from knowing that help is only a button-push away".

It is important to consider the claims of McWhirter and Cameron in the broader context of social alarms, the issue of social contact being one which still safeguards the position of resident wardens, especially where the alternative is a system either without a mobile warden or where such mobile wardens have no responsibility for routine visits. Elsewhere (1982, p 15) Cameron pointed to visits as having the purpose of surveillance, stating that:

> As a minimum, fortnightly visits are made, many [users] are visited weekly, some as much as two or three times a day and during the night if necessary. If the client resists this then a once a month 'check of equipment' visit is made in order to gain such access.

The monitoring and response centre for the service was initially located at a hospital in Larbert where calls were handled by the telephone operators (Cameron, 1979, p 5), reflecting the interest of the health board and the fact that they had financially supported the setting up of the service (p 12). Eligibility for the service, excepting for those living in sheltered housing, was determined according to a joint social work/health board procedure as follows (p 13):

Priority was to be given to those who were aged 75 or over for whom there was some evidence of risk such as a history of falls, medical condition such as chest or heart trouble, etc. Some younger disabled people also came into this category. At the next priority level were those who were at risk by virtue of living alone or being left alone, or those elderly couples where the partner could not cope in a crisis.

The objectives, as well as providing 24-hour support to such users, were to help people live in their own homes 'for as long as possible'; to delay hospital admission; and to facilitate hospital discharge (McWhirter, 1987, p 244).

The health board's involvement and a generally high level of awareness of the scheme ensured the interest of local GPs. Some, it was noted, were initially resistant to the scheme fearing that it would generate more work (Cameron, 1982, p 13). In the event some 14 per cent of what were deemed genuine calls to the monitoring and response centre resulted in a GP being called, with a further 10 per cent resulting in requests for routine GP visits (McWhirter, 1984, p 21). The initial resistance of some GPs faded and a postal survey (with a remarkable 90 per cent response rate among the 147 GPs in the MECS area) found that 97 per cent considered that MECS had been useful in summoning emergency help, and with 87 per cent of them having requested an alarm device for one or more of their patients.

As noted in Chapter Three, McWhirter, who was senior registrar of the local health board, undertook a comprehensive evaluation of the service. He started by: (a) posing the fundamental question as to why there was an envisaged need for alarm systems; and (b) gathering whatever evidence was available regarding their application.

In answer to the question 'why the need for alarm systems?', McWhirter suggested (1984, p 32) that:

Any member of the population may become acutely ill, fall or have some other problem. However, the elderly are more likely to be placed in particular difficulties by such emergencies because (i) they are more likely to live on their own and to be isolated; (ii) they are more likely (than the general population) to suffer from acute problems like falls, cerebro-vascular accidents (strokes) and cardiac problems; and (iii) the mobility of the elderly is often poor which may create acute problems or restrict the elderly person from seeking help by themselves.

Unsurprising, but relevant nevertheless, is his emphasis on social alarms being able to respond to essentially medical emergencies. Moreover, he was clear in his assertion (p 43) that "it is obvious that alarm systems are only part of a package of services provided if the objective of helping the elderly to remain in their own homes is to be achieved".

He concluded (p 118) that "it is obvious that MECS has a very much broader function than responding to emergencies" and noted that the evidence pointed to the objectives concerned with giving 24-hour support and helping keep people in their own homes both being achieved. With regard to delaying hospital admissions he was, however, cautious, stating that "a number of indirect measures suggest that there may have been some achievement of this objective". McWhirter posed questions (p 245) about the reasons for what were deemed false calls and judged that "many people simply wanted human contact, or needed help for some simple task to which they would not admit". He suggested that for some users alarms gave rise to a false sense of security (p 247).

By the end of 1987 MECS had grown to cover 1,006 households dispersed in the community, 1,302 people in sheltered housing and 1,021 others in grouped housing (Duncan, 1988, s 6.1). The monitoring and response centre had moved to the Regional Council's offices and mobile wardens had been employed. Notable, by this time, was the acknowledgement that a radio-based system was not, on its own, adequate to meet the council's needs. New social alarm equipment to operate via the telephone network was therefore purchased and a planned withdrawal of the radio equipment took place.

By 1990 the service had been extended to cover most of the remoter areas within the region (Duncan, 1993, s 6.1). However, financial support from the health board had ceased. But with responsibility for the service remaining with the Regional Council, the emphasis continued to be on meeting social welfare objectives. By 1996, 2,200 households with dispersed alarms and 3,300 households in groups were covered (Dick and Pomfret, 1996, Appendix).

Significantly under the MECS scheme, some people with dementia were linked and activity monitoring devices were tested. This initiative was discussed by Macnaughtan (1997) and is further examined in Chapter Thirteen.

With local government reorganisation, the MECS service has been divided between its constituent authorities. As noted by Marshall (2001, p 134), however, the use of social alarms for people with dementia continued. Hence there has been ongoing provision of social alarms linked to certain sensors concerned with gas, smoke, temperature and outside door monitoring. Close links and collaborative working with health agencies have also been maintained.[1]

The wider Scottish picture

The interest generated in other Scottish authorities by the establishment of MECS in Central Region was substantial and as a consequence several sought to follow their example. There was, however, no rush. The pace of development was such that just one new Scottish service was established in each of the seven years from 1980 to 1986 (Duncan, 1993). The caution of authorities reflected:

- a desire to await and consider the outcomes of the Central Region initiative;
- a recognition of the high capital cost of equipment, this being added to where equipment in sheltered or amenity housing schemes might require replacement because of its incompatibility with that at the monitoring and response centre;
- concerns regarding likely additional costs of providing for the needs of users in rural areas;
- uncertainty as to whether or not mobile warden services were appropriate;
- the dilemma regarding the appropriateness of speech and/or non-speech systems and their implications for service management; and
- different views as to who (social work or housing authorities) should lead and finance such initiatives.

One of the services that emerged faced the biggest challenge of all with regard to serving a widely spread rural population, that of the Highland Regional Council.

HIGHLAND REGIONAL COUNCIL

By 1982 the then Highland Regional Council had established a speech-based service operating through the telephone network. The service, Highland Helpcall, became a further initiative against which other Scottish authorities could judge the potential of social alarms.

The need for a speech link and the use of the telephone to facilitate this had been envisaged by Highland Region from 1980 when initially giving consideration to the project (Sewel and Wybrow, 1985, p 17). The service was conceived as a social work project with social workers responsible for assessing eligibility for carephones. Of note was that the support of the Scottish Ambulance Service was obtained and as a consequence the monitoring and response service was operated from their headquarters at Inverness (p 15).

Symptomatic of the experimental nature of the initiative was the expectation that it would use what were described as "different levels" of equipment. One level envisaged a short-distance radio transmitter worn as a wristwatch or pendant device to signal the need for help to a "good neighbour" (Sewel and Wybrow, 1985, p 19). Another level required a telephone in the home of every user, enabling a signal to be sent to a monitoring and response centre and a speech channel opened. The response, where necessary, would be made by local nominated contacts and key-holders, that is, friends and relatives living nearby.

Difficulties arose in developing the service due to pressures on social work staff. As a consequence of this, responsibility for assessments of eligibility was transferred to the project supervisor and was adjudged in relation to information obtained from local medical and nursing professionals. By mid-1984 the service was providing for 450 users, 130 of whom lived in sheltered housing schemes (Sewel and Wybrow, 1985, p 25).

The successes of the scheme were beginning to be apparent through, among other things, documentation of the emergencies dealt with. Local-level equipment was, however, being replaced. For most users the service was also benefiting from a partnership with the Women's Royal Voluntary Service whose volunteers undertook monthly visits "to carry out a battery and equipment check and also to check that the client still understands the equipment and is using it in such a way that it would be readily available in the event of an emergency – i.e. the pendant or wrist-watch is being worn and not hung-up or put in a drawer and that pull cords are left hanging down" (Sewel and Wybrow, 1985, p 26).

By 1991 the Highland Helpcall service had expanded to cover 2,000 households (920 dispersed and 1,080 in grouped dwellings) and had been decentralised to 18 mini-centres that switched through to the Inverness headquarters out of hours. The mini-centres were based at local social work resource centres in residential homes for older people. Bilingual Scots Gaelic/English services had been established from those mini-centres in the Gaelic-speaking heartland.[2]

Over 2,000 households were linked by 1996, a few in remote areas without electricity. Some users on the island of Eigg, for instance, had carephones that were run off batteries charged by wind power. Volunteer involvement had remained high.[3]

The Strathclyde debate

The debates that took place about service configurations were exemplified by that involving the former Strathclyde Regional Council and its constituent housing authorities including Glasgow City. A working group chaired by the author of this book was established in 1983 to examine the issue. It reported on the technical inadequacies of the telephone-based speech systems that were being marketed at that time manifested in the inability of manufacturers to offer equipment that was compatible with more than a limited range of systems installed within sheltered housing schemes. The issue was discussed by Fisk (1984, p 23). He argued that authorities should "stand firm in their demand for equipment to conform to specific management briefs including the need to link economically to a range of warden alarm equipment".

Glasgow District Council, it should be noted, had 10 different types of warden call system installed in some 40 sheltered housing schemes and would have had to spend substantial sums in their replacement to effect compatibility with the monitoring and response centre equipment being then proffered. The same situation did not, however, apply to all other housing authorities within Strathclyde. There was, at the same time, a strong wish to develop a social alarm service that would reach those older people who did not live in sheltered housing.

Having considered the issues, Strathclyde Regional Council moved to develop a social alarm service in collaboration with both Motherwell and Glasgow District Councils, this retaining the notion of a comprehensive service that was part of a network of social welfare services and fitted in to existing networks

(FORMER) STRATHCLYDE REGIONAL COUNCIL

The Strathclyde Alert service commenced operation in 1985, with a number of housing authorities funding most capital items, especially the equipment at the monitoring and response centre. The social work authority funded revenue items, such as staffing at the monitoring and response centre and mobile wardens. There was no financial input from health boards.

By 1988 the service had extended to include over 2,000 users in five districts: Renfrew, Cunninghame and Cumnock and Doon Valley in addition to Glasgow City and Motherwell (Duncan, 1988, s 0.1). Five mobile warden response teams were operational. They carried out programmes of visits, the latter being regarded as adding (s 0.1) "a vital social element to the service, visiting people who may be isolated" and being "an occasion to check that the equipment is functioning correctly and to ensure that the user continues to understand how to operate the alarm. The general well-being of the user can also be monitored over time".

By 1993 the Strathclyde service had expanded to cover 16 of the 19 district councils within the region (Duncan, 1993, s 0.1). Crucially, however, Kilmarnock and Loudoun, Bearsden and Milngavie, and Glasgow District Council all set up their own social alarm services, justifying their actions by reference to both their particular management requirements for sheltered housing services and, in the case of Glasgow, the desire to provide a service that placed greater emphasis on home security.

The Glasgow initiative is particularly worthy of consideration in that it brought into focus the dilemma concerning social welfare and housing functions of social alarms. It followed a frustration that arose from the Regional Council's emphasis on users in the wider community to the possible exclusion of older people with similar needs who were living in sheltered and amenity housing.

GLASGOW CITY (FORMERLY DISTRICT) COUNCIL

The new social alarm service in Glasgow had the objective of providing an integrated housing service to 'special needs' groups and was to be installed in 30,000 dwellings over a three- to four-year period. Linking sheltered housing schemes was not a priority. Non-users, that is without a relevant need for a social alarm device, would therefore be living in a minority of dwellings. The broader purpose of the service was apparent when the standard facilities were considered. These comprised:

- ability to summon help by pulling a cord located in every room or a pendant worn around the neck;
- smoke detectors;
- temperature detector to prevent hypothermia;
- inactivity monitor; and
- intruder alarm.

The service was not established without a certain amount of acrimony. The Regional Council chair referred to discussions with Glasgow District Council where there was a feeling that the City was overemphasising their property management needs (*Glasgow Herald,* 24 January 1989). He affirmed that "We're anxious to keep the focus on people rather than on property", adding that "What Glasgow is talking about would not be compatible with what we already have and we're worried that Glasgow appears to be going its own way". The reasons for Glasgow going its own way were stated by the convenor of their housing committee as the functional limitations of equipment used by the Strathclyde Alert service, which did not meet the district council's specifications, and the unwillingness of the Regional Council to expand their service sufficiently quickly.

The dispute remained unresolved and the new Glasgow service went ahead. As well as for its emphasis on property management, the service is important because of the way that its management was originally configured. Like the Highland Regional Council service, this involved monitoring and response centres being operated, during working hours, by local offices. Housing officers would then respond as appropriate, making home visits if necessary. Out of hours, any calls would be taken at the main monitoring and response centre, which also operated as the location for receiving and accommodating homeless people, with mobile wardens attending where needed.

That users of the Glasgow service were generally satisfied with their social alarm service is clear from a survey undertaken by the Council (Glasgow City Council, 1993). As well as endeavouring to establish the extent of satisfaction, this survey explored use of the service in its first areas of operation, Anniesland and Drumchapel. The views of next of kin and emergency contacts as well as direct service users were sought. Some 2,000 dwellings had had alarms installed in these areas and from the one in five selected, 357 interviews were completed, representing an 81 per cent response rate (Glasgow City Council, 1993, p 6).

Evidence indicated the effectiveness with which the service was targeted at those with support needs, there being a higher proportion of respondents unable to undertake various tasks such as using public transport, getting in and out of bed or preparing a hot meal, than in the Scottish population as a whole (p 8). Over one in five had used the social alarm system in an emergency (p 19) with non-emergency use being dominated by calls where users informed the monitoring and response centre where they were going (p 21). Such notifications were essential for the system to operate as an intruder alarm in the absence of the user.

The telephone survey of 79 next of kin and/or emergency contacts found generally positive views about the service, but more than a quarter were unaware of their own status as nominated contacts (p 24). Sheltered housing schemes, though not initially part of the scheme, were increasingly linked as and when their warden call systems required replacement.

The Glasgow service was subsequently extended with some 7,000 to 9,000 households linked by the end of 1993 (Duncan, 1993). By 1996 this had risen to 13,000 and in 2002 to 14,000. At 2002 the service was provided free of charge to the City's local authority tenants and was being expanded to embrace more private sector users and people at risk of domestic violence.[4]

of support of family, friends and neighbours. It sought in addition, and with an eye to obtaining further funds, to bring about collaboration with the health board.

Later initiatives in Scotland

The choices and actions of other housing providers in Scotland were undoubtedly influenced by developments in the authorities featured above. The dilemmas encountered by Central and Highland Regions were relevant from the points of view of the merits of different technologies and the problems of serving very rural communities. The differences of view between Strathclyde Regional Council and Glasgow District brought into focus the dilemmas relating to property or social welfare perspectives on service provision. Relevant here, however, is the size and resources of both authorities, which enabled each to drive forward in ways that would ensure that their respective positions and their objectives for their social alarm services would be satisfied.

The role of health boards in relation to funding or accommodating social alarm monitoring and response centres has been noted for Central and Highland Regions. This role has been particularly apparent for the islands councils.

In the Orkney Isles the social alarm service, established in 1983, was mostly funded by the health board, with the response centre being based at the main hospital in Kirkwall (Duncan, 1988, s 2.1). Particular attention was given, in setting eligibility criteria, to ensuring the inclusion of those needing social alarms as part of respite care or for those recently discharged from hospital.

In the Shetland Isles as in Orkney the monitoring and response centre for the social alarm service, set up in 1987, was based at the main hospital. The health board and social work authority shared monitoring costs (Duncan, 1988, s 2.2). Both the services used telephone rather than radio links and used local named contacts to visit in the event of an emergency or other necessitous circumstances.

By 1993 the Orkney and Shetland services had expanded, based on their original patterns of provision. User numbers in the Orkney Isles had grown

COMHAIRLE NAN EILEAN SIAR (WESTERN ISLES COUNCIL)

For a decade the Western Isles remained the only Scottish authority without a social alarm service that operated via a monitoring and response centre. By the mid-1990s, however, some 60 older people had been provided with alarm devices that dialled directly to a sequence of responders (Dick and Pomfret, 1996, p 10). These direct dial devices were supplied and installed by the occupational therapy department of the local health board. A number of problems were, however, encountered. These included:[5]

- the lack of any guaranteed response with the equipment ringing round to each programmed number up to the limit of its call capacity;
- the inability of the equipment to relay the nature of calls when activated by virtue of frequent power cuts; and
- the necessity of people to respond for fear of emergency in the event of calls generated by power cuts.

The authority did establish a monitoring and response centre in 1997 under the auspices of their social work department. *Faire*, the name of the service, means watching in Scots Gaelic. Nine of the 11 staff at this time were bilingual Scots Gaelic/English speakers. Responses were made via nominated contacts, with the emergency services acting as a reserve.

As well as serving the needs of people assessed as potentially benefiting from a social alarm by social work professionals, monitoring was undertaken for the small number of sheltered housing schemes in the Western Isles. At 2000, 100 households in sheltered housing and other designated accommodation were served together with 550 households where carephones had been provided.

from 66 to 244 (Duncan, 1993, s 2.1). The number of users of the Shetland Isles service had increased in the same period from about 160 to 570 (s 2.2).

Housing association services in Scotland

Duncan (1993) noted five social alarm services that were operated by housing associations in Scotland in 1993. One of these was set up in the mid-1980s by Hanover (Scotland) with Kirk Care Housing Association, though responsibility for management was vested in the former. Bield Housing Association, which was to have been part of the same joint initiative, set up on their own (see below). A primary consideration in the establishment of each of these housing association services was to obviate the need for assistant wardens.[6]

At 2003 there are only two housing association social alarm services operating in Scotland, based in Glasgow and Edinburgh. Both operate throughout the country and primarily meet the needs of residents in housing association sheltered housing schemes, although there is a minority of users with carephones who may or may not live in housing association dwellings.

The overall picture of housing association activity in social alarms was documented by Duncan and Thwaites (1987). They noted, following initial activity by local authorities, the interest of some housing associations in setting up their own services which, together with those established by social work and housing authorities, would offer an "increasing diversity of schemes" (p 7) characterised by different kinds of response services. Most housing associations were, at that time, either linked to local authority services or were considering so doing.

The work of Duncan and Thwaites involved successive interviews with the same sample of tenants. These took place first in 1986 and then again after a six-month period in the spring of 1987 (Duncan and Thwaites, 1987, pp 22-3). The total sample included 113 households, some linked to the Strathclyde Regional Council Alert service, some to that of the Grampian Regional Council. Other interviews were undertaken with interested parties including wardens, volunteer responders and a good neighbour organiser.

The Duncan and Thwaites report was important for the guidance it gave to housing associations who, at that point, were often unsure as to the best course of action to take. Conclusions were drawn that might be interpreted as implicitly critical of the sheltered housing model in that they noted that allocation of tenants to the schemes bore little relationship to the need for an alarm service (p 33). Alarms were noted (p 47) as not influencing people's decisions to move to dwellings with such provision but most respondents testified to a greater sense of confidence since knowing they had 24-hour alarm cover.

BIELD HOUSING ASSOCIATION

In 1993 the Bield Housing Association service, BCAS (Bield Community Alarm Service), linked 4,820 households including residents in developments managed by some 15 other housing associations. The service was set up in mid-1988 with objectives that included:

- improving cost effectiveness;
- improving services to tenants;
- giving 24-hour a day cover to their sheltered housing schemes; and
- giving cover to amenity housing schemes and those in other non-sheltered dwellings.

By 1991 there were 3,700 households linked. As in the Barnsley service in England, different sets of receiving equipment were used because incompatibility problems were experienced. The sets, however, were linked to a single computerised database.

A postal survey of service users found emergency use of the social alarm had been made by approximately a quarter of respondents, this either resulting in connection to the sheltered housing warden or to the BCAS response centre (Rosenburg and Wang, 1992, p 64). Remarkably the survey found that there had been a decline in the proportion of respondents (in comparison to a similar survey in 1986) who had experienced an emergency "in the previous year" (Rosenburg and Wang, 1992, p 63). This was ascribed to the "general improvement in mobility and fitness within the tenant population."

Notable also (p 64) was the extent to which the alarm was not used in some emergencies – in almost half of emergency events, service users telephoned the doctor directly. Of concern to the association was the fact that, for tenants who had lived in Bield Housing Association schemes both before and after the advent of BCAS, a proportion felt that the overall quality of service had declined. Over a third of respondents said that the reductions in warden's hours had made the service worse (p 65).

Other notable findings of the report (pp 48, 50-1) were that just 20 of the 54 tenants who were provided with pendant triggers were wearing them at the time of their interview.

Other Scottish services

As with the local authority services noted above, others had some health board support. In Angus, for instance, a contribution was made towards capital costs of their radio-based system, with the monitoring and response centre being housed in the ambulance service headquarters in Dundee (Edward, 1989, pp 97, 99). That such support sometimes coincided with concerns about meeting the needs of a dispersed rural population has been mentioned. But for part of Scotland, especially in the central belt linking the Clyde and Forth valleys, rurality is not a major issue. Furthermore, population levels are such that the greater number of sheltered housing schemes made it more likely that housing authorities would develop social alarm services for management reasons. A number of social alarm services managed by housing authorities and associations were, therefore, established in this area.

The position in Glasgow has already been discussed. The social alarm service developed by Edinburgh District Council, established in 1983, is also worthy of attention because of that authority's original insistence that the equipment should, as noted in Chapter Four, meet a requirement that included an activity monitoring capability (Duncan, 1988, s 7.3). Remarkable, in addition, in relation to the technology developed for and used in Edinburgh is the commercial intent that was associated with its development. European patents were taken out for the technology whose development had cost some £500,000 (*Glasgow Herald*, 4 March 1986). It was stated that the equipment "could soon be in use by housing authorities in Europe", with housing directors from the continent being invited to see the technology in operation. This optimism proved unfounded, with the manufacturer concerned withdrawing from the field.

Few private social alarm services in Scotland have been developed. Some, such as Community Careline in Lanarkshire, removed social alarms from a wider portfolio of their services. The indication is that private services in Scotland have been consistently unable to compete with those established by local authorities and housing associations.

Discussion

It is clear from the above that the initial impetus for the development of local authority social alarm services in Scotland was with the social work authorities. This then shifted so that a similar number of services, particularly in the Central Belt, were developed by housing authorities. The reasons for this shift have been well documented and in part followed the strong housing orientation of services in England and Wales.

More recently, however, the position may be changing. What appeared to be some kind of balance between social welfare and housing interests may be shifting back to the earlier position. This is reflected in the strengthening emphasis on what Dick and Pomfret termed welfare services (Dick and Pomfret, 1996, p 11). Hence, of the 17 full-time monitoring and response centres operative in 1996, 10 were managed by the social work departments of the authorities concerned (Dick and Pomfret, 1996, p 4). Notable, relating to these, was the number and proportion of social alarm users who had carephones.

Dick and Pomfret also commented on the increasing predisposition of social alarm services to embrace people who were not elderly but had a support need. Respondents to their survey of service providers (pp 7-8) reported on the inclusion of people with learning difficulties, mental health problems, terminal conditions and degenerative illnesses, vulnerable single mothers and people at risk of domestic violence.

There are, however, different perspectives on the issue of service orientations. It has, for instance, been claimed by one housing association service provider that a somewhat narrow service ethos concerned with assessment characterises the approach of at least some social work authorities. As a consequence, they may be paying too little regard to the wider role of social alarms in providing reassurance and associated benefits to people who do not need or do not want formal packages of care.[7] Nevertheless, the pointers are such that social alarm services provided by local authorities in Scotland will increasingly address social welfare issues. The involvement, albeit peripherally and only for some services, of health boards and ambulance services suggests that they are, furthermore, well poised to adjust to agendas relating to medical care and healthcare at home. Such developments are discussed in Chapter Twelve.

The distinctive character of Scottish social alarm services that was signalled in the earliest period of their development has been maintained. The involvement of social work authorities as the main service providers has ensured a strong social welfare ethos. This is reflected in the number of carephone users as opposed to those with call systems. The former, by 1996, totalled nearly 49,500 and the latter some 30,000, suggesting around 80,000 users in Scotland overall (Dick and Pomfret, 1996, Appendix).

Notes

[1] Correspondence with Linda Macpherson (Falkirk MECS).

[2] McLeod, F. (1989) in paper to seminar on social alarms, The Planning Exchange, Glasgow.

[3] Piper, C. (1996) in paper to conference on social alarms, Torquay.

[4] Community Care Bulletin 190A (1996), Nuffield Centre for Community Care Studies, University of Glasgow and correspondence with Dave Buckner (Glasgow Housing Alarms Service).

[5] Correspondence with Ian MacPherson (Faire Community Alarm Service).

[6] Conversation with David Gordon (Hanover Scotland Housing Association).

[7] As above.

SEVEN

Social alarms in Ireland

Introduction

This chapter details the position of social alarms in Ireland, covering both the Republic of Ireland and Northern Ireland. Social alarm services in each have different characteristics that reflect the respective perspectives on housing, social welfare, healthcare and security matters, and are partly determined by the extent of state subsidies and the agencies through which those subsidies are channelled. Almost all social alarm services, however, operate via nominated contacts, that is without the use of paid response staff such as mobile wardens. Social alarm services in the Republic, furthermore, appear to be unique when considered in relation to services in all other countries in the relatively narrow emphasis placed on security.

The differences in broader policy frameworks reflect, of course, the concerns, priorities and views of the governments of the United Kingdom and the Republic of Ireland. For Northern Ireland, therefore, there is much in common with the three countries of Great Britain, albeit that there are variations in administrative frameworks and the responsibilities of local authorities. In Northern Ireland there are joint health and social services authorities. This, it might be considered, could result in greater attention being given to healthcare agendas when endeavours are made to develop the potential of social alarms, but that it is not notably the case reflects a shared perspective with the rest of the United Kingdom whereby social alarms have tended to be promoted by housing rather than social welfare agencies. In the case of Northern Ireland, however, the main developments of social alarm services resulted from housing association, rather than local authority, initiatives. They took place in a context where the provision of social housing has not, since 1971, been a responsibility of local authorities.

Statutory services relating to the needs of older people in the Republic of Ireland are less well developed. Local authorities are providers of social housing at a modest level when compared with Great Britain, with the amount of provision being substantially diminished by virtue of high numbers of sales to tenants. But the heritage of social welfare services has much in common with Great Britain and is characterised by a widespread provision of institutional care. A vital need to extend community services has, however, been recognised (Crosby, 1993, p 136).

The development of particular forms of housing for older people in the Republic has tended to follow the approach in Great Britain and Northern

Ireland insofar as the main model adopted as an alternative to residential care is that of sheltered housing. Such housing is normally provided with social alarm systems, albeit they are often not linked to a remote monitoring and response centre. The level of provision of sheltered housing is relatively low and what has been provided is due to the activities of just some local authorities and a selection of voluntary bodies.

As with Northern Ireland, both social welfare and health functions in the Republic are undertaken by joint health boards. On the social welfare side of things the needs of older people in the Republic may not be very well catered for. Concerns regarding this were well explored by Ruddle et al (1998) in their review of a nationwide policy framework that promised much more. In the words of Power (1993, p 291) there was an "innovative and ambitious programme of housing for the elderly" introduced in 1987 which promised more than it delivered. What is more, Power noted (p 291) that this programme sought to integrate older people within communities in order to "avoid any hint of segregation".

Ruddle et al (1998, p 4) a few years later lamented, in relation to a range of unfulfilled service objectives, that "the legislative framework has not been created, and in general services for older people are still provided on a discretionary basis". To try to redress matters they went on to point to (p 9) the need for a duty to be placed on local authorities and/or health boards to provide such services as home help, meals on wheels, day care, respite care and sheltered housing.

Northern Ireland

In Northern Ireland, in contrast to the position in Great Britain (examined in Chapters Five and Six), the rate of development of social alarm services was relatively slow. This reflected the different local government context (noted above) and was partly a consequence of housing powers being transferred from local authorities to the Northern Ireland Housing Executive (the Executive).

The circumstances of this transfer related to the civil disturbances of that time. The focus of some of the resentments and fears that led to those disturbances followed discrimination in housing allocations and in access to public sector housing – hence the perceived need to bring housing under the aegis of a single agency (Boal, 1995, p 50). But after the formation of the Executive the Troubles, as they had become known, intensified and the issues relating to allocations became one of a broader range of concerns about remedying poor housing conditions and providing accommodation for people from both communities who were being displaced through violence and intimidation (see Maginnis, 1991). For such reasons it is understandable that little attention was given to social alarms.

This, together with the reference point offered by Scotland, might have helped sustain the initial view of the Executive that social alarms were a matter for the welfare authorities, not housing. Having said this, the Executive did manage some sheltered housing schemes, the demand for which almost certainly increased during the Troubles on account of the fears of older people in or close to those communities most affected.

Given the geographical proximity of Northern Ireland to Scotland and its similar mix of urban and rural areas it was perhaps natural, therefore, that ideas about service development would focus on health and social welfare rather than housing needs, although investigations were made by the Executive into the nature of social alarm service provision in England.[1]

Interestingly, and reflecting both the rurality of much of Northern Ireland and concerns regarding security, the notion of developing a service with a mobile warden facility was not countenanced. Some interest was, however, shown in the idea of supporting a charitable organisation, Age Concern, who would operate a monitoring and response centre were one to be established.[2]

The first attempt at setting up a social alarm initiative in Northern Ireland was by the Northern Health and Social Services Board. This planned radio-based service had a commitment of support from the Executive. It stumbled, however, by virtue of difficulties encountered in obtaining approvals from the Home Office for the use of radio frequencies and problems with the supply of the necessary hardware. The system was to operate without speech since in the early 1980s no manufacturer was seen as being able to provide adequate radio signal transmission over a minimum of 10 miles without recourse to cables or landlines.[3]

But while there were difficulties in developing a social alarm service with a primarily social welfare orientation, this was not the case for housing associations who, with their representative body, the Northern Ireland Federation of Housing Associations, decided to develop a service. The objective was, however, only loosely concerned with social welfare issues since it was primarily aimed at providing cover for wardens in the sheltered housing schemes of their member associations. This initiative resulted in the establishment of the James Butcher Helpline. The approach often taken by housing authorities in Great Britain (as discussed in Chapters Five and Six) was, in other words, pursued.

JAMES BUTCHER (NOW OAKLEE) HOUSING ASSOCIATION

The James Butcher Helpline was established in 1983. It was located in Belfast and benefited from the support of the Department of the Environment (Northern Ireland) as well as that of the Northern Ireland Federation of Housing Associations. It was managed by the James Butcher, now Oaklee, Housing Association and quickly grew to cover many of the approximately 3,000 dwellings within sheltered housing schemes throughout Northern Ireland. The service supported seven housing associations in all. Responses to calls were made via scheme-based wardens and/or nominated contacts. By 1993 the James Butcher Helpline linked 4,700 households in sheltered housing schemes.

As the technologies developed to include carephones, and with security as well as broader welfare considerations in mind, the James Butcher Helpline engaged in a joint initiative with Help the Aged (Northern Ireland) to provide a service to "particular tenants living near interface areas in Belfast" (Northern Ireland Housing Executive/Northern Ireland Federation of Housing Associations, 1993, p 23). This was in order to provide "a lifeline to elderly people, living alone, who feel at risk because they live in particular sectarian interface areas in Belfast".[4]

By 1995 most housing associations in Northern Ireland were served by the James Butcher Helpline. The service had extended, mainly as a result of working with Help the Aged (Northern Ireland), to include 5,000 households in the wider community in addition to 6,000 in sheltered housing. Help the Aged had, it should be noted, been particularly active in Northern Ireland in providing carephones (Tout, 1996, p 25). Some users were provided with an activity monitoring facility consisting of pressure mats and/or infrared detectors, the latter also acting as an intruder alarm.[5]

Further development of the James Butcher Helpline service was facilitated as a result of sales and marketing being assigned to Aid-Call, the private service based in England. Aid-Call (see Chapter Five) was later taken over by Age Concern Enterprises, a trading arm of the charity Age Concern.

In May 1999 the James Butcher Helpline ceased operation. Users of the service at that date were transferred to Aid-Call's own monitoring and response centre in England. Some 1,000 individual users who had been linked from the Republic of Ireland were transferred to the Eircom (Irish Telecom) service. At the time of closure, the James Butcher Helpline had grown to serve over 14,000 households.

FOLD HOUSING ASSOCIATION/HELP THE AGED (NORTHERN IRELAND)

Fold Housing Association and Help the Aged (Northern Ireland) split from the James Butcher Helpline in 1993 to set up Fold Help Careline. Fold Housing Association was, and remains, one of Northern Ireland's largest housing providers (the largest being the Executive). Fold Help Careline now serves about 16,500 households, mostly with carephones, many provided by Help the Aged (Northern Ireland). Over 1,000 households are linked from the Republic of Ireland including those managed by the CallCare (Ireland) service. The Fold Help Careline service with Help the Aged (Northern Ireland) is a partner to CallCare (Ireland), a service operating from the Republic border town of Clones, County Monaghan (discussed below).

Fold Help Careline benefited from the closure of the James Butcher Helpline in terms of the transfer of several corporate, mainly housing association, customers. It was left as the only service in Northern Ireland not within the private sector. In little more than 18 months, the number of households linked to the Fold Help Careline almost doubled from the 8,400 served in 1998.

Other social alarm services in Northern Ireland are all in the private sector. They operate as adjuncts to primarily security services. One is based in Newry and is understood to serve some 2,000 households including clients of the Newry and Mourne Health and Social Services Board.

Discussion

The particular circumstances in Northern Ireland have meant overall that today's social alarm services are less tied to housing than might otherwise be the case. They are, therefore, dissimilar to their counterparts in England and Wales. By virtue of the higher proportion of carephone users they are, arguably, better positioned to respond to social welfare and healthcare agendas. Both Age Concern and, more emphatically, Help the Aged (Northern Ireland) helped promote the use of carephones and to nurture, therefore, the development of social alarms in Northern Ireland. Indeed, between 1987 and 1996 Help the Aged were responsible for the provision of some 5,000 carephones in the Province (Tout, 1996, pp 24–5). Their work was, and remains, supported by volunteer visitors who assessed need and also were able to "counsel, install alarms and give continuing guidance" (p 25).

Some 24,500 people representing about 10 per cent of older people in Northern Ireland are estimated to have social alarms.

Republic of Ireland

In the Republic, in contrast to Northern Ireland, most social alarm services are in the private sector. The exception is the service operated by Dublin Corporation. The proportion of older people linked to such services is, however, less than Northern Ireland. Some 30,000 people, representing about 6 per cent of older people in the population of the Republic, are estimated to have social alarms.

The reason for the lower usage of social alarms in the Republic when compared to Northern Ireland lies in a combination of factors:

- the late development of a specific interest by local authorities in the housing needs of older people and the lack of widespread development of sheltered housing (O'Connor et al, 1989, p 63ff; Garavan et al, 2001, p 49);
- the lack of any factual assessment nationally of housing needs of older people and ipso facto any consideration of the potential role of alarms (Ruddle et al, 1998, p 129);
- the low ownership of telephones in many rural areas (Power, 1979, pp 72-3);
- the poor development and limited availability of domiciliary support services within which social alarms might be included (Working Party on Services for the Elderly, 1988, p 80; Garavan et al, 2001, p 33);

- the fragmentation of housing and support service providers and the inclusion of a contribution by voluntary organisations (National Council for the Aged, 1985, p 41; O'Connor et al, 1989, p 63); and
- the failure to implement a clear statutory framework within which social alarms might be seen as having a role (Ruddle et al, 1998, p 4).

The first social alarm service established in the Republic was at Wexford in the early 1980s. This linked 13 older people who lived alone, by radio, to receiving equipment installed in the local general hospital (National Council for the Aged, 1985, pp 61-2). The hospital and nominated contacts held keys in order to facilitate a response in the event of the alarm being activated.

The users had portable devices with which to activate the alarm. Some also had a timer-based passive alarm facility that they cancelled each morning and night. For half, however, the passive alarm facility was disconnected because they were allegedly "unable to cope with it" (O'Connor et al, 1989, p 58). This service later ceased operation with the users being transferred to what has become the Republic of Ireland's largest private sector service, Emergency Response, based at Bunclody, County Wexford (see below).

DUBLIN CORPORATION

The first social alarm service of any size in the Republic of Ireland was established by Dublin Corporation in 1984. This linked the corporation's sheltered housing schemes via the telephone network to what was described as an aid centre "supplied and manned by a commercial firm" (National Council for the Aged, 1985, p 61). The system cost £300 per household, this high price being "one of the major drawbacks of the system" (National Council for the Aged, 1985, p 61). Subsequently O'Connor et al (1989, p 74) noted that the Dublin Corporation social alarm service linked 15 of its sheltered housing schemes after their bell and buzzer systems had been replaced by what the National Council for the Aged (1985, p 61) then described as "sophisticated talk-back systems".

By 1999, 60 sheltered housing schemes comprising over 3,000 dwellings had been included, enabling Dublin Corporation to replace most resident wardens with community wardens. The remit of the community wardens included visits to sheltered housing tenants with each of them covering some 120 or more households. Responses to emergency calls were made through nominated contacts. No charge was levied on the corporation's tenants for the service.

A broader overview

The earliest report that provided information about social alarm services in the Republic of Ireland (National Council for the Aged, 1985) placed them within a broader overview of older people's housing and noted related security issues. It recommended (p 62) that research be carried out regarding the potential of social alarms and that health boards should work with local authorities and the Garda Siochána (the Irish police force) to examine their merits. The context was one where there was growing interest in such technologies but uncertainty as to their potential role and likely benefits. Indeed, Telecom Eireann (now Eircom) was reported to be developing a system to help older and disabled people to summon help "without the need to lift a telephone" using a portable transmitter and/or sensors placed by doors and windows (National Council for the Aged, 1985, p 60).

These initiatives signalled a consciousness of the role of such technologies as being important for personal security and responded to concerns about the vulnerability of older people to crime rather than medical emergencies. The National Council for the Aged (1985, p 60) noted that a powerful rationale for the provision of social alarms related to the fear among older people "of being attacked in their own homes and not being able to call for help". This followed both particular and well-publicised incidents and reports that highlighted the isolation of many older people, especially in rural areas.

The vulnerability of older people living alone became a regular theme in discussions of social alarms. It helped to stimulate a comprehensive research report that documented possibilities for social alarm service development (O'Connor et al, 1986). This report had a remit to explore "the application of new technology to the development of suitable communications networks for urban and rural elderly" people (p 9). The stimulus for the research was noted (p 20) as relating to "some particularly alarming cases of burglary and assault in rural Ireland in the winter of 1984".

Media attention may, however, have resulted in fears being unduly raised among older people. (O'Connor et al, 1986, p 14) reported on the range of needs that they expressed. These included:

- social contact;
- needs arising out of medical emergencies;
- personal and environmental accidents;
- breaches of security; and
- the after-effects of breaches of security.

A study involving one of the report's authors on the needs of older people in rural areas was quoted, this concluding (p 16) that "fears about security are primary and that a second, much less common fear, is about health, specifically of not being able to care for oneself due to illness or disability". Fear of break-ins was noted (p 24) as affecting the willingness of older people to go out, be it locally or on holiday. Such fears were, they considered, instrumental in reducing the amount or frequency of social contact.

In signalling the role of social alarms in the medical context the report stated that "of the emergency services there is a general consensus that the ambulance service is the most appropriate to respond to elderly alarms *(sic)*. The Gardai do not want to assume this role other than possibly as a back up service when other contacts cannot be reached" (O'Connor et al, 1986, pp 68-9). The omens for speedy development were, however, poor by virtue of the call for caution and the need to avoid ad hoc decision making (pp 50-1); and the invocation that it would be necessary to coordinate services across professional and departmental boundaries at local and national levels to ensure a comprehensive approach.

The report by O'Connor et al followed on from that of the National Council for the Aged (1985). Together the reports heralded a growing appreciation, among those professionals in the Republic of Ireland who were concerned for the welfare of older people, of the potential of social alarms to cover both security and healthcare needs. The ensuing *Years Ahead* report (Working Party on Services for the Elderly, 1988) helped a little in further pointing to the merits of social alarms (see Ruddle et al, 1998) but the recommendations of the O'Connor et al report were only taken up to a limited extent.

Nevertheless, most health boards in the Republic became involved with social alarms if only in a small way. In most cases, for instance, they now fund the provision of carephones to enable people to link to private services. One, the Eastern Health Board, set up its own small social alarm service operating for the benefit of 65 older people linked to a monitoring and response centre at St Vincent's Hospital, Athy (Ruddle et al, 1998, p 186). This no longer operates. The availability of free telephone rental for people aged over 65 and some tax concessions available on carephones also stimulated growth in their usage (Ruddle et al, 1998, p 187).

Today, the involvement of health boards in social alarms may, it is considered, increase as a result of the recommendation in the health promotion strategy developed by the Department of Health and Children (Brenner and Shelley, 1998, p 64). This argued the need for "provision and monitoring of telecommunication personal alert systems for use in medical and security emergencies". The *Years Ahead Review* (Ruddle et al, 1998, pp 185-6) of the same year noted that all health boards, at that time, had "undertaken some initiative in relation to alarm systems for older people, whether for medical emergencies or security reasons". But the authors exhibited some uncertainty as to how things should progress.

Most of the expansion in social alarm service provision in the Republic of Ireland has taken place in the private sector. And, in a way that cannot be overstated, it is the private sector social alarm services that have, over recent years, experienced a major boost because carephones have been included in the government's Scheme of Community Support for Older People (see below). This scheme provides 90 per cent subsidy towards the cost of such devices for eligible older people.

The Scheme of Community Support for Older People

The Scheme of Community Support for Older People was launched in 1996. Following the suggestion of a task force established to investigate security issues affecting older people, it linked to networks of locally based organisations established via the community alert and neighbourhood watch programmes (Task Force on Security for the Elderly, 1996, p 28).

The community alert programme had been launched by Muintir na Tire, that is locally based women's organisations. It was established to "stimulate community care and encourage low key neighbourly vigilance following recent attacks on the elderly". The neighbourhood watch scheme was established by the Garda Siochána to help crime reduction (O'Connor et al, 1986, pp 33-4).

Eligibility for help under the scheme was, and remains, restricted to people aged 65 or over and living alone or with others who are older people or "other dependent and vulnerable people *(sic)*". Assessment for eligibility is "supposed to take account of the vulnerability of the older person" but in practice it is not monitored (Fitzpatrick Associates, 1999, p 12).

Numerous agencies benefit from the scheme, often in relation to small sums of money. Apart from community alert and neighbourhood watch groups, Societies of St Vincent de Paul have featured quite strongly in the listings of beneficiaries. Social services agencies are also present. A dramatic increase in grants awarded to the charitable body, Security for the Elderly, is also notable in the period of the scheme's operation to 2001.

Social alarms were considered "to have counted for more than half the total spending" under the scheme in a review of the 1998 release of funds (Fitzpatrick Associates, 1999, p 14). There were, however, suggestions that outside of rural areas there was generally poor targeting and that the channelling of social alarms through community groups had resulted in a bias towards middle-class neighbourhoods. Differences in service accessibility between the poorest and wealthiest areas may, therefore, have been reinforced.

Other concerns were noted as:

- the lack of expertise of many local groups (Fitzpatrick Associates, 1999, p 26);
- the fact that, due to variable take-up, many areas of the country remained uncovered by the scheme (p 16);
- poor links with local authorities and health boards (p 27); and
- the lack of agreed standards for equipment (p 32).

Added to this, a total of over a £IRL million had gone to an organisation which had direct links to a private social alarm service, Emergency Response, whose income was substantially increased through their ability to levy monitoring charges on those for whom social alarms were provided.

Regardless of the above, the overall grants scheme in the Republic has achieved considerable success in the provision of social alarms through the Scheme of

Community Support for Older People. The provision of carephones will undoubtedly have given reassurance to many older people and will have been used, with appropriate responses having been made, in a number of emergencies. Indeed, a survey undertaken of users of the CallCare (Ireland) service (reported on later in this chapter) testifies to some such benefits.

There has, in addition, been the added value of stimulating community activity through the formation or refocusing of community groups and helping the achievement of broader regeneration objectives. Anecdotal information, however, suggests somewhat high drop-out rates where an alarm user decides not to or is unable to continue paying for a monitoring and response service after being provided with a carephone and after the initial monitoring period has expired.

As a means of beginning to overcome some of the shortcomings of the scheme the review pointed to the potential benefits of it being transferred in part or in whole to the Department of Children and Health (Fitzpatrick Associates, 1999, pp 40-1). Such a move, it was suggested, would make the scheme more proactive and could ensure better targeting, for instance, through the use or support of public health nurses. This has not taken place. But adjustments have been made to application forms for grant funding such that community groups are required to be specific about the criteria they propose to use in order to target those with the greatest needs.

It is also apposite to note that the Department of Social, Community and Family Affairs appears content to permit the purchase of different types of carephones, including direct dial devices. They have stated that they "are generally satisfied that [the] type of equipment sought is warranted ... the Department could not be seen to endorse the mandatory selection of 24 hour socially-monitored equipment where in fact small scale security devices may suffice".[6] They added that "it is the responsibility of the voluntary groups to ensure that equipment purchased conforms to national/international standards".

Private services

Overall, some 10 social alarm services exist in the Republic with about half operating their own monitoring and response centres. The largest by far is Emergency Response, which was operated in association with Cable and Wireless and the charity Victim Support.

The Emergency Response service had a particularly high profile, its founder being a former presidential candidate. By 2001 the service had 18,000 households linked, including those of the Cable and Wireless service (*Irish Times*, 19 November 1999). Users of the Emergency Response social alarm service were mainly older people, with the largest number of users living in the counties of Mayo, Galway, Dublin, Wexford, Waterford and Kilkenny.[7]

The service emphasis has clearly included personal security, but the extent to which a security emphasis will remain is an open question since the service was wholly acquired in 2001 by Tunstall Telecom.

Another private national service is Eircom's Medi System, with between

3,000 and 4,000 users. A sudden increase in the number of its users came about when, as noted earlier, customers of the Age Concern Aid–Call service were transferred from the James Butcher Helpline.

Other private services in the Republic of Ireland are smaller and probably serve anything from a few hundred to a few thousand households. Several do not have their own monitoring and response centre but buy that facility from another agency. Most have arisen and survive by virtue of links with local community alert and neighbourhood watch groups. An example of a new service in Dundalk is of interest by virtue of its medical focus and the incorporation of activity monitoring. It was set up under the auspices of the Dundalk Planning Partnership in 2001 and quickly grew to have some 30 users.

Crossing borders

The geography and social history of Ireland, together with the more recent establishment of increasing numbers of agencies linking the Republic with Northern Ireland, makes a cross-border perspective particularly pertinent. This is not, of course, to deny the importance of the different legislative and administrative frameworks that apply and have an impact on the configuration of social alarm services. There is, however, common cause. Agendas concerned with meeting the needs of older people are in essence the same, as are the opportunities arising through the development of technologies. An added aspect of that common cause relates, regrettably, to the shared experience of security problems. The security issue has been noted as one of the drivers for the promotion of social alarms, notably in the Republic.

Of particular interest, therefore, was the establishment of the CallCare (Ireland) social alarm service, insofar as it was conceived as specifically addressing the needs of older people in border areas and, perhaps, more at risk for security reasons. Any notion of supporting independent living in this context could be construed as having yet a further dimension to that normally encountered. Certainly, a difference in emphasis is apparent from services in Great Britain.

CALLCARE (IRELAND) LTD

CallCare (Ireland) Ltd operates in both the Republic and Northern Ireland. It was established in 1997 as a joint venture between Clones Development Society, Fold Help Careline, Help the Aged (Northern Ireland) and Helplink South (a private social alarms agency). Its establishment was assisted through financial support from Co-operation North, which became Co-operation Ireland, a body established to foster cross-border initiatives.

The intention was for CallCare (Ireland) to focus on serving the needs of older people in border areas. These included the six counties of the Province plus a further six counties in the Republic. The expertise of the partner agencies was to be used to help develop markets on both sides of the border. Apart from Clones Development Society, the parties to the venture all had prior interests in social alarms. Help the Aged (Northern Ireland) and Fold Housing Association jointly owned the Fold Help Careline, while Helplink South operated a social alarm service through Fold Help Careline. CallCare (Ireland), like Helplink South, was and remains contracted in to the latter.

An evaluation of the CallCare (Ireland) service was undertaken over the period from 1999 to 2000. This documented its growth and explored the nature of the markets within which it was being developed. It noted that service growth was particularly strong in the Republic but had taken place in a rather erratic manner due to the way that funds were released by the Department of Social, Community and Family Affairs (discussed earlier). Growth of the service in Northern Ireland was weaker and essentially confined to initiatives focused on the security of older people in County Fermanagh, that is that part of Northern Ireland closest to Clones. By January 2000, the CallCare (Ireland) service was being provided to 966 households, 62 of which were in County Fermanagh and most of the remainder in the counties of Cavan, Monaghan and Donegal.

As part of the evaluation a personal interview survey of 33 CallCare service users, both living north and south of the border, was undertaken in July 1999. This found that 27 respondents lived alone and nearly half (16) were aged 80 or over. Two thirds (21) of respondents lived in the Republic, mostly in County Monaghan. Over half (18) received some kind of support such as home care, home nursing or help with shopping. Four out of 10 (14) claimed to have become users through the activities of community alert groups, though the true number is certainly higher by virtue of such groups sometimes operating via a third party.

The community alert groups in question were in the counties of Cavan and Monaghan. The former users benefited from carephones as a result of the 1997 release of funds from the Department of Social, Community and Family Affairs and represented, therefore, early CallCare (Ireland) service users. The latter users benefited from carephones as a result of the 1998 and 1999 releases of funds.

Half (17) of the respondents lived in single-storey cottages or bungalows and most (20) were in rural areas. Over half (20) had lived in their present home for some 40 years or more, that is since 1960 or earlier. Six had lived in their present home since 1930 or earlier. The vast majority (30) were owner-occupiers.

For all but one this was their first experience of having a carephone. Six out of 10 at the time of interview had been linked to the CallCare (Ireland) service for more than a year. Only one respondent, who had experienced a heart attack when her daughter was present, had used the service in an emergency.

Of particular interest is that two thirds (21) of respondents indicated that they had a carephone at least in part at the behest of others, usually family members or a representative of a community alert group. A clear majority (28) however, cited reasons to do with living alone, peace of mind, security, health and/or fear of falls. The benefits stated of having a carephone were roughly equally divided between summoning help, peace of mind and security. All but one respondent felt confident about using the service if the need arose; and four out of five (27) felt confident or very confident about getting a prompt and efficient response.

Crucially, half (17) of respondents felt that having a carephone would or had enabled them to stay put for longer than would otherwise have been the case, although just three had been considering moving at the time they joined the service. The indications were, therefore, that the objective of supporting independent living was being satisfied. Respondents had difficulty in indicating any problems to do with carephones. Three did, however, recognise that a problem would arise if telephone lines were down; and five did not like the pendant transmitter device.

Worrying is the fact that nearly a third (11) of respondents claimed to have had no information about the CallCare (Ireland) service. Heartening is the fact that most of those who had had information were able to name the individuals who provided it. This showed that the service had managed a personal touch, at least in its formative period. Half (17) claimed to have read the written information they had on the service.

Discussion

The nature of social alarm services in Ireland has been shown to be different from that which characterises provision in Great Britain. Further differences have been noted, as would be expected, between Northern Ireland and the Republic. With regard to the Republic it is significant that most social alarm services are in the private sector and that they are profoundly affected by the framework of financial support administered by the Department of Social, Community and Family Affairs.

Also notable is the fact that social alarms in the Republic have developed in large part due to concerns about security. This emphasis probably makes the Republic unique among countries that have relatively high numbers of social alarm users. But as noted in the review by Fitzpatrick Associates (1999, p 34), no measurable reduction in crime can be attributed to the scheme. This simple statement, however, misses an essential point that relates to the broader benefit that might be attributed to social alarms in terms of providing reassurance.

The study by Garavan ct al (2001), furthermore, pointed to the fact that 89 per cent of older people living in the community felt safe or very safe. This finding emerged from personal interviews with over 900 older people split between the Eastern Regional Health Authority and Western Health Board areas. Out of these 177 (19 per cent) had the use of a "fully functioning personal alarm", presumably with pendant-type radio triggers, and clearly gave their users some reassurance. Garavan et al (2001, p 145) noted, however, following focus group discussions in which the role of such devices was considered, that "most described its usefulness in terms of obtaining help in the event of a medical emergency rather than for the purposes of safety *per se*".

In Northern Ireland private sector social alarm services are few in number and, in fact, provision is now dominated by one provider, Fold Help Careline. Although in many respects this service operates in a manner akin to those in Great Britain, it is distinctive because of its social welfare and security orientation. This different perspective arises through the influence of Help the Aged (Northern Ireland) and the particular focus that was directed at areas experiencing security problems during the period of the Troubles.

The cross-border service, CallCare (Ireland), in some ways synthesised the perspectives that characterise the Republic and Northern Ireland. The survey of users pointed to many of the purported objectives of the service having been at least to some extent fulfilled.

The foregoing suggests that social alarms in Ireland will continue along an evolutionary path that is somewhat different to that in Great Britain, with particular differences applying in the Republic. The most crucial question relates to the future of the Scheme of Community Support for Older People that operates in the Republic and whether a review of it, and a growing consciousness of the potential role of social alarms in relation to social welfare rather than security, will lead to that social welfare role being more strongly developed.

Notes

[1] Correspondence with Victor Blease (Northern Ireland Housing Executive).

[2] As above.

[3] As above.

[4] Correspondence with James, C. (Northern Ireland Housing Executive).

[5] McCandless, F. (1995) in paper to conference of the International Federation of Housing and Planning Conference, Belfast.

[6] Correspondence with Laura McKenna (Department of Social, Community and Family Affairs).

[7] Conversation with Derek Nally (Emergency Response).

EIGHT

Social alarms (PRS) in North America

Introduction

As noted in Chapter Four, the main difference in the evolutionary path for social alarms or personal response systems and services (PRS) in North America arises from the fact that their development was almost entirely a private sector phenomenon, with such services being promoted on the basis of cost savings in healthcare. This contrasts markedly with the position in Great Britain where, as was noted in Chapters Five and Six, development predominantly took place within the public sector and was concerned with housing and social welfare agendas.

This is not to suggest that there was no overlap or common ground between the respective experiences. Both, as with other developed countries, experimented with bell and buzzer systems in the context of different types of accommodation, such simple technologies becoming particularly commonplace in institutions. However, the ensuing paths were divergent.

In Canada, common ground has been evident mostly with the United States and relates to the fact that social alarms (PRS) were seen as relevant, at least in part, to private sector healthcare services. There is also, however, some common ground with Great Britain relating to the recognition that social alarms are also relevant to the needs of older people in public sector housing.

The Canadian context is one where there are relatively high levels of public sector housing provision in some areas. In 1992, for instance, there were 46,000 public sector dwellings for older people in the province of Ontario (Hobbs, 1992, p 24). PRS installations had at this time already been made in the context of healthcare facilities and nursing homes, reflecting the nature of developments in the United States. The Rainycrest Home for the Aged at Fort Frances, Ontario, for instance, had PRS installed in 1985 and was an early example of the use of such technologies in what was a typical setting. The service providers saw it as an addition to their programme of support for older people, which included homemaker services, transportation services and a 'call a day', and helped older people in an area stretching over a 150 km radius stay in their homes as long as possible (Ontario Ministry of Community and Social Services, 1986, p 3). This service is profiled below.

In the United States, early initiatives like those in Canada were generally small and localised. One, at Woodbury, some 30 miles east of the City of New

York, was described by Schantz (1992). This service, based at the United Presbyterian Nursing Home, was established in 1983 and was seen as central to their planned support outreach programme. In 1991 it had grown to embrace "over 1,300 active subscribers" (Schantz, 1992, p 229). The development of PRS in the United States and Canada is explored below.

Dibner's dream

That Andrew Dibner can be recognised as the creator of carephones and is the main claimant to having initiated social alarms (PRS) was noted in Chapter Four. The potential that the technologies offered demanded attention, albeit within somewhat specialist fields, hence a flurry of activity took place to evaluate Dibner's invention and to establish "if such systems could contribute to independent living while saving tax dollars" (Sherwood and Morris, 1981, p 1). There was, in other words, a powerful motivation on the part of governments to explore any means by which PRS could minimise the cost of care and support for older people that fell to them. The evaluators acknowledged this in the graphic language of their opening remarks, "Skyrocketing costs of nursing home care ..." (Sherwood and Morris, 1981, p 1).

Along with the imperative to save costs, however, the issue of independent living did receive attention and there was some consideration, albeit implicit, of the impact of such technologies on people's quality of life – notably with regard to their self-confidence. The concern of skyrocketing costs was, therefore, accompanied by a "concern for quality of life for older persons" (Sherwood and Morris, 1981, p 1). Elsewhere, Lerner and Stevens (1986) identified the potential additional role of PRS as security devices. They stated (p 2) that "These devices could play an important role as environmental and security alarm systems, although the size of this role and its effectiveness have yet to be fully explored".

The anticipated benefits of the technology for frail older people explored in the study by Sherwood and Morris were reflected in their choice of users. These numbered 551 in total and comprised "frail, functionally impaired, medically vulnerable elderly residents of public housing" (Sherwood and Morris, 1981, p 1); 234 of these were assigned to a control group and were not as a consequence provided with a carephone. About 30 per cent of the sample were aged over 80, the great majority being female (Ruchlin and Morris, 1981, p 71).

For the most part the technologies accorded with the commonplace pattern of equipment and service provision that later became evident for social alarm users in Great Britain. Distinctive in the United States, however, was the incorporation, as standard, of a passive monitoring facility using a timer, which could be used to send a digital signal to the monitoring and response centre. This then required the operators to telephone the user to establish if there was a problem and to alert responders in the event of an identified problem or there being no response. Systems operating in this way were at that time nonexistent in Great Britain and, as noted in Chapter Four, were seen (at least by housing service providers) as unnecessary in view of the presence of wardens.

The evaluation methodology used in the work of Sherwood and Morris (1981, pp 8-10, identified 157 comparable matched pairs of older people and followed their progress over three years towards four service goals:

- to help ensure that emergency services would be provided when necessary for health emergencies and environmental emergencies such as break-ins, fires, etc.;
- to reduce anxiety about living alone because of fear of medical and/or environmental emergencies;
- to help increase the likelihood of maintaining independent living; and
- to increase the person's willingness to extend him/herself to perform normal activities when alone.

Progress towards these goals was assessed for three target groups (Sherwood and Morris, 1901, p 4ff). These were older people who were severely functionally impaired and socially isolated; older people who were severely functionally impaired and not socially isolated; and older people who were medically vulnerable and/or moderately functionally impaired and socially isolated. The findings served to justify Dibner's dream in that they were generally positive or neutral in relation to the target groups for many of the goals stated.

Notable was the consistently positive outcome for Goal 1. This was reflected in users feeling more likely than the control group to be able to get help should the need arise (p 11). A reduction in anxiety (Goal 2), however, was only evident for those with severe functional impairments but who were not socially isolated. They, it was noted, were more likely to be generally satisfied with their living circumstances and life in general (p 11). Given the negative findings in relation to some anxiety measures for the others, the role of alarms in providing reassurance for users was, at least in this initial study, not established.

Feelings about independent living (Goal 3) were, as with Goal 2, more positive for those with severe functional impairments but not socially isolated, justifying the cautionary line taken elsewhere by Fisk (1989, p 117) that although "for most, it appears that alarms bring psychological benefit" there was, perhaps, a paradox that indicated that those in greatest need might be psychologically harmed. This was acknowledged by the evaluators who stated that (Sherwood and Morris, 1981, p 14):

> For the socially isolated person less in touch with the help system, this intervention may have been a shock, bringing them realistically in closer touch with helping resources but, at the same time, heightening their awareness of their medical vulnerability.

The finding was also signalled in later work in Baltimore by Lerner and Stevens (1986, pp 11-12) who noted that "socially isolated subscribers had ... an appreciable decline in their sense of mastery and an increasing feeling of vulnerability, fearing that their independence had been undermined".

As far as service costs were concerned there were substantial savings ($7.19 for each $1 spent on the service) for users with severe functional impairments but who were not socially isolated. There were, however, no net benefits or additional costs identified for the other groups (Sherwood and Morris, 1981, p 15). Savings, where evident, mostly derived from a reduction in the number of days spent in nursing homes for those who were provided with a carephone (Ruchlin and Morris, 1981, p 73). No value was ascribed to non-monetary benefits resulting from enhanced personal security (p 72).

The evaluation of this pilot resulted in a range of recommendations and suggestions from Sherwood and Morris (1981, pp 19-23) as to how PRS technologies and services might appropriately be configured. Much valuable knowledge was also gained regarding the nature of emergencies, as users as much as the evaluators explored their usefulness in relation to users' needs.

Encouraged by this generally favourable evaluation, Dibner set out to further develop and market his product. In so doing his company tapped a powerful stream of emotions that ran through an increasingly geographically mobile American society, which was concerned for growing numbers of older people perceived to be at risk. Part of the assessment of the market potential was facilitated by the organisation of an international symposium.

In the Forward to the book edited by Dibner (1992) that followed this symposium, it was stated (p ix) that:

> ... the Dibners were ahead of the times in several ways. When children at a distance contemplate the danger for a frail parent living alone, they understandably consider restricting the freedom of the parent in the interest of safety. The resulting restriction, sometimes leading to institutionalization, is the price frail parents are expected to pay for giving risk-aversive children a sense of security.

Dibner's company, Lifeline Systems, subsequently grew rapidly and remains North America's leading supplier of social alarm equipment (PRS).

Early PRS development

By 1984 there were 57 PRS services in the state of Massachusetts alone, where Lifeline Systems were based, with an average of 30 carephones linked to each (Devins, 1984, p 4). Some indication of the spread of services elsewhere was given in a survey by Stafford and Dibner (1984). This included 335 Lifeline programmes, that is those using the equipment supplied by Lifeline Systems, in 47 states. The survey established (p 6) that 91 per cent of such programmes were based in hospitals, reflecting the main thrust of Lifeline System's marketing. Most programme coordinators reported (p 6) that they had achieved savings in in-patient days. Interestingly, though Lifeline Systems had a good knowledge of the international position, they did not market their wares outside North America.

Reports of more evaluations of the benefits of PRS fuelled the establishment of systems throughout North America, with increasing numbers being established outside hospital and healthcare facilities. Datlen (1988, p 7) stated that by May 1987 there were over 2,000 programmes using Lifeline systems across North America, 30 of them in Canada (particularly in the provinces of Ontario and Alberta).

Further evidence of the merits of PRS came with a study by Koch (1984). He found (p 31) in his work relating to 46 patients at the Royal Alexandra Hospital in Edmonton, Canada, that "the sharp increase [in hospital utilisation] during the year immediately preceding Lifeline installation is followed by a decrease (to near zero) in the ratio of admission to patient months. A decrease in the total of in-patient days is apparent as well". The programme, Koch noted (p 31) met with the "overwhelming acceptance by hospital staff, patients and families and the community at large". Though Koch urged caution in relation to his results because of the relatively small sample size, they appeared to be confirmed in other research.

Cain (1987, p 26), in evaluating a service covering 70 people linked to the Jerry L. Pettis Memorial Veterans Administration Hospital in Loma Linda, California, found that in the year after admission to the programme there was a 48.4 per cent decrease in hospital admissions and a 69.3 per cent decrease in in-patient days. She noted (pp 29-31) that "the cost of one Lifeline unit is little more than the average cost per day of hospitalization" and concluded that "the program should be utilised to the fullest extent and extended as needed; since the obvious advantage of the cost of the Lifeline equipment and the comparison with hospitalization expense is irrefutable".

Gatz and Pearson (1988) evaluated the Emergency Alert Response System (EARS), a service that worked with various hospitals in Los Angeles. This was set up in 1981 and by 1987 had 700 subscribers. Importantly this evaluation attempted to measure benefits in terms of subjective well-being of users rather than cost savings (p 3). Both service users and their families were interviewed. While the researchers had difficulty in pinning down clear results, they found (p 27) very positive opinions about EARS and noted numerous statements regarding the extent to which people's sense of security had been increased. Families, they noted (p 17) gave several examples where independent living was attributed to the presence of EARS although, interestingly (p 16), subscribers "did not change significantly in their rating of the probability that they would be institutionalized within the next year".

At the opposite side of the United States a pilot project relating to 172 people living in six districts of New York City found that PRS enabled a reduction in homecare hours, higher levels of user satisfaction and savings per person of $565 per month (Dixon, 1987, p 2).

The case for PRS was, in other words, being reinforced by varied pieces of research in different parts of North America. The marketing endeavours of

Lifeline Systems and a growing band of competitors meant, furthermore, that there was increasing awareness of the technologies among potential users, their relatives and carers. Stories in the press, as noted in Chapter Four, fuelled interest and helped to sell the products.

Given the rapid expansion of PRS services and the publicity being given to them, they became the focus of some attention by the American Association of Retired Persons, a voluntary organisation representing the interests of millions of older Americans (AARP, 1987). In their 1998 report appraising such technologies they found (p 1) that some 15–20 companies were by that time in the market. They also noted (p 5) that some health insurance companies were willing to pay for PRS where they had been recommended by a doctor, and concluded (p 8) that social alarms were "a powerful tool that promotes independence and provides security to thousands of older Americans".

With some private insurance companies willing to invest in PRS as a means of reducing their healthcare expenditure for policy holders, the implications for public spending through the US government's Medicare and Medicaid programmes were, therefore, becoming apparent. Indeed Lerner and Stevens (1986, p 4) noted that the Medicare payment system gave hospitals a powerful incentive to minimise in-patient days and promote PRS.

Medicaid is means tested and is administered by each state. It covers over half of all nursing home payments and supports about two thirds of all nursing home residents (see http://www.careguide.net/careguide.cgi/eldercare). Medicare is a large health insurance programme administered by the federal government. The medical insurance element for Medicare requires payment of a monthly premium; and the hospital insurance element requires both payment of a fee on admission and shared payments for extended stays in a hospital or nursing home. The Medicare system, it should be noted, covers hospital care. PRS in this context is therefore excluded, despite the potential cost reductions that might be achieved.

Twigg (2000, p 123) observed that Medicare provided medical cover for all older citizens regardless of income though "it is compromised in terms of coverage – no prescription drugs – and by co-payments and deductibles". Medicaid is also in some ways compromised in that it is not always readily accessible for those in the greatest need. In the particular context of PRS Benson (1992, p 223) noted that "the criteria are often so rigid it raises questions as to whether those who can get coverage are the ones who would benefit most from it".

In Canada, the attention being given to PRS during this period continued to be broadly based. The context was one where a number of government and municipal authorities were very conscious of the desire of older people to stay put and, while there was investment in public housing projects for older people, this was counterbalanced by the support being given to accommodation alternatives. Having said this, the potential role of PRS in a key period of service development was totally overlooked in a substantial study of the public sector options for older people in Ontario (Denton and Davis, 1986).

Datlen (1988, p 23), however, in her examination of the options in Ontario, recognised the potential role of PRS as part of broader care packages and recommended them in public housing schemes for those older people "who want or need them". She noted (p 10) their potential in relation to security and argued that they "may be more relevant for senior citizen public housing tenants in major urban centres ... than in small communities across the province". She summed up by stating (p 33) that social alarms "are of considerable emotional and physical benefit to elderly people since they provide the security of knowing that help is on the way to a stricken senior, and emergency help actually arrives within a short period".

By 1992 in the United States there were, according to the American Association of Retired Persons (AARP, 1992, p 2), about 450,000 people with PRS, of whom about a quarter had had to use them in an emergency. Several companies were noted as having their own monitoring and response services operating nationwide. Having said this, well over half of users were linked to local centres (American Association of Retired Persons, 1992, pp 9-10).

The growth in services included, however, a few rogue traders. The AARP (1992, p 12) reported that there had been scams with PRS service providers skipping town after pocketing monitoring fees. They reported that they had had many complaints about exorbitant prices and inappropriate sales practices. One company, Life Alert, was noted as having faced legal action in California, their sales staff allegedly having been "trained to wear down the older consumer, spending as many as six hours inventing horror stories about what might happen without a PERS" (p 13). Elsewhere it was noted that "several states had taken action against PERS manufacturers and sellers for high-pressure sales techniques, misrepresentations regarding the product, faulty equipment and over-pricing" (see www.consumerlaw.org/consumer/emergen.html).

The United States

The phenomenal rate of growth of PRS in the United States reflected the importance of the message arising from early service evaluations. PRS were seen as in the interests of a wide array of agencies concerned with nursing or hospital care in the private and voluntary sectors. They could subscribe to or develop such services for themselves, thereby reducing occupancy rates and manage their facilities more efficiently. Given the nature of their establishments, with staff on duty 24-hours a day, a response service using nominated contacts could be established and would normally operate from their emergency room/ department. Further attractions of such services included their ability to operate over wide areas and the benefits indicated for service users. The vast majority of households, furthermore, had telephones and could therefore be linked readily.

An early picture of services in the United States was provided through a survey of 689 PRS services at the end of 1983 (Stafford and Dibner, 1984, p 1). This sought to establish the stability of such services and was also seen as guiding Lifeline Systems in their future marketing strategy. About half the services (335) responded. These linked a total of 11,598 users. The average number of users per service was just 36 with the largest 285. Most (as noted earlier in this chapter) were based in hospitals. Half of these were not-for-profit and some were owned and run by churches and voluntary organisations (Stafford and Dibner, 1984, p 2). It should be noted that government and municipal funds were in some cases elicited to help establish and/or run the services. A considerable emphasis was placed by most services on the use of volunteers.

Given the small numbers of users linked to most services, their experience of dealing with emergencies identified through the PRS was limited. Summing the experience of different services, however, enabled a broad guideline to be established that "a program of 50 subscribers can expect approximately 30 emergencies in a year" (Stafford and Dibner, 1984, p 3).

Expansion in the number of services in the United States continued. PRS became, as a consequence, the subject of further attention. Other companies joined Lifeline Systems in the race to garner business from what they perceived as a growing and sizeable market. Some operated their own monitoring and response centres and encouraged organisations to subscribe to them as opposed to setting up their own service. A 'starter package' from Lifeline Systems with a receiving device and carephones for 20 subscribers was available, in 1986, at $15,000 (ECRI, 1986, p 3).

Some services used what Lerner and Stevens (1986, p 14) described as tape-dialler (direct dial) devices, which called predetermined numbers and played a recorded or synthesised message when answered. They noted, however (p 18), that these were not, strictly speaking, response systems, since there could be no direct response via the communication link established. Rather they were simply emergency alarms. It was argued (p 25) that a monitoring service was more appropriate if users were to receive "some measure of assurance that the person receiving the alarm is prepared to deal with an emergency situation".

In a 1986 review, Lerner and Stevens identified 11 manufacturers of PRS, although only eight featured in a brief relating to such devices (ECRI, 1986). The products of 12 companies were featured in a review in 1987 by the American Association of Retired Persons (AARP) although this included the proviso that other devices not featured, were "available in only certain regions of the country and several manufacturers chose not to participate" (American Association of Retired Persons, 1987, p 7). By 1992 the AARP were able to report that there were more than 30 brands available (American Association of Retired Persons, 1992, p 2).

Lerner and Stevens (1986, p 1) sought simply to document the role of PRS in "improving the quality of life of elderly persons living alone". They offered (p 39) what might be considered to be the first independent appraisal of such services in the United States and called for a wider, more all-embracing, research agenda. They argued (p 2) that:

When integrated properly with community-based or health-related home care services, PERS may help prolong an elderly person's independent, non-institutionalized life. In summary, increased use of PERSs among elderly persons living alone can, for large numbers, improve the quality of life, reduce the number of avoidable deaths, and eliminate unnecessary institutionalization of those who wish to and indeed can live alone.

Noting the potential role of PRS in relation to home security, Lerner and Stevens (p 4) saw the main group of potential users as likely to be "those elderly somewhat-to-moderately disabled individuals who currently live alone or with another elderly or disabled individual, and who suffer from chronic conditions requiring medical assistance".

The strong medical and healthcare orientation of services was therefore apparent from the early period of social alarm service development in the United States. At the same time, little or no reference or consideration appears to have been given to any role that such devices might have in common with those hard-wired systems that were present in some developments for older people.

The applicability of this medical/healthcare orientation was reinforced by the experience reported by Lerner and Stevens (1986, pp 19-20) of a homecare project managed by the New Jersey Hospital Association involving 58 hospitals throughout the state. A frequent comment of service coordinators was to the effect that "the best people to respond to an emergency are the people who have to respond to emergencies every day". Having said this, different requirements were recognised and great diversity noted among services (pp 25-6).

Though there is clearly much overlap, Lerner and Stevens attempted to broadly classify those different requirements. The labels have been chosen by the author to encapsulate what were rather long-winded descriptions by the researchers. These were:

- medical services – hospital based but also involved in homecare service delivery and including convalescence after hospital treatment;
- emergency services – involving ambulance personnel and seeking to respond to acute events requiring immediate medical attention (heart attacks, strokes, etc); and
- contact services – which involve routine contact with response staff or by volunteer workers attached to the services in question.

The range of requirements was such that Lerner and Stevens (1986, p 26) stated that "no single emergency response service will adequately satisfy the entire population of potential users (or their families or communities) and thus be considered uniquely successful".

Lerner and Stevens (p 27) also attempted to quantify the number of PRS services and service users. They quoted a survey undertaken in 1985-86 throughout the United States by the American Hospital Association, which pointed to over a third of responding hospitals operating some form of PRS service. If extrapolated upwards to include the more than 7,000 hospitals involved this suggests that there were at least 2,500 services. The distribution of such services was, however, uneven and uncontrolled, reflecting concerns about the extent to which services were available to those most in need of them (Lerner and Stevens, 1986, p 37). Adding to the number of services were the activities of many security companies which, by the mid-1980s were beginning to offer PRS as adjuncts to their other activities (Montgomery, 1992, p 203).

An idea whose time had come?

A company that marketed carephones via retail outlets throughout the United States suggested in 1995 that the PRS market was growing at 8-10 per cent annually and that social alarms was "an idea whose time had come" (see http://w972.com/ers860/ers863f.htm).

This opinion, although coming from a commercial source, has some resonance, arising not so much from the increase in the numbers of services and users but in the recognition that had begun to emerge within state governments about the contribution that PRS could make to what that appraisal referred to as the economics of healthcare. It was noted, for instance, that New York State and Georgia had been the first of 26 states to reimburse the cost of PRS for those older, and poorer, Americans assessed as in need of the service. Just three years earlier the AARP had reported that in most states neither Medicaid or Medicare were available for PRS and that such cover was also absent from most private health insurance policies (American Association of Retired Persons, 1992, p 12).

In 1992, Montgomery noted (1992, p 209) that 19 states included PRS under their Medicaid programmes, especially where a written recommendation had been received from a doctor. She stated that some 8,000 people were covered this way. However, as noted by Chumbler et al (1997, pp 125-6; 1998, p 210), in the context of Arkansas eligibility for Medicaid did not guarantee payment on account of the limitations of state budgets and inefficiencies in service targeting.

Despite such difficulties, the key point is that statutory bodies in the United States, regardless of any consideration of supporting independent living, were increasingly convinced that social alarms could bring cost savings and that there was the potential to reduce or contain that element of healthcare spending that fell to the public purse.

Although pointing to difficulties in service targeting, the work of Chumbler et al (1997 and 1998) provided further evidence of the merits for service providers of PRS. The primary purpose of the programme that they studied in Arkansas was to limit older people's use of nursing homes (Chumbler et al, 1997, pp 118-19). Arkansas, it should be noted, is one of the poorest states in the United States.

Chumbler et al (pp 123-4) studied 553 older adults in rural communities and found that although there was a strong correlation of PRS provision with living alone, being cognitively intact and experiencing difficulties in the activities of daily living, there was also a correlation with being white. They concluded, among other things, that there was the need to explore why PRS were less readily prescribed to African-Americans and the need for specific interventions to ensure, more generally, that appropriate home-based services were available to them (Chumbler et al, 1997, pp 124-5; 1998, p 224). With regard to the potential cost savings available to service providers they noted that for in-home health and support services overall under the Arkansas Medicaid programme, costs were about half as much as nursing home care (1998, p 209).

Ensuing work in the United States relating to social alarms is that of Roush and Teesdale (1997). They examined the record for one year pre- and one year post-admission for 101 patients of the Talahassee Memorial Regional Medical Center, Florida, and found a reduction in the number of in-patient days (from 10.45 to 6.16 per annum) after the provision of a PRS device. They concluded that "PRS programs can be effective in reducing hospital utilization" (pp 360-1). They found, however, no significant change in the number of visits to the emergency department.

While Roush and Teesdale urged some caution in interpreting their results because other sources of variance might not have been identified, they argued (pp 362-3) that "if quality of care can be maintained in conjunction with marked reduction in hospital usage by older PRS users, then perhaps a reduction of some magnitude in Medicare expenditure would follow".

An overall picture

The overall picture is one in which social alarms (PRS) are now well established in the United States. Their operation, while originally most closely associated with hospital-based services, is now complemented by often large national services administered by the main manufacturers, and a wide array of small services proffered by local security companies. ECRI (1998, p 3) noted a trend towards hospital services being replaced by links to national services or to other locally based service providers, this being driven by the need for further cost savings.

Finally, the listings of services for older people in the Americas Guide provided further information on PRS in the United States (see www.americasguide.com). This revealed something of the distribution of services and appeared to signal, as noted by ECRI (1998), a reduction in their number. The information must, however, be treated with caution in view of the fact that it is not known what proportion of services are listed. It is suggested that some services relating to local hospitals and healthcare facilities were probably omitted since these were normally provided just for users of hospital services.

Nevertheless, in September 2000 there were 551 services listed that operated in all but three states (Alaska, Nebraska and North Dakota). This represented a reduction of 47 listed services in the period from November 1999. Particularly high numbers of services operated in New York State, Florida, California and Texas (see Table 8.1). Only one state, Virginia, recorded an increase in the number of services in the 10-month period considered.

The types of PRS service were difficult to divine from the names and addresses alone. Sometimes it was clear that the services operated from hospitals and in other cases from security companies. At random from among the former, for instance, would be the service based at Wallkill Valley Hospital, Sussex, New Jersey; and from among the latter the Central Security & Electric service at Rolla, Missouri. Many other service names related to nursing services, heathcare and answering services. Several carried the name 'Lifeline' including seven of the 64 services in New York State.

A random telephone interview survey was undertaken by the author with 19 of the PRS services listed. Care should be taken in interpreting the results of this since a very high rate of refusals was encountered. Such refusals are attributed both to the fact that social alarms were a peripheral activity for many of the agencies approached, their primary interest being in security matters; and (despite reassurances) there were concerns regarding commercial confidentiality. As an incentive to participate all were offered, and those services that collaborated were provided with, a summary of the survey results.

Table 8.1: Social alarms (PRS) in the United States

	November 1999	September 2000	Change
ARIZONA	18	18	0
CALIFORNIA	47	46	−1
CONNECTICUT	23	23	0
FLORIDA	66	56	−10
GEORGIA	13	12	−1
ILLINOIS	12	11	−1
MARYLAND	13	11	−2
MASSACHUSETTS	10	10	0
MINNESOTA	14	10	−4
NEW JERSEY	26	19	−7
NEW YORK	67	64	−3
NORTH CAROLINA	18	18	0
OHIO	26	25	−1
PENNSYLVANIA	43	39	−4
TEXAS	36	34	−2
VIRGINIA	23	26	+3
WASHINGTON	11	11	0
ALL OTHER STATES	132	118	−14
ALL USA	**598**	**551**	**−47**

Listed are states with 10 or more social alarm (PRS) services at September 2000.

Source: www.americasguide.com

The services surveyed extended across the United States and included 12 states from California to Maine and New York State. Notable from the results was that all 19 had been established before 1992 – one was over 20 years old. Nine were based in hospitals or nursing homes, these tending to have relatively few households links and, where stated, were invariably below 2,000. One service had been based at a hospital but had recently moved out. The smallest of the hospital based services linked just 30 households. Six services did not operate their own monitoring and response service, contracting to other agencies. Three would not say whether they operated their own centres and might reasonably be added to the six.

With regard to service users, invariably three quarters or more were aged 65 or over. Many services claimed that all their users were of this age. Five services attested to some of their users benefiting from Medicaid or some form of state aid. In other words, most were reliant on users who used their own private resources, albeit in some cases helped by health insurance policies, to purchase the service.

Users of most of the services lived within a 50 mile radius of the location of the monitoring and response centres. Several services, however, operated over extensive areas. Two services surveyed operated nationally, the largest of these having over 90,000 users.

The local, regional or national remits of the services surveyed clearly had an impact on the kind of responses that could be provided to emergency calls. In most cases and for most services it seems that responses were made through the contacts nominated by the user. However, for many of the services operated from hospitals or nursing homes, staff were also used.

One of the PRS services surveyed was the hospital-based Lifeline, operated by the North West Texas Healthcare System, covering 26 counties of the Texas panhandle. The operational objectives were noted as being the same as those for other hospital-based services and aimed at providing speedy responses to emergencies and reducing long-term care costs. Responses to calls involved hospital staff and/or nominated contacts. The service, based at Amarillo, was one of "over 150 Lifeline programs in Texas" and was established in 1982.[1] By early 2001 the service embraced 1,300 subscribers in 42 cities within the panhandle area. A satellite PRS service operating for the benefit of subscribers in Boise City, Oklahoma, was started in 1990.

In conclusion, the survey of services, albeit relatively small, appears to have captured the rich variety of social alarm services that operate in the United States. It included extremes in terms of size, from 30 to 90,000 users. It included different types of service, both based within and outside hospitals and nursing homes, operating both nationally and in different states from the west to the east coasts.

The fact that most of the PRS services surveyed were well established may reflect something of a sample bias, though the fact that there is an ongoing reduction in the overall number of services, both noted earlier and evident in the numbers on the Americas Guide website, supports the notion that relatively few new services may have been established in the last few years. A further possible bias, towards hospital- and nursing home-based services, may have taken place by virtue of such organisations being less sensitive about providing information.

Canada

As noted at the beginning of this chapter, in the matter of PRS the United States and Canada can in most ways be considered together. Certainly the main manufacturers of PRS saw Canada as the natural and easiest extension to their market in the United States and Lifeline Systems, being located in Massachusetts, was well placed geographically to quickly market their wares in the most populous of Canada's provinces (Ontario and Quebec). The technologies in both countries were therefore essentially the same, albeit operating within different regulatory frameworks.

The emphasis in both countries that was placed on private sector provision has been noted, although counterbalanced by the interest of public sector bodies, notably in Alberta and Ontario. The provincial government in Alberta, for instance, funded a PRS programme, the Seniors Emergency Medical Alert Program, as part of its efforts, through health and social welfare provision, to support older people in the community (Watzke and Birch, 1994, p 30). This meant that potential users were eligible for a grant towards the cost of buying a carephone, which could be linked to one of a number of approved monitoring and response services.

The early interest in PRS within Ontario was noted in various studies undertaken in the 1980s. The first study of note simply sought to gather information. It identified and explained the different types of device and reported on some of the research and evaluations that had been undertaken up to that time (Ontario Ministry of Community and Social Services, 1987). Five systems were identified (p 6) as being available in Ontario and used by different PRS services. For Canada as a whole the study noted (p 11) that 40 using Lifeline equipment operated in eight of the country's 12 provinces. Various services were summarily described including the Rainycrest service (see below) and hospital-based services at Guelph and Fort Erie.

THE RAINYCREST SERVICE

The Rainycrest Service was established at a home for older people at Fort Frances, Ontario. Alongside the PRS service were pre-existing domiciliary care and transport services that helped to maintain people in their own homes. These were supplemented by daily check-up telephone calls that both enabled monitoring of well-being and provided social contact (Ontario Ministry of Community and Social Services, 1986, p 3).

Both service users and a control group were studied, 50 people in total, each group being drawn from the overall applicants for the service. Carephones were randomly assigned. Those not allocated carephones were advised that they were on a waiting list (p 10). Details of users, their calls to the service and action taken were noted in writing on file cards. Personal interviews were administered twice, once with the older person at the time the carephone was installed and again three months later, via telephone; 50 and 43 interviews respectively were achieved (p 15).

Being an early scheme, various technical problems were encountered and the confidence of some service users was, as a consequence, undermined (p 16). The period of study was, furthermore, relatively short and it was not possible to draw firm conclusions regarding system usage, the nature of emergencies, and so on. In fact, only four service users experienced emergencies in the study period (p 23). Despite this there was a clear understanding of the purpose of the service, even if some did not fully understand how it operated. This pointed to the major service benefit as providing an increased sense of security and worrying less about accidents and emergencies. Paradoxically, and perhaps arising out of the temporary unavailability of the service to them, the control group, without carephones, showed a tendency to worry more than they had initially.

Crucially, the study found that the service resulted in users becoming more independent and facilitated a reduction in direct support that was received. The reverse was true for the control group, a finding which it was suggested indicated the extent of reassurance given to both users and caregivers, though whether this had any implications for social contact was not discussed (p 24). The study concluded that social alarms were "a valuable tool in providing emergency assistance ... increasing peace of mind ... and enhancing independence" (pp 25-7) although with a number of provisos concerning the reliability of the equipment, the users' understanding of it, and the nature of any wider community support. In 1998 the Rainycrest service remained operative, although with just 65 users.[2]

An ensuing Canadian study explored the broader potential of PRS and involved interviews with service providers, some service users and a range of manufacturers (MacLaren Plansearch, 1988). The context was one where considerable emphasis was given to the search for alternatives to institutionalisation. The study sought to examine the use of PRS and consider their potential future role in helping "elderly people maintain independent lifestyles in the community, thereby reducing demand for institutional care" (p 1/1). MacLaren Plansearch, identified over 70 services throughout Canada (p 3/16). The motivation of the commissioners of the research, the Canada Mortgage and Housing Corporation, related to concerns about older people being unattended in emergencies and its consequences in terms of institutionalisation and the additional costs of care (p 1/1).

MacLaren Plansearch noted that call systems as well as carephones were part of many services and that activity monitoring was included. A service entirely based on activity monitoring (using PIRs, passive-infra-red sensors) and linked to a monitoring and response service in Toronto was cited (p 2/4). Direct dial devices were also noted as sometimes being used by healthcare organisations to "aid patient discharge planning" (pp 3/4, 3/17).

A range of services, including private sector, voluntary and some municipal providers was evident with the former (generally security services) having the largest number of users and more than half the total estimated Canadian market (p 3/18). The majority of services offered by municipal authorities were via hospitals, the strong justification being (p 3/20), "With an emergency response system elderly patients can be sent home earlier than [would be] possible if they had no direct emergency communication with the hospitals".

Such services tended to have more frequent social contact with their users. These users tended not to be guided in the way that appears to have been typical of services proffered by security companies, who advised "to only use the system when there is a serious emergency" (p 3/19).

Interviews with 23 service users established that half had decided to join a PRS service on the recommendation of a health professional (p 4/2). A majority felt that social alarms had given them greater feelings of security and there was no evidence of any decrease in social contact (p 4/4). There was, however, criticism of the portable transmitters as heavy, bulky and/or irritating, with only one in five actually wearing the device when interviewed (p 4/4). MacLaren Plansearch (p 10/8) concluded that:

> If technology can permit affordable, safe, independent living to continue, the government should, by all means possible, support the development of emergency response system programs suitable to community and social support contexts in Canada.

Wider perspectives

By 1992 it was estimated that about 25,000 people had social alarms (PRS) in Canada (Rodriguez, 1992, pp 9-12). While many of these had carephone devices others were noted as living in congregate housing. Congregate housing comprises grouped dwellings for older people, sometimes in the form of retirement villages with central services that may include healthcare provision (pp 12-15).

Various PRS services were described by Rodriguez, these bearing testimony to the associated public policy initiatives concerned with helping people to stay put and to a replication of the pattern of service provision based in hospitals that was to be found in the United States. He noted (p 12), for instance, a programme based in St Peter's Hospital at Melville, Saskatchewan, that served 225 people across an extensive rural area. By contrast he noted (p 16) the more urban focus of the Elizabeth Bruyère service in Ottawa (described further below), which grew from 100 subscribers in 1990 to 450 just two years later. By 1994 the latter service served 750 (Fisk, 1995, p 146). Overall Rodriguez (1992, p 17ff) noted the range of hospital-based PRS services with as few as 45 people linked, and several initiatives being taken by provincial and municipal governments.

One of the latter was described by Hobbs (1992, p 26). She observed that by 1989 the Ontario Ministry of Community and Social Services had helped to fund nine PRS services (including the Elizabeth Bruyère service). These mostly operated from homes for older people and, in total, served approximately 500 people. The Ontario Ministry of Health were subsidising a further 32 services linked in total to some 5,000 people. In all Hobbs estimated (p 25) that, taking account of private sector services, 8,500 people were served by PRS in the province of Ontario alone. She also suggested (p 25) that "47 per cent of seniors may be in need of a PRS" by virtue of disability, advanced age or living alone. This pointed to a potential Canadian market of some 440,000 people.

The interest in social alarms of some of the regional governments was reflected in the concerns that had arisen about equipment standards and manufacturer monopolies. Hobbs, herself a provincial government employee, put forward a model specification reflecting the Ontario perspective. This strongly argued the need for PRS to be used within broader frameworks of care and support services and recognised activity monitoring as an important feature (pp 27–30).

The interest in bringing PRS within the frameworks of healthcare insurance and government-supported social welfare programmes in Canada was also affirmed by Watzke (1994, p 162). He noted that, despite the initiatives in Ontario:

> To date, in Canada (and in the U.S.), there has been very little support for PERS from government health authorities. This is remarkable given that it is known that the vast majority of real PERS alarms are related to medical emergencies.

Subsequently, Roush et al (1995) cautiously endorsed the findings of some of the research undertaken in the United States. They noted (p 919) that for a sample of 106 people enrolled on the PRS programme at the Langley Memorial Hospital, British Columbia, there were clear reductions in hospital admissions and in the number of in-patient days. The former had reduced from an average of 1.2 admissions in the year before PRS to 0.9 in the ensuing year. In-patient days reduced from an average of 14.4 to 5.9 in the same period. Interestingly, however, the number of visits to the emergency department slightly increased, suggesting that quicker responses to medical emergencies may have enabled more effective interventions that did not require admissions. Roush et al (1995, p 921), however, quoted an unpublished study in the United States, which, for a sample of 240 mostly male patients at the Indianapolis Veterans Affairs Medical Centre, found no significant differences in admission rates or in-patient days. Both Roush et al (p 922) and Fisk (1995, p 150) testified to the extent to which users of Canadian PRS felt a greater sense of security.

A further example of a Canadian PRS service is that of the Edmonton Lifeline. This service was managed by the Good Samaritan Society and set up by Lutherans on a non-profit making basis with the help of government grants (Gott, 1995, p 86). In January 1993 there were nearly 1,000 users of the service in five communities in northern Alberta. Most were elderly but younger users were also included. The response to emergency calls relied upon 500 volunteers.

Finally, studies by Fisk (1995) and Watzke (1994) provided information regarding the characteristics of PRS users for services in Ottawa and Edmonton respectively. The former, as noted in Chapter Five, was part of a comparative study with the Oldham Helpline service in Great Britain and is profiled below. The latter study, of the Lifecall of Canada service by Watzke (1994), is of importance by virtue of its claim (p 161) to being "probably the most thorough analysis of a large PRS sample to date". They studied 5,221 users.

SISTERS OF CHARITY OTTAWA HEALTH SERVICE

For the Elizabeth Bruyère Helpline service (managed by the Sisters of Charity Ottawa Health Service) in Ottawa, Fisk (1995, pp 149-52) interviewed 20 users in western Ottawa. While primarily concerned with comparing the nature of the service with one in Great Britain and the way in which the needs of service users were addressed, this also provided some information on the users themselves and the ways in which they interacted with the technologies. For the Ottawa service it should be noted that the users interviewed were considered typical except by virtue of living in an urban area of the city as opposed to its extensive rural hinterland.

The average age of those interviewed was 79, although the overall age range was from 45 to 94 (Fisk, 1995, p 150); 14 were aged over 80. Some indication of their support need was given in the finding that 14 stated they had difficulty in walking about outside their homes and seven within them. Most, it should be noted, lived in dwellings all on one storey, many in condominiums (apartment blocks).

By virtue of subscribing to the PRS service they were not, of course, a representative sample of older people in the community. Significantly, all but two reported that as a result of having a social alarm they felt able to live at home longer (p 150). Although a question regarding security was not posed, spontaneous remarks were frequently made by service users about feeling more secure. Notable was the finding (p 151) that users saw the purpose of the service in different ways including security, the ability to access help when needed, and giving respite to relatives. Usage of the PRS had been made in an emergency by eight of those interviewed when they had:

- fallen or were stuck (5)
- difficulty breathing (1)
- a nosebleed (1)
- overdosed on medication (1)

Distinctive features of the Ottawa service were noted as it being bilingual (English/French) and the extensive use that was made of volunteers who helped by visiting service users and undertaking some administrative tasks and in-service promotion (p 146). Regardless of these distinctive features, however, the Elizabeth Bruyère service is considered as broadly typical of hospital- or healthcare-based services both in Canada and other parts of North America.

The study of the private Lifecall of Canada service (based in Edmonton) was undertaken with information provided by the users when initially subscribing to the service and from details of calls made by them to the service and their outcomes (Watzke, 1994, p 153). Notable among Watzke's findings was the propensity for women to make more calls that were deemed 'false alarms' although in other respects no gender differences were apparent (p 162).

Discussion

There are many similarities in the contexts of PRS developments within the United States and Canada, both with regard to their nature and the manner of their operation. The technologies are essentially the same, reflecting the fact that Canada is the obvious first foreign market for many products manufactured in the United States.

Throughout North America, Lifeline Systems were for some time the only manufacturer of PRS operating to a monitoring and response centre. By virtue of this fact, and through astute marketing to hospitals and healthcare providers, they established a large market presence. By 1994 it was estimated that there were 450,000 users of PRS in North America (Watzke and Birch, 1994, p 2). And while Lifeline Systems dominated there were, by that time, considered to be between 25 and 30 companies marketing their wares in the United States and 10 in Canada.

Substantial emphasis in both countries was placed on private sector service provision, this being complemented by some provision by charitable and voluntary organisations. This reflects the way that PRS services were developed in relation to agendas concerned with supporting those with medical needs. These were sometimes powerfully driven by a belief, substantiated by research in both countries, that cost savings were to be made through reductions in hospital admissions, in-patient days, and earlier discharges.

Only in parts of Canada, particularly Ontario, was there any strong sense in which the private sector ethos was balanced by the interests and activities of public sector bodies concerned for housing or social welfare services. In both countries, however, the growing pressures to have PRS included within medical insurance services and government-supported social welfare programmes has, as noted in this chapter, begun to bear fruit.

A further characteristic of PRS services in both the United States and Canada is their size in terms of the number of households linked. The way in which such services developed meant that many were small. This remains the case today. Indeed, the telephone survey undertaken in 2000, found one service in the United States with just 30 users. The small Rainycrest Service in Canada, which, while operational in the 1980s, was noted as having hardly grown in over a decade.

Where PRS operate alongside other services or have, in any case, staff available on a 24-hour a day basis, then services would appear to some extent sustainable at that small size. This is true within hospitals and nursing homes. But the fact that conflicts can arise is one probable reason why some rationalisation in the number of services appears to be taking place. Such conflicts would occur when staff are utilised to respond to calls and are therefore drawn away from other tasks. This might be the norm, however, only for a small proportion of services and generally speaking would only arise after failing to reach nominated contacts or, where appropriate, eliciting the support of emergency services. A further reason relates to the costs of receiving equipment at the monitoring and response centre, especially as functionality increases and services seek to replace increasingly aged technologies.

For the United States, it was noted from the Americas Guide database, the number of services listed had reduced by 45 in a 10-month period to September 2000. The telephone survey found one hospital-based service that, just a month before, had contracted out. At the other end of the scale, however, there are a few massive services. As noted earlier, one was picked up in the telephone survey, which had over 90,000 households linked and which operated nationwide.

Taking such matters into account it is estimated that, at 2003, the number of people with social alarms in North America is around 840,000, of which over 800,000 are in the United States.

It has been demonstrated that PRS services in North America have a number of distinctive characteristics that set them apart from their counterparts on the other side of the Atlantic. Such differences and their importance are discussed in Chapter Ten.

Notes

[1] Correspondence with Jim Kiper (North West Texas Lifeline).

[2] Correspondence with Kevin Queen (Rainycrest).

NINE

Social alarms in the rest of the world

European Union (excluding Great Britain and Ireland)

The development and growth of social alarm services within countries of the European Union has been extremely variable. This is unsurprising given the different national contexts; their particular heritage and idiosyncrasies in relation to housing, social welfare and health/medical services; and the mixed array of equipment that has been developed and marketed.

And despite the gradual moves towards the adoption of more shared perspectives among EU countries and some shared trends away from forms of institutional provision for older people, it should not be assumed that a common approach is either appropriate or necessary. Indeed, the contrary is probably the case in view of the varied frameworks of service provision and different built forms to which they relate. Such differences become evident in this chapter.

What is clear is that in all countries the role of social alarms crosses professional boundaries. The effectiveness of the technologies and the services that depend on them is, therefore, frequently compromised as a consequence of poor coordination (King, 1993, p 13). This is, perhaps, an inevitable outcome of the promotion of care in the community in contexts where existing service frameworks had been established with other objectives in mind. The old perspectives associated with more institutional forms of provision are being discarded with difficulty. The discussion (in Chapter Two) of the potential for such technologies to liberate their users seeks to redress such matters and, where endorsed, can help underpin changes in approach.

Some generalisations can be made and become evident from the ensuing descriptions for a selection of countries in the European Union:

1. In almost all of the EU countries examined in this book, as with Great Britain and Ireland, there is emphasis on the development of care in the community (Walker, 1993, p 5). The prerogative is, in essence, the same as that in Great Britain and Ireland, that is to respond to agendas associated with enhancing the rights of individual older people and to redress their marginalised position.
2. A call is being made in all countries for the greater effort of families and communities to support their relatives or neighbours. This signals the need, acknowledged to a greater or lesser degree, for new policy frameworks to support informal carers (King, 1993, p 13). The decline of the extended

family, evident to a varying degree in the different countries, also points to the need to harness volunteer workers in support of service provision (p 12).

3. For those countries with a strong tradition of municipal services, for instance the Netherlands, Denmark and Great Britain, there are strong efforts being made to invoke greater use of private and/or voluntary, not-for-profit agencies.

4. The configuration of social alarm services and the agencies of service provision vary substantially. Municipal provision and/or financial support is more commonplace in the Netherlands and the Scandinavian countries. Voluntary bodies are particularly well represented in Germany. Private sector agencies, though few in number, appear to predominate in Italy and some of the emerging nations of central Europe such as Slovenia and the Czech Republic.

5. The objectives of social alarm services are generally associated with social welfare agendas. The agencies of provision, commonly municipal authorities and/or voluntary bodies, reflects this. This means that for most European countries the role of services fits between the more medically oriented services of North America and the more housing oriented services of England and Wales.

While it is difficult to provide an estimate of the total number of users of social alarms in Europe as a whole, a figure for the European Union is suggested as 2 million. Each European country for which some information on social alarms is available is examined below.

Denmark

Underpinning the frameworks of care and support in Denmark is a belief in self-determination. As in other European countries, this has resulted in a strong emphasis on developing the means of supporting older people independently in their own homes. Indeed, Denmark has been credited within the European Union as having the widest variety of social welfare and other services aimed at maintaining older people at home. This has involved discarding the notion of sheltered housing (considered too institutional) in favour of well-designed flats with flexible support provision (Crosby, 1993, p 63).

The approach has involved the promotion of special forms of housing provision for older people and the encouragement of integration between service providers (Friediger, 1992, p 35). Social alarms have played a part in achieving these objectives and are a statutory requirement in specialised accommodation for older people (Organisation for Economic Co-operation and Development, 1996, p 125). A particular form of specialised housing, congregate housing, without a warden or nursing support has been promoted with a government subsidy (Leeson, 1992, p 44). The call systems used are generally akin to those in Great Britain but often allow for activity monitoring. Calls are monitored by ambulance and/or domiciliary care staff (Ministry of Social Affairs, 1990, pp 10-11; OECD, 1996, p 125; Singlelenberg, 2000, p 24).

The perceived need for social alarms is clear from publications produced by the Danish government. The Ministry of Social Affairs (1990, p 10), for instance, noted the relevance of both active and passive systems. Within the latter they referred to systems that operated with a timer device, requiring to be periodically reset, as "semi-active". Older people who require social alarms are entitled to them free of charge through a scheme funded by local authorities, where this enables them to remain at home (Crosby, 1993, pp 68-9; Cullen and Robinson, 1997, p 128).

The first social alarm service in Denmark linking people in their own homes (that is with carephones), was established in 1978 by the Viborg municipal authority (Leeson, 1992, p 43). By 1985 there were 230 users of this service, most of whom had carephones but 45 of whom had radio units.[1] During normal working hours, responses to calls were undertaken by homecare staff who in any case had responsibilities for supporting service users as part of their homecare duties. Out of hours the monitoring and response centre would use other local contacts or emergency services.

In 1982 a social alarm service was set up by one of Denmark's largest authorities, Næstved. This was integrated within a broader range of homecare functions. Other authorities followed, encouraged by the perceived benefits, both from user and provider perspectives, identified in local service evaluations. The five years prior to such developments were characterised by experimentation with social alarm technologies including consideration of the best means of activating alarms, including the use of pull cords and touch strips, and the merits of activity monitoring.[2]

At 1992 it was estimated that 20,000 people in Denmark had a social alarm device. There was resistance to the extension of passive and activity monitoring, it having been affirmed that "users think the passive system both controls and puts them under tutelage" (Friediger, 1992, p 37). While potentially able to bring help more speedily in the event of a medical or other emergency, important questions about surveillance were raised in one review of developments in Denmark (Leeson, 1992, p 46).

Social alarm services in Denmark have been considered as well developed (Hansen, 1999, p 15). A number of area-based services are operated by municipal authorities and there is at least one national service, Falck, owned by an insurance company and essentially focused on medical needs. Responses to alarms are made by ambulances this, according to Friediger (1992, p 38), being "very often ... an over-reaction" and adding to service costs.

A social alarm service in Århus is operated by the social welfare department of the municipal authority in collaboration with the fire department.[3] In 1997 some 5,000 households were linked, most within care homes and sheltered housing. Responses were made, when necessary, by care staff based at 37 centres throughout the municipality.

An example of a small social alarm service is that of the city of Horsens. In 1999, 380 households were linked including six dwellings in grouped housing for older people.[4] Carephones were provided free of charge to those assessed by a nurse or occupational therapist as needing them due to medical and/or mobility problems, with people's needs being kept under regular review.

France

Social alarm services in France are less well developed than in many European countries although there has been an emphasis on care in the community, including the provision of varied forms of sheltered housing for older people with high levels of support need (Crosby, 1993, pp 83-5). The emphasis on community care rather than institutional care has been evident since the 1960s (Tester, 1996, p 17).

Social alarm services in France normally operate within broader strategies for older people drawn up by the municipal authorities (Randall, 1999, p 16). Most have been managed by municipal authorities or voluntary organisations. Monitoring and response centres have frequently been based with emergency services or homes for older people. Volunteers have sometimes being used as responders. The public telephone authority (PTT) fits telephones and carephones free of charge for older people on low incomes (Crosby, 1993, p 86). Financial support by municipal authorities is discretionary (Cullen and Robinson, 1997, p 130).

An example of a municipal service is that provided by the city of Nice. In 1978 Nice was one of the first cities in France to establish a social alarm service, which was subsequently complemented by another operating throughout the Alpes-Maritimes area and linked to a monitoring and response centre based with the ambulance service at St Roch hospital.[5]

The city of Niort in the Deux-Sèvres administrative district, in experimenting with different forms of housing for older people, developed a scheme of warden-assisted flats in 1991 to serve the neighbourhood of Clou-Buchet (Weiller and Laumonier, 1993, p 123). These benefited from the continual presence of a warden and were equipped with a range of technologies including a social alarm (p 130). For older people throughout the city, however, a service known as SERENA operated, which provided home assistance, telephone counselling, social alarms and surveillance. The service was set up in 1992 and was funded by a teachers' mutual benefit fund (Weiller and Laumonier, 1993, pp 131-2).

A further example is the Présence Verte social alarm service in the Département de l'Herault. The municipal authority of Lot-et-Garonne (near the Pyrenees) funded Présence Verte for older people living at home who need a high level of support (see http://www.presenceverte.com/presentation.html and http://www.lot-et-garonne.fr/html/cell2000/pages_so/solid1.htm).

In 1991 it was estimated that there were between 75,000 and 80,000 users of social alarm services in France.[6]

Germany

By the end of the 1980s some 170 social alarm services had been established in West Germany. These served about 17,000 mainly older people (Prass, 1992, pp 58-9). An unofficial survey in 1988 had identified 100 services with between 40 and 370 users and overall nationwide provision for "at least 13,000" (Zoche, 1994, pp 63-4). Zoche (p 59) noted that the first scheme was piloted at St Willehad Hospital in Wilhelmshaven, Lower Saxony, in 1980 with government financial support. This offered outreach services to hospital patients.

The 1988 survey identified the extent to which social alarm services were being established by voluntary bodies, a pattern which has continued. Zoche (p 64) noted that "it is the welfare organisations which are the classic operators of private emergency call services in Germany. The Red Cross, the Malteser Hilfsdienst, the Johanniter-Unfall-Hilfe, the Arbeiter-Samariter-Bund and the Caritas-Verband are the most important", with other services being operated by hospitals, security companies and other agencies. The largest service, he affirmed, operated from Frankfurt am Main. An example of a larger service was that in Berlin, run by St John's Ambulance (Löckenhoff, 1988, p 46).

The smallness of some earlier services led to a process of rationalisation and the setting up of umbrella organisations (Prass, 1992, p 60). This meant that some services were operational during daytime hours only, then switching through to one or other of the monitoring and response centres that were staffed 24-hours a day. The provenance of social alarm services reflected a continuing emphasis on the part of the German government on supporting older people outside institutions, promoting self-help and family support (Crosby, 1993, p 99). They were helped, also, by the availability of reduced telephone rates for pensioners (p 105).

The operation of social alarm technology in Germany is essentially the same as that in Great Britain. The apparent absence of services run by municipal authorities means that responses are first through local contacts. Health insurance companies have, it appears, not been involved in the promotion of social alarms. Zoche (1994, p 64) noted that according to service providers between 20 and 80 per cent of users "would have to go into an institution" but for their social alarms.

FREIBURG HOME EMERGENCY CALL SYSTEM

An evaluation of a social alarm service in Freiburg in the Black Forest noted similar benefits to those identified in other studies (Löckenhoff, 1988). This research was undertaken among both service users and their carers.

The Freiburg service was set up in 1984 under the auspices of the Caritas organisation, a charitable body. Its aims included integration of the service with social welfare and healthcare services, it being affirmed that it was concerned with more than just emergencies (Löckenhoff, 1988, p 38). To this end it was considered (p 39) that the service could help enhance social networks, encourage help between neighbours who were recipients of the service, and improve the quality of life for carers. The service incorporated two-way speech and responses to calls were made by nominated contacts or volunteer workers.

A survey of users of the Freiburg service elicited a number of comments about its benefits (p 41). Though the number of interviews undertaken was unspecified the figures quoted point to 30 users being involved. Among the purported benefits were:

- enabling people to stay put in their own homes and yet able to obtain help in emergencies;
- engendering a feeling of security; and
- greater peace of mind for relatives.

It was noted that the service had assisted many older people to live alone in their homes after the death of their spouse. The service appeared to help them, and others living alone, to feel reconnected with their community (Löckenhoff, 1988, p 42). Importantly, when considering the extent to which such technologies might liberate individuals, a further advantage was specified – that the service substituted for the otherwise continuous presence of a carer, in so doing giving the user a greater sense of independence and autonomy (p 43).

Set against these benefits Löckenhoff noted (pp 43-6) a number of barriers to taking up or using the service. These included:

- people's unwillingness to accept the need for a social alarm, a feeling that is exacerbated, perhaps, by the requirement (p 39) that users wear the portable radio trigger;
- fear of, or uncertainty about, the technology and of releasing personal information to be held on a computerised database;
- the difficulty for some potential users of finding suitable responders to whom house keys could be entrusted; and
- service costs, the Freiburg scheme being considered relatively expensive.

To these were added the problem of lack of awareness of the service and Löckenhoff (p 44) called for more active marketing of social alarms to centres of activity of older people, doctors' surgeries, and so on.

Interestingly, the average period during which users were linked to the service was just five months (Löckenhoff, 1988, p 45), reflecting a substantial emphasis on meeting the needs of people discharged from hospital. Such people were of all ages with the overall range of users being noted as including young people with acute illnesses (p 47).

EMERGENCY HOME CALL SERVICE IN NORDRHEIN-WESTFALEN

Information for a social alarm service in Nordrhein-Westfalen, including the City of Dortmund and other major urban communities, has clearly demonstrated its operation within a broader array of services concerned for the welfare of older people. Most pertinent, perhaps, is the provision of on-line advice and the option of videophone links to the monitoring and response centre. Objectives were shared with other services, these focusing on supporting independent living and affording users greater security.

In Dortmund in 2001 there were nearly 21,000 users of the service aged 65 or over.[7] Over 8,000 calls were dealt with in 1999. Medical staff were engaged to facilitate the provision of appropriate help when medical emergencies occurred. Responses requiring home visits were made through service staff and/or nominated contacts of the users.

The service was operated by a church organisation (Evangelischen Johanneswerk eV) based in Bielefeld and was supported by a range of charitable bodies. The cost of receiving the service was met for many users by the state government according to their assessed needs and means. Many users were self-funding (Adam, 1995, p 112).

Italy

Most social alarm users in Italy subscribe to services in the private and voluntary sectors. There appear to be no services provided directly by municipal authorities though some, notably the Veneto province, contract with a private service, TESAN, to provide for older people throughout the area for which they have responsibility (see below). This accords with the overall position in Italy where social welfare service frameworks are determined locally and are often complemented by services provided by private and/or voluntary agencies (Tester, 1996, pp 8-19, 81). Indeed, private and voluntary agencies have been noted as replacing public sector service provision (Crosby, 1993, pp 152-4). The context is one where there is a recognised need to support older people in the community and a concern on the part of government agencies about disproportionately high numbers of older people in rural areas (Crosby, 1993, p 145).

Most of the responsibility for health and social welfare services rests with regional governments who have a duty to prepare periodic health and social care plans. A core element of these addresses mechanisms for the delivery of care in the community services and is concerned to help, where appropriate, with the resettlement of older people from institutional care (Crosby, 1993, p 147).

TESAN

TESAN is by far the largest social alarm service in Italy. It operates nationally and in San Marino, though most service users are in northern Italy. A sizeable proportion of these are those for whom TESAN are contracted to provide a service on behalf of the Veneto municipal authority. By the end of 1998 TESAN had 25,000 households linked, with numbers at that time increasing by about 3,000 a year (Allen et al, 1997, p 25).

The service, while similar in many respects to those operated in other countries, is distinctive by the emphasis given to maintaining social contact with service users. This involves regular check calls to users, these being seen as important to their overall well-being. The frequency of such calls was determined by the user's needs but typically took place weekly (Allen et al, 1997, p 25).

The importance of such social contact was reaffirmed in a study of the TESAN service. This study found, over a four-year period from 1988 to 1991, and in relation to 1,875 deaths among service users, that there was just one suicide – where seven would have been expected based on mortality rates in the general population of older people in the Veneto region (De Leo et al, 1995, p 633). The suicide was of a 67 year old single woman who was living alone and referred to by her relatives as depressed and isolated She drowned herself just three and a half months after joining the service.

Given the potential importance of the finding of the research by De Leo et al, note must be made of the nature of the contact made by the service with its users. This took place as part of the contract to the Veneto municipality and required the service "to contact each client on an average of twice a week to monitor their condition through a short, informal interview and to offer emotional support" (p 632).

De Leo et al (p 634) implied that it might have been expected that suicide rates among the service users would have been higher than the general population in view of their being nominated to the service on the basis of related predisposing factors. They affirmed that "it is reasonable to assume that factors important in suicidal behaviour were particularly concentrated in the elderly subjects we studied because in most cases general practitioners and social workers were the ones to ask that their needier clients or patients be connected to the service".

In addition to the main monitoring and response centre at Vicenza, TESAN operated a number of regional response centres. These were staffed during normal working hours, switching through to Vicenza when closed. Responses requiring home visits were undertaken by nominated contacts and/or, if required, via local emergency services. The service was being developed to include telemedicine facilities for users newly discharged from hospital (Allen et al, 1997, p 33).

Also notable in relation to this service is that it was the subject of a rigorous economic evaluation by a team at the Universita di Padova (Tamborini et al, 1996). Among wide-ranging conclusions this study found (p 133) that, in a personal interview survey of 684 service users, between one in 10 (10.2 per cent) and a third (33.4 per cent) considered that moves to residential care had been avoided through their use of the TESAN service (p 133). Respondents also considered that having a social alarm reduced the risks associated with living at home.

Tamborini et al (1996, p 13) concluded that the impact of the service was such that public investment in social alarms should be countenanced. They calculated (p 134ff) that the cost savings associated with the reduced need for residential care for older people in the Veneto municipality would fund substantial numbers of users living at home, with (p 118ff) associated psycho-social benefits for the individuals concerned and their families.

The Netherlands

The Netherlands is particularly well advanced in the use of social alarms despite a tradition that is reflected in the high level of provision of forms of institutional care (Crosby, 1993, p 175). Social alarms were introduced in 1978 with central monitoring services emerging from 1984 (van Berlo et al, 1994, pp 69-70).

Tester (1996, p 91) noted that alarm services in the Netherlands were part of a range of services offered via local authorities and often were proffered by voluntary and charitable bodies. The Dutch equivalent of sheltered housing she noted (p 19) as "usually linked by alarm to nearby residential homes".

Hielkema (2001, p 600) summarised the position more recently, noting that "social alarm services in the Netherlands are provided by homecare organisations … welfare foundations and national and regional emergency centres" and adding that "health insurers often enter into contracts with these organisations on behalf of those they insure". Gott (1995, p 81) observed that social alarms were considered by the Dutch government as "one of the ways to support independent living" and an integral part of welfare policy albeit, not at that time, adequately integrated with medical and social services.

The promotion of social alarms in the Netherlands has to some extent been associated with the need to reduce the cost of health insurance. This has led to a number of concessionary schemes for social alarm devices as part of a broader range of policies concerned with helping people to stay in their own homes (Crosby, 1993, pp 179-180; van der Leeuw, 2001, p 11).

In 1986 it was estimated that there were about 15,000 older and 1,500 younger people in the Netherlands with social alarms. The 15,000 represented about 1 per cent of those aged 65 or over (Vlaskamp, 1992, p 107). By the end of 1993, van Berlo et al (1994, p 69) affirmed that around 200 organisations were providing services to some 63,000 people. The smallest systems had fewer than 20 households linked to them (van Berlo et al, 1994, p 71).

Vlaskamp (1992, p 113) noted that most social alarm services in the Netherlands operated to staffed monitoring and response centres. Many smaller services were run by volunteers and had fewer than 50 people linked. In keeping with government policy to promote care in the community and to reduce the proportion of older people living in institutions, grants were provided to assist the establishment of local alarm organisations (p 114).

Notable was the medical orientation of many services. This was particularly the case for those services managed by charities and voluntary organisations, their monitoring and response centres usually employing staff with nursing qualifications. This enabled them to mediate with doctors, ambulance services and others when urgent medical help was required (Vlaskamp, 1992, p 115). Some social alarm services were integral parts of wider service frameworks providing homecare support.

A smaller role in social alarm provision was maintained by the private sector. Private services did not, however, benefit from public subsidy. They tended to operate over wider areas, many being national, and offer portfolios of services that included property security, intruder and fire alarms (Vlaskamp, 1992, p 115). Service expansion was particularly noted as taking place in the charitable and voluntary sector based at centres that offered a range of homecare and related services (Gott, 1995, p 82).

The little evaluative work done with services in the Netherlands was noted by van Berlo et al (1994, pp 71-2) as pointing to the importance of social alarms in combating the fear associated with falls or medical events and their complications. By the late 1990s about 3 per cent of people aged 65 and over had a social alarm (van Berlo, 1998, pp 390-3) and by 2001 the national percentage was estimated by van der Leeuw (2001, p 14) at between 3 and 4 per cent. A higher percentage of older users (11.8 per cent) was noted, however, for Amsterdam, this comparing with just 2 per cent for the Rivierenland region (van der Leeuw, 2001, p 12).

Slovenia[8]

Slovenia was part of the former Yugoslavia. Its service frameworks, as a consequence, were moulded by the philosophy and ethos of that communist state. This was reflected in an emphasis on institutional provision for older people with care needs (Rudel et al, 1995, p 1503). Following Slovenia's independence in 1991 this emphasis has been redressed and social alarms have been included in government policy documents that endeavour to foster more community-based service frameworks.

Rudel et al (p 1504) have described the first social alarm service in Slovenia. This was established in 1992 in Ljubljana and benefited from government financial support. After 16 months operation, and various publicity and promotional efforts, there were 65 service users provided with carephones. A service evaluation stated that "all clients reported positive psychological effects" (Rudel et al, 1995, p 1504). Hojnik-Zupanc (1996, pp 188, 191) noted that some two thirds of users were aged 70 or over and that 86 per cent were women. Of over 2,000 calls received just 2 per cent were deemed emergencies. Service users had grown in number to 120 by the end of the second year (Premik and Rudel, 1996, p 224) and 150 by 2001 (Rudel and Fisk, 2001, p 735).

The most recent study of the service revealed the average age of users as 85. These were characterised by "almost identical health problems to their institutionalised colleagues" (Rudel et al, 1999, p 204). Most interesting, however, was the thought given to the role of operators at the monitoring and response centre. This revealed the extent to which social alarms were seen as more than facilitating responses in the event of medical emergencies. The service also offered advice (see also Hojnik-Zupanc et al, 1998, p 192). The medical orientation was, however, clear from the fact that it is nurses that were employed at the monitoring and response centre. Rudel et al (pp 204-5) grouped the operators' tasks as follows:

* consulting, provision of advice, chatting;
* mediating in relation to doctors, nursing care and emergency medical services;
* coordinating care services between different providers; and
* monitoring both service provision and giving reminders to users regarding medication.

In the early period an evaluation took place that reported very positively on the Ljubljana social alarm service (Rudel et al, 1995, p 224). As a result of this evaluation, plans were made to develop a number of regional centres. Such plans did not, in the event, come to fruition. Nevertheless, some positive outcomes of the initiative are evident in addition to the fact that some 150 users at any one time are served by the current service.

Hojnik-Zupanc et al (1998, p 193) noted that much emphasis was placed on service development rather than a "mass recruitment of users". Nevertheless, awareness of social alarms in Slovenia is increasing and their place in the range of community-based services is becoming better established. Also private health insurers are recognising social alarms as a means of their avoiding some of the costs associated with institutional care. Development has not taken place to the extent anticipated, however, because of the absence of sufficient financial support. Premik and Rudel (1996, p 224) lamented that "all parties are in favour of the system but nobody is willing to pay for it". A further problem noted by Hojnik-Zupanc et al (1998, p 194) was the relatively low numbers of older people with telephone lines to their homes.

At 2003 there are three other social alarm services in Slovenia. One, established in 1997, operates from a residential home for older people in the city of Celje. It benefits from financial support from the Ministry of Work and Social Affairs and, in 1999, had fewer than 20 users. Despite the low user base, the service at Celje has helped in the development of homecare services in that region, with the service manager also having responsibility for a team of homecarers.

The two remaining services are more security oriented, with their monitoring and response service being staffed only during the daytime, with someone 'on call' out of hours. One of these schemes operates in the town of Maribor. When a call is received that relates to health or social welfare needs an appropriate worker is informed who then phones the user to check their circumstances before deciding on the most appropriate response.

The potential for the further development of social alarm services in Slovenia has been noted by Rudel and Fisk (2001, p 736). They affirmed that "paradoxically, the absence of well developed personal response systems in Slovenia can be viewed as advantageous", explaining this by adding that "the reason is that such systems and services in more developed economies are often constrained with long established bureaucratic and funding frameworks". There was, they considered (p 737), an "opportunity for Slovenia to develop new and holistic service frameworks" in which social alarms and related technologies could play an important part.

Sweden

Social alarm systems are a commonplace feature of flats in Sweden. Östlund (1994, p 48) pointed to their being introduced in 1973 as part of the standard range of equipment in service houses, roughly equivalent to what in Great Britain is known as very or extra care sheltered housing. Early systems included both active and passive features but with use of the latter subsequently diminishing in a context where their appropriateness was questioned (Östlund, 1994, p 49). Regarding the passive feature Östlund (p 49) argued that "since the development of care is directed towards less control of the individual, the usefulness of such alarms is decreasing".

The Swedish government, recognised the value of social alarms when in 1982 it described them "as a complement to care and support for the elderly and for persons with disabilities" and "making it easier for old people to stay in their own homes" (Östlund, 1994, p 51). Achievement of the latter, Östlund noted (p 51), was claimed in a local study published in Swedish by Wallengren and Samuelsson in 1988, which stated that "39 per cent of users would not be able to stay in their own homes if it were not for the safety alarm". Testimony to the smallness of some services was given by Wenger (1986, p 20). She reported on a social alarm service in the community of Klippan that had just 65 subscribers.

Later in the 1980s social alarm services became more widespread in Sweden, with initiatives being taken by most municipal authorities. By 1991 there were some 130,000 users of social alarms, 80,000 of whom were living in service houses or other forms of specialist housing (Stenberg, 1992, p 137). Some services had several thousand users with carephones linked to them. Social alarm services operate in all municipalities. Private services are rare (Östlund, 1999, p 55).

One of the municipal social alarm services was operated by the Social

Emergency Department of the Stockholm municipality. It commenced in 1980 and by 1993 had expanded to include the provision of about 3,000 carephones out of an estimated 4,000 users of such devices in the capital. The Stockholm municipal service was the largest in Sweden.[9] Responses to calls were made by locally based staff or via standby staff based at the monitoring and response centre. The role of the service related to both medical emergencies and assistance with personal care needs.

A study of the municipal service in the city of Linköping established the views of 74 users, living in their own homes or in a service house (Östlund, 1994, pp 55-7). It concluded that:

- the presence of an alarm positively influenced moving choices;
- relatives were reassured;
- users felt safer; but
- some changes took place in the extent of contact with others.

Regarding the last of these, Östlund found (p 55) that some users lost some of their daily contacts. She remarked (p 56), however, that the behaviour of older people with social alarms generally did not change, and noted that, although telephones could help in relation to social contact, such technologies were not always appropriate when there were needs that related to befriending or emotional support.

In summary, and noting the various service evaluations in Sweden, Östland saw the merits of social alarms but remained concerned about their potential to sustain dependency. She stated (p 54) that "safety alarms increased safety and flexibility in terms of users' time and space. The elderly could choose where to live and the home help service could keep in contact" and "from this perspective, safety alarms can be regarded as a technology that contributes to increased independence". But she added that "the safety alarm may be a person's only alternative to reach help – and in that perspective, dependency remains".

Other European countries

Austria

An overview of social alarm services in Austria was provided by Kirschner (1994). She found (p 23) that in 1993 some 15 organisations offered services including some municipal authorities. Financial support for such services was at the discretion of the nine federal states (Cullen and Robinson, 1997, p 126).

The first Austrian service was established in Salzburg in 1983 (Kirschner, 1994, p 30). It operated from an ambulance station. Kirschner noted (p 32) that eight further services were established in the ensuing three years partly stimulated by "the aggressive marketing strategy of an Austrian sales company". She calculated (p 33) that the 11 services that operated from ambulance stations served some 1,500 users. Two services were operated by what she referred to as social organisations, and all but one provided other care and support services, including medical care and home meals. The largest service had 1,100 users and operated with the help of volunteers.

In 1994 there were an estimated 2,600 users of social alarms with hardly any in the private sector (Kirschner, 1994, p 38). The potential of such services had, however, been established as had their role in providing security and a means of obtaining help in the event of falls or illness. By 1999 it was claimed that one in every 500 people aged 65 or over in Austria were linked to a social alarm service (Leichsenring, 1999, p 15).

Czech Republic

A social alarm service known as AREION was established in the Czech Republic in 1992. Its origins were in a voluntary organisation called Life90. The service was, in part, staffed by volunteers (Kasalová and Mellanová, 1998, p 258). Some grant aid was received from the Ministry of Social Affairs. The service was provided free of charge, by 1999 linking some 200 users in Prague, Hradec Králové and elsewhere.[10]

The service has included passive features including monitoring door opening, with Kasalová (1994, p 30) noting that "the system has already proven its merits not only for health emergencies but also for criminal assaults". But take-up was lower than anticipated due, according to Kasalová (p 30), to "the psychology of older people who have proven surprisingly reluctant to use these devices". Incorporated in the service were daily outgoing calls to its users (Kasalová and Mellanová, 1998, p 258).

A survey of service users found that most valued it highly. Telephone calls to users were particularly appreciated by those who appeared to be socially isolated though they were criticised by others who appeared to have extensive local and family networks (Kasalová and Mellanová, 1998, p 259). Kasalová and Mellanová (p 259) judged AREION to have been a success and pointed to the desirability of the service being extended throughout the country. The investment for service development, they suggested, might be forthcoming from state funds and/or from insurance companies.

Finland

According to Vaarama and Kautto (1999, p 46) social alarm services have been available in Finland since 1984. They are provided throughout the country following national legislation that required each municipal authority to make such provision. The services were free to eligible users (Cullen and Robinson, 1997, pp 11, 129). Some experimentation has taken place in Finland to consider the wider role of social alarms in relation to the needs of older people with dementia (Leikas et al, 1998). There are approximately 120,000 social alarm users in Finland.[11]

Greece

What were described as pilot services were established in some urban areas of Greece. Services in Athens and Thessalonika were understood to be free to eligible users (Cullen and Robinson, 1997, pp 11, 132).

Hungary

A social alarm service was established in Budapest, which reportedly linked 90 per cent of the municipal authority's homecare clients (Széman, 1998, p 458). It operated via a radio link to a monitoring and response centre managed by a charity. Care workers of the charity responded to calls.

Norway

Social alarm services in Norway are operated both by municipal authorities and private sector organisations. They have been noted as available in most municipalities (Daatland, 1999, p 29).

There have been concerns in Norway regarding carephones and their functionality. This resulted in tests, on behalf of the Norwegian Consumer Council (Forbrukerrådet) being undertaken by the Research Institute for Consumer Affairs in Great Britain (*Forbruker Rapporten 5*, 1990).

Malta

Only one social alarm service operates in Malta. It was set up in 1990 and grew to serve all three islands of the Maltese archipelago (Wright, 1998, p 51). By November 2001 the service had grown to have 8,350 users.[12] All had carephones, there being no sheltered housing in Malta. The service is provided through a collaborative arrangement between the government's Secretariat for the Care of the Elderly and Maltacom, the islands' telecommunications company. The service is focused on social welfare needs with medical certification being required prior to provision.[13]

There has been no charge for equipment installations and a reduced charge for new telephone line installations. Responses to calls are made through nominated contacts, doctors or emergency services as appropriate (Wright, 1998, p 51). Outgoing calls are made to service users on their birthdays and service staff undertake home visits.[14]

Wright noted (1998, p 51) that problems encountered by the Maltese service appeared to focus on mains failures and the flood of calls to the monitoring and response centre that these generated; and the lack of understanding of the system by some users. Emphasis, he noted, was placed on maintaining good personal contact with users, with the benefits of the service being seen as not just providing a means of obtaining help in medical emergencies but as giving additional security and peace of mind for the users and their relatives.

Switzerland

A mosaic of social alarm services is understood to be managed by municipal authorities or contracted by them to private sector organisations. According to Cullen and Robinson (1997, p 107) social alarms have been installed free of charge for eligible users. By 1997 they provided for perhaps 4 per cent of older people in Switzerland.[15]

Spain

Several social alarm services operate in Spain mostly under the auspices of voluntary or charitable organisations. The number of users has been estimated at around 45,000, with the Red Cross serving nearly half. A private sector social alarm service is Eulen, which provides social alarms to some 4,500 users and domiciliary support services to a larger number on behalf of municipal authorities.[16]

Some municipal authorities have provided social alarms and, according to Cabrero (1999, p 22), have reported favourably on them. A social alarm service, Magna Careline Espana, aimed mainly at the expatriate market on the Costa del Sol was established in 1997 by a British housing association. It closed, however, due to lack of take-up.[17]

Other countries

Aside from the foregoing, social alarm services are known to operate in the following European countries: Belgium, Croatia, Cyprus, Iceland, Luxembourg and Portugal.

Outside Europe and North America

Outside Europe and North America, the development of social alarms has been concentrated in relatively few countries, the most notable being Australia, Israel and Japan.

Australia

The need for initiatives in Australia involving the use of "low cost emergency telephone devices" was noted by the Bureau for the Aged (1986, p 71). Subsequently, various initiatives were pursued including a pilot social alarm service, established in 1991 in the city of Geelong. Other schemes at the time were also operative in New South Wales (see http://www.zorro.com.au/vitalcall/new.html).

An appraisal of one initiative, provided by the Heidelberg Repatriation Hospital, was undertaken by Farquhar et al (1992). This studied 125 people (pp 3-4) who were assessed by an occupational therapist as needing a social alarm, initially by reference to their assessment reports and then, 15-22 months later, by a telephone survey. The minimum criteria for eligibility for the service were that applicants should have been living alone; have medical or physical problems that constituted a major risk; and should have had sufficient physical and cognitive ability to use an alarm.

Farquhar et al found (p 4) that the average age on assessment was 79, with the commonest source of referrals (65 per cent) being doctors. Most (88 per cent) users admitted to having had a fall in the previous year. By the time of the telephone interviews 56 of the original 125 were unavailable. Of those 'lost', 30 had died, 13 were institutionalised, nine were in hospital, and four had ceased using the alarm. Of the remaining 69, 26 had used their carephone in the previous year, most usually (that is, in 54 per cent of occasions) because of a fall, 12 requiring hospitalisation as a consequence.

Farquhar et al (p 5) noted that "most clients felt the alarm was of major (74%) or moderate (20%) importance to their lifestyle" and that they generally ascribed the importance of their alarms in terms of the peace of mind and confidence it gave them (p 6). However, the researchers expressed concern (p 4), that 39 per cent of users stated that they were not wearing their pendant transmitters at the time of their telephone interviews, asserting (p 6) that "agencies could check, during their visits, that subjects are wearing their alarms and, if not, could remind them of the importance of doing so", adding that "it is ... important to periodically monitor the clients to ensure their optimal compliance".

Notable is the fact that the first nominated contacts of service users were also interviewed (pp 4-5), these being mainly relatives (46 per cent) and neighbours (33 per cent). While details of the latter were not reported, the researchers pointed to a strong positive correlation with the views expressed by the service users (p 5). Finally, Farquhar et al (p 6) remarked that "emergency alarms are a moderately inexpensive and well tolerated facility that can be provided to selected at risk patients". They were unable to state whether they were cost effective.

In the ensuing period social alarm services developed throughout Australia though they were arguably "insufficiently integrated into overall service planning" and "grossly under applied in the area of care in the home".[18] Most were private sector services but with several not-for-profit services operating in South Australia and Victoria. Victoria was the only state with a clear public sector funding commitment through their Department of Veterans Affairs. This covered the full cost for eligible service users. One regionally based health insurance company was willing to pay for social alarms as part of healthcare programmes.[19]

Detailed research on social alarms in Australia has been undertaken in the state of Victoria by the Department of Human Services (1998). This offered a thorough and comprehensive review of the state's own social alarm service (VICPACS, see below) in the context of other services operated in the state. Outside Victoria a similar variety of services operate. In Western Australia a social alarm service is managed by Silver Chain, a voluntary body contracted to various state departments with responsibility for health and social welfare services. The service is based at Osbourne Park, serves about 2,000 people, and operates in 31 shires and some very remote areas of the state.[20]

That the nature of social alarm services in Australia might change is, however, signalled by the clear social welfare orientation of many services and the recognition of the role that sensors and smart technologies might play in the future. British Telecom (1996, p 144), for instance, noted the work being undertaken at the University of New South Wales using a number of sensors as part of a system for activity and lifestyle monitoring, ideas relating to which emerged in their later initiative with Anchor Trust (see Porteus and Brownsell, 2000) in Great Britain. This is discussed in Chapter Thirteen. At 2003, there were estimated to be between 90,000 and 110,000 social alarm users in Australia.[21]

VICTORIAN PERSONAL ASSISTANCE CALL SERVICE

The VICPACS service was set up in 1988 and became operational statewide in 1989. It grew to become an important component of homecare services in Victoria. The context is one where the Victorian government had also promoted what it called a telelink service for housebound clients so that they could participate in group activities. The government were also conscious of the potential benefits that might come via the Internet (Department of Human Services, 1998, pp 9-10).

While originally administered internally, the VICPACS service was contracted out to two private sector providers. One of the services utilised was Vital Call in Sydney. The service was provided free of charge to those assessed as in need of the same (Department of Human Services, 1998, p 10) and, at 1998, some 6,200 users were being funded (p 84). The government's vision of the role of social alarms was clearly broad. The report affirmed (p 17) that "PRS could be directed ... to prevent inappropriate use of the homecare service system. PRSs could also complement existing homecare provision".

Likely cost savings and the possibility of resource reallocation were indicated (Department of Human Services, 1998, p 26), it being noted that "some homecare services have directly introduced the PRS into their homecare delivery to offset existing homecare costs". More specifically the department's evaluation led them to suggest (p 37) that "considerable fiscal savings can be achieved in the acute care and rehabilitation sectors if PRSs are provided at discharge" from hospital. Broader benefits of social alarms were noted through their providing support for carers, enabling them to return to work and reducing domestic tension (pp 23-4).

With regard to the inclusiveness of the service, concerns were voiced about underrepresentation of ethnic minorities and smaller language groups (pp 43-4). Separate services for such groups were not, however, advocated but rather the employment of multilingual staff, staff training on cultural awareness issues and the use of party line or conference calling facilities at the monitoring and response centres. The conference calling facility would enable three-way conversations to take place including the service user, the operator at the monitoring and response centre, and a translator.

Finally, in looking at broader agendas, the department (p 40) recognised the potential of social alarms, together with associated technologies (including activity monitoring and smoke detection) for people with some dementia. In fact a very inclusive approach was advocated, it being stated (p 32) that this could facilitate development of a more preventative role. Issues of age (p 62) and social isolation (p 33) should not, they considered, compromise eligibility.

Evident from supplementary information provided with the evaluation of the VICPACS service is the extent to which social alarm services had developed, at least in Victoria. The report (p 80ff) noted that "over 10,500 consumers in Victoria are receiving services". While some services were noted as having a security orientation, others were more oriented to healthcare. The Vital Call service, for instance, employed nurses at their monitoring and response centre (Department of Human Services, 1998, p 80). Others, such as the service at Geelong, use community-based volunteers (p 81).

Israel

The position regarding social alarm services in Israel was first documented in a government-sponsored survey in 1989. This was reported on by Cahn (1992, p 69ff). Among other things Cahn noted (p 80) the survey's recommendation that such services should be encouraged and the role of such technologies in relation to healthcare needs recognised. Emergency medical services or the police were seen as appropriate responders, it being suggested that such a framework could help develop a better understanding between the police and the communities they served.

The survey found that 10 social alarm services operated throughout Israel (Cahn, 1992, p 69). Local services were run by voluntary organisations such as

Yad Sarah in Jerusalem, which provided, according to their brochure, "medical emergency radio-alarms to the homes of the needy". They were the first organisation to operate a social alarm service in Israel (Cahn, 1992, p 74). In 2001 wrist-worn radio triggers were being assembled by Yad Sarah at the rate of 30 a day (http://www.yadsarah.org.il/News/jparticle.html).

A range of other organisations now offer social alarm services in Israel. One is Shahal but for whom social alarms are part of a broader range of services and technologies that include cardiac monitors, respiratory monitoring systems and an Internet medical service (see www.shahal.co.il and Chapter Twelve). This service was established in 1987 and developed to include operational bases in several countries. Its operation, in association with medical diagnostic devices, was noted by Yatim (1997, p 27). With regard to social welfare agendas, social alarms have been seen as an increasingly important component of domiciliary service provision (Cahn, 1992, pp 79-80).

More recently there were some nine companies concerned with homecare services supported by social alarm and related technologies with "approximately 3 per cent of adults in Israel (some 150,000 people aged 25-90) being users of some form of tele-based homecare service" (European Commission, 2001, p 184).

Japan

Japan has one of the most rapidly growing populations of older people and by early in the 21st century "probably will be the oldest nation in the world" (Clark and Ogawa, 1996, pp 443-4). This presents that country with a substantial challenge if care in the community agendas are to be pursued. Such agendas are central to the government's Gold Plan, launched in 1989, and have underpinned developments aimed at supporting older people subsequently (Organisation for Economic Co-operation and Development, 1996, p 147; Kose, 1997, p 137). The Gold Plan was revised in 1994 but apparently has had limited initial impact.[22] Housing options for older people include 'silver housing' projects that include social alarms and are based on the British model of sheltered housing (Kose, 1997, p 132).

The starting point for social alarms in Japan is considered to be the service established in 1981 by the Musashino Corporation, Tokyo in 1981 (Abe, 1992, pp 85-6). Other municipal authorities followed suit and, by 1988, some 230 had developed social alarm services. Some include activity monitoring. It was estimated at the time that together with private services 26,000 mainly older people had social alarms (Abe, 1992, p 87).

In many cases, services were managed by the fire departments of the municipalities in question. In some, responsibility was contracted out to private companies or voluntary organisations. About 6,000 people with social alarms subscribed to private services, these often being provided as an adjunct to property security or in one case to a taxi service, with taxi drivers responding when an emergency arose, providing help and determining if there was a need for an ambulance or the police (Abe, 1992, pp 87, 98). In 1997, such a service based on a cooperative of taxi companies operated "in forty areas throughout Japan", with 4,800 paying customers. Users could also, naturally, use the service to obtain a taxi for ordinary purposes (see http://www.jinjapan.org/trends/honbun/ntj970818.html).

More recently, a trade mission from Great Britain to Japan reported on a number of initiatives where social alarms featured within smart home developments (Gann et al, 2000, p 17ff). More traditional social alarm services were also apparent including one, SECOM, which served some 42,000 people and operated alongside a property security monitoring service (pp 36-7); and another, Anzen, operating on a partially devolved basis in regional centres. This served 27,000.

After reviewing three social alarm services in Japan, Abe (1992, p 98) affirmed both the need for their further development and for them to broaden their role to increase the extent of human contact with users. This, he suggested, required an extension in capacity to give advice on a broad range of issues concerned with independent living. Also suggested was the need for technological developments that would ensure more prompt reporting of medical conditions where someone was unable to set off the alarm.

MIYAGI PREFECTURE

The Miyagi prefecture covers 71 municipalities over a sizeable region around and including Sendai City. Its social alarm service, established in 1988 jointly with the Miyagi Prefecture Medical Association, saw its purpose as being focused on the medical needs of its users (Abe, 1992, p 92).

Alongside the need to respond in the event of medical or other emergencies was an advisory service that gave guidance on medical services and treatments. A passive monitoring facility was incorporated, many users having sensors attached to their toilet doors and relating to which information was sent, once daily, to the monitoring and response centre (p 93). Some problems were encountered in relation to the latter but there appeared to have been broad acceptance of this feature. By February 1990, 35 out of the 71 municipalities were subscribing to the service and there were over 700 older people (aged 65 or over) living alone supported by it (p 93).

Other countries outside Europe and North America

China

The existence of social alarms in China has been noted in an overview of housing for older people in Hong Kong.[23] Projects providing specialist housing for about 2,500 older people were described, each having "emergency alarm and warden services". Such alarms were introduced in Hong Kong in 1991 and, as well as being installed in specialist forms of housing provision, by 1995 they had extended to include over 1,000 households in the wider community.[24]

New Zealand

The first social alarm service established in New Zealand was in 1983. This was operated by a not-for-profit organisation, the New Zealand Disabilities Resource Centre. Subsequent initiatives were mostly taken by commercial organisations (Herman, 1992, p 131). One scheme, the Palmerston North Telephone-linked Alarm System, was the subject of a favourable evaluative study in terms of its ability to meet the "emergency needs of at-risk individuals" (p 132).

The role of private sector social alarm services has been indicated in a government reference to the fact that "many older people choose to increase security by personal and house alarms, security and smoke alarms" (Ministry of Social Development, 2001, p 61).

Singapore

The existence of social alarms in accommodation for older people in Singapore was noted by Harrison (1997, p 30). The manner of their operation involving calls being switched over to a monitoring and response centre managed by the police is described elsewhere (see http://www.dpa.org.sg/DPA/publication/hdmj97/p19.htm).

Other countries

Aside from the foregoing countries outside Europe and North America social alarm services operate in Costa Rica, Mexico and South Korea.

Discussion

Social alarms are now widespread throughout the Western world and have begun to spread to a number of less developed countries. While the research evidence is often limited there are clear indications that service configurations are primarily concerned with healthcare and social welfare objectives.

The impetus for using such technologies appears to relate most closely to fears of the consequences of demographic change and a desire to reap the benefit, in terms of cost savings, that social alarms are seen as offering. That it is not necessarily easy to exploit that potential is illustrated by the case of Slovenia where, although there is agreement as to their benefits, government agencies are unwilling to support new initiatives to the extent that might be considered appropriate (Premik and Rudel, 1996, p 224). At the same time the extent of wealth among potential private service users remains constrained.

For richer countries, however, there is often uncertainty and a clear difficulty attached to social alarms because of their not seeming to fit within established departmental and service structures. The original patterns relating to service providers have as a consequence largely been maintained. In some countries such as Germany, Spain and Israel, voluntary organisations are major providers, sometimes with public sector support and often in competition with the private sector.

The general lack of specific attention given to social alarms was noted by Cullen and Robinson in their review of assistive technologies in countries of the European Union. They observed (1997, p 122) that:

> Although most countries have provisions under social policy to provide some form of financial support for disabled and elderly people to acquire assistive technologies, in many countries this support is better defined for assistive technology to be used in occupational and educational settings than for the more general purpose home use.

But at the same time as social alarms are becoming more established in many parts of Europe, so the agendas relating to them are changing. The evolution of social alarms within frameworks concerned for smart homes is one that is signalled (see Chapter Eleven), there being innovative projects and high levels of awareness of their potential in such countries as the Netherlands, Norway, Japan and Australia. A further line of evolution is signalled by the pursuit of healthcare and medical agendas, this strongly featuring for services in Israel, some of which operate worldwide.

In the private sector, by contrast, social alarm services seem more anchored to the simple role of obtaining help in an emergency. The context in which these are proffered appears similar in many countries, with social alarms often aligned with security services.

The message is that social alarms are seen by increasing numbers of governments and public sector institutions as important to policy and practice agendas and will remain, therefore (at least in relation to those with an assessed need), the subject of attention and subsidy. Social alarms are, however, also seen as a commercial opportunity that may be offered alongside other 24-hour services. Many security companies and, interestingly, a Japanese taxi cooperative, have clearly recognised this.

Notes

[1] Møller, K (1985) in paper to conference on bio-telesurveillance, Annecy.

[2] As above.

[3] Correspondence with Carl-Johan Skovsgaard (Municipality of Århus).

[4] Correspondence with Hans Bronfeld (Municipality of Horsens).

[5] Mayer, M. (1983) in paper to telecities workshop, Nice.

[6] Conan, M. (1994) in paper to conference on information technologies, Glasgow.

[7] Correspondence with Ines Weidhase (Evangelisches Johanneswerk eV, Bielefeld).

[8] Correspondence with Dr Drago Rudel (MKS Electronic Systems Ltd. and University of Ljubljana).

[9] Landegren, M. (1993) in paper to telecities workshop, Nice.

[10] Correspondence between Hana Kasalová (University Hospital of Králové Vinohrady, Prague) and Dr Drago Rudel (MKS Electronics and University of Ljubljana).

[11] Correspondence with Hans-Aage Moustgaard (International Security Technology, Helsinki).

[12] Correspondence with Mary Ciantar (Maltese Telecare Centre).

[13] Correspondence with Paul Mifsud (Planning Authority, Malta) and Maryanne Gauci (Department for the Care of the Elderly).

[14] As above.

[15] Correspondence with Luis Ruiz (CSEM, Swiss Centre for Electronics and Microtechnology, Neuchâtel).

[16] Correspondence with Dr Guillen Llera (Eulen, Madrid).

[17] Correspondence with Gill Clark (Magna Careline Ltd, Dorset).

[18] Bruce, I. (1997) in paper to conference on technology for people with disabilities, Canberra.

[19] Correspondence with Ian Bruce (Home and Community Services and Strategies, Brighton).

[20] Correspondence with Deida Nicholls (Silver Chain).

[21] Correspondence with Ian Bruce (Home and Community Services and Strategies, Brighton).

[22] Correspondence with Satoshe Kose (Building Research Institute, Tsukuba).

[23] Fung, T.T. (1995) in paper to conference of the International Federation of Housing and Planning Conference, Belfast.

[24] As above.

TEN

Social alarms: international comparisons

The current position

Social alarms, as documented in Chapters Five to Nine, are now established in most, if not all, countries of the Western world. They are particularly well established in Northern Europe including the Scandinavian countries, and also in North America, Israel, Japan and Australia. They are also increasingly evident in a number of less developed countries such as those within former Eastern Europe and the former Yugoslavia.

The evidence for this wider distribution of social alarms is limited in the sense that there are, as emphasised in Chapter Three, few published articles and reports emanating from many of the countries in question. The main manufacturers meanwhile have been understandably guarded about where they have marketed their wares lest they signal commercial opportunities to others.

Despite such provisos, the information presented in this book makes it possible to list both the countries where social alarms are well established and those where some social alarm services are evident but the markets remain poorly developed. Social alarms are well established in many of the former in the sense that they are underpinned by public sector subsidies and sometimes legislation that encourages or requires such provision. Alternatively there are commercial markets within which services can actively compete for the custom of older people and/or agencies that provide support services for their benefit. A number of smaller countries can also be included where the markets may be limited in size but where social alarms are used by several thousand older people. Table 10.1 provides those listings of countries with established or developing markets.

Themes and issues

Making comparisons between the contrasting countries with social alarms is difficult. The paucity of specific information regarding them has been noted. And even when some information is available it may only be passing mention.

Few central or regional government departments or agencies have specifically addressed the issue of social alarm services and their role. Accolades must go, therefore, to the Victoria State government in Australia in their review of the VICPACS service discussed in Chapter Nine (Department of Human Services,

Table 10.1: Countries with social alarms

Established markets		
• Australia	• Great Britain and Northern Ireland	• Netherlands
• Austria	• Iceland	• New Zealand
• Belgium	• Ireland	• Norway
• Canada	• Israel	• Spain
• Denmark	• Italy	• Sweden
• Finland	• Japan	• Switzerland
• France	• Luxembourg	• United States
• Germany	• Malta	
Developing markets		
• China	• Czech Republic	• Portugal
• Costa Rica	• Greece	• Singapore
• Croatia	• Hungary	• Slovenia
• Cyprus	• Mexico	• South Korea

1998) and, for earlier studies, to Scottish Homes (Duncan and Thwaites, 1987), the Ontario Ministry of Community and Social Services (1987) and the Canada Mortgage and Housing Corporation (MacLaren Plansearch, 1988).

Other relevant work, to be fair, has been funded by government departments or agencies but wherein social alarms have been noted within wider ranges of services or technologies. Perhaps the most notable of these, funded through the European Commission, is the work of Cullen and Robinson (1997).

As indicated in the Appendix, this book has had to rely on a disparate range of information from a multiplicity of published and unpublished sources. But by this means it has been possible to make informed observations by which similarities and differences in approach between countries towards social alarms and their role in supporting independent living among older people become clearer.

A useful starting point for such observations on social alarms was provided in Chapter One through its reference to, and preliminary discussion of, the demographic, political, social and technological contexts. In furthering this discussion it is appropriate to take matters in a different order, reflecting the different influences of a number of factors. This is not to say that such influences applied equally in all countries. Things are far more complicated than that. They are affected by the happenstance of technological innovation; the cultural, linguistic and historic affinities of a particular country; the marketing strategies of the main manufacturers and suppliers; the political predisposition of governments and their propensity or not to support social alarms through public subsidies; different views as to the role and purpose of social alarms; and geographical location.

Technological context

In considering the countries where social alarms are most prevalent, the technological context relates to both the location of initial innovations and the way in which products were subsequently marketed. The advent of social alarms, albeit in different forms, both within the United States and Great Britain has been discussed in Chapter Four. What followed was the aggressive marketing of the products in those countries in ways that responded to what were seen as the greatest market opportunities, that is the private healthcare and sheltered housing markets respectively.

For the United States the main early drive came from Lifeline Systems with any additional marketing effort outside that country being confined to Canada. For Great Britain the main drive came from Tunstall Byers (now Tunstall Telecom) and Davis Security Systems (now, through acquisition, Attendo Systems Ltd), with the focus being essentially confined to Great Britain and Northern Ireland. The main factor was, in other words, technological push. And on both sides of the Atlantic there were circumstances that were receptive to the marketing messages purveyed by the companies in question.

For the United States and Canada the message aimed at healthcare providers in hospitals and nursing homes was concerned with cost savings through such things as the earlier discharge of patients or, in the jargon, discharging people "quicker and sicker" (Fisk, 1990, p 11). Social alarms were also promoted as a means of supporting outreach services, this message having a particular appeal to those seeking to provide services to older people in rural areas.

For Great Britain and Northern Ireland the message, aimed almost exclusively at local authority service providers, was concerned with cost savings through reducing or obviating the need for sheltered housing wardens. However, it was a message laced with a generous dose of ageist sentiments and imagery that saw local authorities as patrons or benefactors needing to be seen to be doing good for the older people in their areas.

Manufacturers were, in fact, less than subtle in their marketing messages. As noted in Chapter One a kind of social alarms icon emerged in the picture of the fallen woman using her social alarm to obtain help (see Plate 1.1). The implied question, not lost on service providers, was: what would have happened if she had not had her social alarm to hand?

The United States, Canada, Great Britain and Northern Ireland are, of course, relatively wealthy countries. The growth of social alarms therefore fed on the private wealth of the former and the public sector munificence of the latter. The context for North America was more open in that carephones could be installed in any home where there was a telephone line. The context for Great Britain and Northern Ireland was clearer in that the call systems would normally replace bells and buzzers or be included as a standard part of, and requirement for, sheltered housing developments.

Social alarm innovation in other countries such as Germany, Japan, Sweden and Australia generally came later. This mostly focused on carephones together with the receiving equipment that would be installed at monitoring and response centres.

While the companies that manufactured and marketed social alarms experienced changes in fortune it is interesting to note the continued dominance, at least in their countries of origin, of Lifeline Systems in the United States and of Tunstall Telecom in Great Britain and Northern Ireland. Other companies of note are Estafette, Antenna and Attendo in different parts of Europe, and VitalCall International in Australasia.

Where such companies operate has tended to relate to cultural, linguistic and geographical factors. Hence Lifeline Systems remain active throughout North America, a huge market in itself, and there is the tendency for most European companies to market their wares in adjoining countries. The exception in the latter case is Tunstall Telecom, which markets its products in different parts of Europe and in several Commonwealth countries, notably Australia and Canada.

It should be noted that several of the countries that are not primarily associated with technological innovation specifically relating to social alarms have been the location of development activity regarding automated and smart technologies in the home. Chapter Eleven bears testimony to some such work.

Political context

With regard to the political context the position is complex. The trend towards care in the community, and ipso facto reducing the emphasis on institutional forms of accommodation for older people, has been noted for nearly all of the countries in which social alarms feature (Organisation for Economic Co-operation and Development, 1996, p 35). This reflects the fact that wherever a country stands in relation to their emphasis on private or public sector mechanisms for supporting services used by older people there is: (a) a common interest in saving public money; and (b) a belief that community-based solutions are cheaper.

Herein lies a political message that strikes a chord with most older people themselves since they, on the whole, strongly affirm their desire to stay put and are very resistant to moving to any form of institution, thereby achieving the objective of at least one basic aspect of independence. If the emphasis within some countries on social inclusion is added then there is a clear rationale for favouring social alarms as one of the mechanisms that can simultaneously help support independence, achieve political objectives, save money and respond to people's wishes.

There is, however, a particular barrier that jeopardises the fulfilment of such political objectives in the very countries where social alarms are most established. This is especially the case where pursuit of the desired objectives is associated with public sector service provision or particular built forms such as sheltered housing. That barrier is enshrined within the established governmental and departmental structures at central and local level, and their associated funding frameworks, these often serving to compartmentalise healthcare on the one hand and social welfare and housing services on the other.

The difficulties are reinforced through territorial battles that are sometimes fought by the professional groupings be they doctors, nurses, occupational therapists, social workers or housing managers. And regarding social alarms, each may lay claim to having particular expertise. But in truth, and as demonstrated earlier in this book, social alarm technologies have potential applications that cross departmental and professional boundaries. One of the problems, therefore, in realising this potential, lies in reconciling different professional perspectives and in responding more closely to the needs and aspirations of users.

In relation to social alarms some battles between professional interests have already been fought. In Great Britain, for instance, the battle between social welfare and housing authorities for control of social alarm services was noted in Chapter Four. This was, however, something of a sideshow in that it resulted from the fact of social alarm services in most cases, certainly in England and Wales, being managed by housing authorities. The real battle is that for which initial manoeuvres have begun more recently. Lined up on one side are the social welfare practitioners. On the other side are healthcare and medical practitioners. And the coming battle between these groups relates not just to different views as to the role of social alarms but to different views of independence and different philosophies of care.

The importance of this battle is not easily overstated since the philosophies of the respective groups are in many respects diametrically opposed. Paradoxically, they both go forward under the banner of care. The difference between them lies in the meaning of that much used and sometimes abused word.

Care

For those working in the areas of healthcare and medicine, care is generally seen in clinical terms. It is a matter of treatment for patients, the success of which is dependent on patient compliance with prescribed courses of medication. While this can be seen in terms of supporting independence, relatively little consideration appears to be given to what independence means. In this context, expert knowledge and decision making is firmly in the hands of the medical or healthcare practitioner, leading to a substantial difference in power between the giver and the recipient of treatment or care. Any aspiration to harness social alarm and related technologies in ways that offer the potential for user empowerment or liberation are threatened by such perspectives.

For those working in social welfare, care is seen increasingly in terms of negotiation and facilitation. It is a matter of support for, not treatment of, service users. And while the recipients of such social welfare inputs may also be patients in the sense that they are in receipt of treatment for medical conditions, they can experience a more equal power relationship with social workers, occupational therapists, homecarers or others whose philosophies are more often concerned not with patient compliance but rather user empowerment, engagement and social inclusion as well as supporting independent living (measured in more than clinical terms).

When social alarms are considered, therefore, a new aspect to the conflict between the philosophies of social welfare and healthcare practitioners emerges. However, it is the medical and healthcare practitioners who are streets ahead when it comes to knowledge of technologies and their application. But, as noted above, their view of care places such technologies in the context of patient compliance. It tends to be focused on institutions, notably hospitals, or localised healthcare facilities. For them, the relevant technologies may be tools for diagnosis and treatment. The possession and use of such technologies, furthermore, adds credibility to their claims to having expert knowledge that might be denied or inaccessible to the patient.

With greater attention now being given to telemedicine (see Chapter Twelve) it is striking the extent to which technological initiatives are focused on the benefits to the practitioners themselves, obtaining and exchanging patient data for consultative purposes. The patient is usually excluded. Where such initiatives reach out to, and endeavour to include, the patient, whether at a healthcare facility or in their own home, the danger is that the philosophies concerned with patient compliance that characterise other contexts will continue.

As noted in Chapter Eight, the healthcare and medical role of social alarms has been well established in the United States and Canada. But in the private North American market there is a high degree of user choice. It is interesting to note, furthermore, that the terminology of research on social alarms in the United States and Canada does not talk about patients, but rather users.

While healthcare and medical practitioners are therefore familiar with various technologies, this is not true to anything like the same extent for those in the social welfare field. The exceptions lie with those workers who have particular specialisms, especially relating to sensory impairments. But otherwise their knowledge of technologies is usually limited and for some social welfare professionals, there may be a tendency to shy away from social alarms and related technologies or to be deferential to the views of medical and healthcare practitioners.

These contrasting approaches to technologies create difficulties when social alarms are specifically considered. On the assumption that professional compartmentalisation will continue, albeit with some blurring at the edges, it means that social alarms will certainly maintain a role that crosses departmental boundaries. In this context, what can be seen as localised spats between housing and social welfare practitioners in Great Britain are likely to fizzle out in favour of the latter. At the same time sheltered housing, where it is retained, will take on a more distinctly social welfare rather than housing role.

For those countries where social alarms are not well-developed, things should be different. Indeed, in terms of harnessing the benefits of social alarms they may have an advantage. With the right guidance, and creative thought on behalf of the governments of those countries, it is conceivable that frameworks for social alarm services might be established that can meet social welfare needs as well as support healthcare agendas. Some of the battles between the interest groups might, therefore, be avoided. In any case the political imperatives associated with care in the community and supporting independence in a broader sense mean that it is the philosophies associated with social welfare that must take precedence.

Social and demographic context

The social context cannot be divorced from the political context noted above. Again there is much in common between the countries where social alarms are present, in that older people's aspirations coincide with the political perspectives that are reflected in care in the community policies. The demographic context is, furthermore, one that has been noted as being shared with all the countries concerned, this reflecting the anticipation of further growth in their populations of older and, in particular, very old people.

What is most interesting to consider, perhaps, is the extent to which the social context is changing not so much by virtue of the increasing numbers of older people but by what might be a greater assertiveness on their part in relation to the services, including social alarms, that they might wish to use. The fact of older people being increasingly recognised as consumers and citizens was noted in Chapter One, as was the fact that some of the worst aspects of ageism, reflected in institutional and separate provision of services for older people, are beginning to be redressed.

That such recognition should come about must be seen as reflecting, at least in part, the increasing political muscle that older people are exercising. Some of the political activism of older people has been discussed by Fisk (1999, p 17ff), including the establishment of political parties in the Netherlands and movements that have been very proactive on older people's issues elsewhere. He noted (p 18) that the American Association of Retired Persons (AARP) could boast a massive 32 million members in 3,600 local groups throughout the United States. This organisation, as noted in Chapter Eight, has published and advised in relation to social alarms.

Such movements of older people respond to the ageism in our societies and the obvious fact that, as the population of fit and active older people grows in all countries, they are a living testament to the unrepresentativeness of negative images of older age that pervade the media. They are, furthermore, bringing about changes in perceptions of the meaning of independence, this increasingly being seen as linked to agendas concerned with social inclusion, participation and engagement. This means that with moves afoot in some countries to bring in more flexible arrangements for the age of retirement, older people should feature more and more in the workplace and the wider community. Their number and spending power may help to ensure that increasing attention is given to their needs, choices and wants both in political terms, in order to win their votes, and commercial terms, in order to win their dollars, yens, pounds, or euros.

The manufacturers and suppliers of social alarms are recognising such changes. The negative portrayals of older people lying on the floor but just able to press their portable transmitters are far less evident and in their place is a growing number of older people, with or without a portable transmitter and a visible social alarm device, who are clearly relaxed, healthy and often engaged in active pursuits (see Plate 10.1). In other words the manufacturers of social alarms and related products are waking up to the spending power of older people. And the marketing strategies that they are now adopting acknowledge the inappropriateness of ageist imagery for a user group that is, or aspires to be, active, engaged and independent. The danger remains, however, that ageist attitudes may only be changing slowly and may continue to be directed towards the very old and to those that can be seen as more closely conforming to long-established ageist stereotypes.

But as evidenced in this book it is some of the frailest and most vulnerable who are among the greatest beneficiaries of social alarms, albeit as part of wider packages of care. This is where that broader vision is necessary to see social alarms develop into second-generation configurations that, along with other interactive services, can serve to engage and involve many of the frailest older people. And by this means key dimensions of independence may become available even to the house-, chair- or bed-bound. More importantly the technologies will serve to benefit all people, regardless of age. Such opportunities have been signalled in the notion of liberation technologies discussed in Chapter Two.

Different perspectives

In examining different perspectives the most appropriate places to start are Great Britain and the United States because of their roles in the initial development of social alarms and the extent to which they use such technologies.

As noted in Chapter Five, social alarms in England and Wales have been largely locked into service frameworks managed by housing authorities. This was contrasted with the position in Scotland (Chapter Six) and Northern Ireland (Chapter Seven) and with the frameworks adopted by virtually all social alarm services elsewhere. Chapter Five noted, however, the interest in social alarms, and occasionally the provision by, social welfare authorities and a tendency to develop less narrowly housing-based perspectives.

Generally, therefore, social alarm services in England and Wales are different from those found elsewhere. As noted by Fisk (1990, p 11) they are in the wrong place – but by virtue of greater attention being given to social welfare issues some change is occurring. Such change it is considered will gain momentum as funding reforms that affect sheltered housing and related service provision are implemented, and as dilemmas relating to healthcare needs are addressed. The last of these is more fully discussed in Chapters Twelve and Thirteen.

Plate 10.1 *Social alarms: a positive image*

Source: IST (International Security Technology) literature

The different legislative framework and devolved government in Scotland is likely to help ensure retention of a more social welfare rather than housing perspective in that country. The devolved administration in Northern Ireland and their shared agenda with the Republic of Ireland will help their service frameworks retain at least some element of their security orientation alongside more general concerns about social welfare.

The context in the United States is less complex by virtue of the private sector and healthcare orientations. While service rationalisation will continue, the essential service emphases are considered likely to stay in place. Most notable, perhaps, is the growing recognition of the potential role of social alarms in saving public money and the associated predisposition of federal and state government agencies to make such services eligible for financial support through their Medicaid programmes. Public funding for social alarms was noted as more commonplace in Canada, with interest in such technologies having been shown by federal government agencies and some provincial governments.

An appropriate backdrop to a discussion of different perspectives on social alarms is, therefore, one that in broad terms notes high public spending and certain idiosyncrasies for Great Britain and contrasts this with the low level of public spending and more straightforward healthcare and private sector service orientations in the United States. Key dimensions concerned with public spending and healthcare, social welfare and housing orientations have, therefore, been identified. The use of social alarms in other parts of the world can also be related to these dimensions.

In examining the position in Europe, excluding Great Britain and Ireland, substantial variation is evident. It was noted in Chapter Nine that there is municipal involvement in social alarm service provision in the Netherlands, Denmark, Finland and Sweden. In the Netherlands and Sweden, a major element of social alarm provision relates to installed systems in sheltered housing or its equivalents. In none of the countries, however, are social alarm services located within agencies that are primarily responsible for housing provision. Rather the orientation is social welfare or healthcare with monitoring and response services often being based at hospitals and/or with ambulance services. Exceptions to the pattern indicated in at least some parts of Northern Europe are to be found in Germany, France and Spain. Here there is greater involvement of charitable and voluntary organisations in social alarm service provision.

For the European countries where social alarm services are best developed, therefore, there is substantial variation in the agencies of provision and in the extent of public subsidy available to services and their users. Differences in emphasis on, or the meaning of, independence in such countries are not evident except by reference to shared agendas concerned with care in the community and an acknowledgement of people's wishes to stay at home.

Given the probability that social alarms will continue to be considered as peripheral to mainstream care and support services, this variation is likely to continue. With some countries, however, there is increasing evidence of internal regulation and specific funding initiatives that suggest that a defined place for social alarms is beginning to be found.

Great Britain is one of these, with the place of social alarms being increasingly strengthened through references in key reports (see Audit Commission, 1998), and the emergence of specific regulatory frameworks. The Code of Practice developed by the Association of Social Alarms Providers (ASAP) for instance, has been endorsed by a number of relevant government agencies. Other countries where frameworks to regulate social alarm services have been developed include Finland, where national legislation promoted social alarm service provision by municipal authorities, and the Netherlands through KBOH, an independent body responsible for standards and the provision of advice in relation to technical aids. All countries that are members of the European Union come within the developing regulatory framework for social alarms that is embodied within the EN50134 series of regulations 1, 2, 3, 5 and 7.[1]

Outside Europe it has been noted that social alarm services are best developed in Israel, Japan and Australia. In Israel the pattern is different and distinctive, with the main services being in the private sector and linked to broader-based medical services. In Japan, it is private sector services that are best developed, with their pattern of provision being most closely akin to that found in the United States. Australia, by contrast, is characterised by both public and private sector social alarm services with the pattern of provision, therefore, being more akin to that in Northern Europe.

Despite much variation, there are identifiable patterns of social alarm service provision. These relate in some part to the accidents of history, the marketing endeavours of the manufacturers and suppliers, and to social and political factors. For many countries for which information is available, therefore, it is possible to identify some elements of those patterns in the context of the dimensions initially identified. These are set out in Table 10.2.

The judgements in the table are guided by the information available but inevitably include a high degree of subjectivity. They should not be seen as definitive. Reference to the main agencies of provision, for instance, does not mean that others are not present. A grey area exists, furthermore, at the interface between healthcare and social welfare. Where these or other orientations are specified, therefore, this partly relates to policy and practice statements extrapolated from information gathered or simply relate to the known agencies of service provision. Service objectives, however, often recognise that such compartmentalisation is inappropriate and can obscure the broader roles and benefits of social alarms.

The variations identified are likely to remain in place, at least in the shorter term. But growing knowledge of social alarms and their potential application in pursuing both healthcare and social welfare objectives suggests that more predictable and possibly convergent patterns of service will emerge. In this context, the agencies of provision will to some extent be immaterial provided that private and public sector service requirements and user needs are being

Table 10.2: Key characteristics of social alarm services by selected countries

COUNTRY	Level of service provision	Main agencies of service provision	Number of installed systems	Public sector funding	Main orientation of services	Estimated number of social alarm users
ENGLAND AND WALES	High	Municipal authorities and housing associations	High	High	Housing	1,185,000
SCOTLAND	High	Municipal authorities and housing associations	High	High	Housing and social welfare	80,000
NORTHERN IRELAND	High	Housing associations	High	High	Housing and social welfare	25,000
DENMARK	High	Municipal authorities and private sector agencies	High	High	Healthcare and social welfare	35,000
FRANCE	Medium	Municipal authorities and voluntary agencies	Medium	Medium	Healthcare and social welfare	140,000
GERMANY	Medium	Voluntary and private sector agencies	Medium	Medium	Healthcare and social welfare	150,000
ITALY	Low	Voluntary and private sector agencies	Low	Low	Healthcare and social welfare	40,000
IRELAND	Low	Private sector agencies	Medium	Medium	Social welfare and security	30,000
THE NETHERLANDS	High	Municipal authorities and voluntary agencies	High	High	Healthcare and social welfare	100,000
SWEDEN	High	Municipal authorities	High	High	Social welfare	200,000
SLOVENIA	Low	Private sector agencies	Low	Low	Healthcare and social welfare	250
AUSTRALIA	High	Private sector agencies	Medium	High	Healthcare and social welfare	100,000
CANADA	High	Private healthcare and private sector agencies	Medium	Medium	Healthcare	40,000
ISRAEL	High	Private sector agencies	High	Low	Healthcare	100,000
JAPAN	Medium	Municipal authorities and private sector agencies	Medium	Medium	Healthcare and social welfare	200,000
UNITED STATES	High	Private healthcare and private sector agencies	Medium	Low	Healthcare	800,000

Note: Estimates of the number of social alarm service users and the level of service provision should be treated with caution as they are based on sometimes dated or incomplete sources. Such sources are noted in the profiles of the countries concerned (see Chapters Five to Nine).

met. Politics will help to determine the extent to which municipal authorities, private sector and voluntary agencies will retain their roles.

Conclusion

The variation evident in the nature of social alarm provision in different countries is considerable. This is attributable to the complex history of social alarms and the host of commercial, social and political factors concerned. It is also attributable to the marginal position of social alarms in virtually all of the countries examined and to the different professional views about them.

Comparisons between countries have shown, however, that there is common ground and that there are a number of dimensions by which social alarms can be considered. These dimensions will stay in place as social alarms develop and as service providers get to grips with successor technologies. The most notable dimension relates to the extent of public sector funding, this in turn pointing to the extent to which governments will seek to regulate and direct service provision.

There appears, in addition, to be some common ground with regard to understandings of independence, although the broadest interpretations appear to characterise European countries with shared social welfare and care in the community agendas. Narrower understandings of independence appear to be associated with those countries like North America and Japan, where medical and healthcare objectives are to the fore.

Insofar as an increasing role for social alarms is evident in all countries, the greater interest of governments and statutory agencies is considered to be essential if healthcare and social welfare agendas using such technologies are to be effectively pursued. An alternative scenario of poorly regulated private sector provision that could prey on fear, and/or exacerbate the vulnerability of service users, cannot be countenanced.

Different emphases will, of course, remain. The United States for instance is likely to continue to rely on private sector provision but with effective regulation increasingly in place. One powerful stimulus for such regulation has been noted in the lobby groups represented by older people such as in the American Association of Retired Persons (AARP). European countries will retain the mixture of emphases though this will be in a context of some convergence, helped by the shared regulatory framework being developed within the European Union.

Most interesting, perhaps, will be the way in which social alarm services develop in the countries where they are not widely used. In such countries the arguments regarding the savings, notably in terms of lower costs for hospital care, will have particular resonance as their economies develop and, at the same time, they seek to minimise the kind of costs associated with the building of institutions. Here there may be opportunities to establish new service frameworks, in part founded on social alarms and their successor technologies.

Importantly these may provide the means by which institutional care can be avoided for a high proportion of older people with support needs.

Ideally, in addition, the technologies might be employed in the pursuit of a wider notion of independence than might otherwise be the case. In other words the basic purpose could have much in common with social alarm (PRS) services in North America. The philosophy and application, however, should draw upon more recent European experience.

Whatever forms the application the new technologies will take as successors to social alarms, lessons must be learned from developments in smart homes, telemedicine, telecare, activity and lifestyle monitoring. These are dealt with in the ensuing chapters.

Note

[1] This EN series of standards has been developed by CENELEC (the European Committee for Electrotechnical Standardization) Technical Committee 79: Alarm Systems. It relates to: 1- system requirements; 2- trigger devices; 3- local unit and controller; 5- interconnections and communications; and 7- application guidelines.

ELEVEN

Social alarms and smart homes

Introduction

Smart homes, when appropriately designed and incorporating suitable technologies, may be an ultimate goal by which older people can achieve independent living. Such a vision is beginning to emerge as smart homes are considered alongside developments in telemedicine, telecare, activity and lifestyle monitoring (discussed in Chapters Twelve and Thirteen). Social alarms can be seen as at the core of smart homes.

As noted by Fisk (2001, p 101) there is no single accepted definition of a smart home. At its broadest, a smart home is one where smart technologies are installed and where those technologies facilitate automatic or user-initiated communication involving a range of appliances, sensors, actuators and switches. Such communication takes place in ways that can empower people and, in so doing, improve their quality of life. Implicit in this definition is the notion that the same empowerment and improvement in quality of life would not be achieved in ordinary homes despite the fact that most of these would have a range of devices that operate independently of each other. Some would benefit from the presence of a social alarm. There is, in other words, something to be gained by communication in a way that adds to that offered by social alarms.

This chapter explores the importance of that new way of communicating, specifically relates it to the needs of older people, and considers its impact on social alarms. In doing so it attempts to capture the ways in which smart technologies can help to promote engagement and social inclusion as well as support the independent living of their users. In addition, however, the chapter points to the danger of such technologies removing choice and control from the user through an over-reliance on automation and the transfer, without proper consent, of personal information to third parties. This latter danger is of particular concern on account of the use of smart technologies to effect what is known as lifestyle monitoring, explored in Chapter Thirteen.

Lifestyle monitoring, it can be noted, was at the heart of an initiative managed by Anchor Trust and British Telecom, which sought to "develop, implement and evaluate a system that could monitor the lifestyles of people in their own homes and look for deviations from a normal pattern of behaviour" (Porteus and Brownsell, 2000, p 26). Such monitoring is now focal to a number of initiatives and is seen as having particular merits when used to assist the management of older people with dementia. It may be an important component of future smart homes.

Also noted in this chapter is the danger that many older people, on account of their relative poverty or disadvantaged social position, may not have ready means of access to such technologies, regardless of any potential benefits. A question will remain, therefore, as to the extent to which public sector funding should be seeking to help their development or influence their configuration.

The context for smart homes

When the needs of older people are considered the context for smart homes is little different to that relating to social alarms. Older people live in a variety of different types of dwellings, virtually all of which can be host to smart technologies insofar as devices can be installed and communication links between them established via radio, dedicated wiring or mains cable. There is, however, the likelihood that smart technologies suited to the needs of older people will be disproportionately installed within sheltered housing schemes in the social rented sector because the private market will be slow to develop.

Several pilot installations of smart technologies have, in fact, taken place in sheltered housing. These have been primarily concerned with the provision of telecare, that is care provided remotely (see Chapter Twelve). A broader range of smart technologies that may or may not give specific consideration to the needs of older people, or people with sensory impairments, characterise other, often new-build, developments.

As a prelude to exploring smart homes and their relevance in relation to social alarms, the fact of such technologies not having been considered in the context of social theories of ageing, as noted in Chapter Two, must be reaffirmed. While this standpoint might have been justifiable in the context of the somewhat simple social alarm systems with which we are now familiar, it is not justifiable for the more sophisticated communications technologies that are coming to characterise smart homes.

The importance of smart homes

The importance of smart technologies lies not just in the linkages between devices in the home but on their ability to communicate outside the home. They will have a dramatic impact on personal communications whether relating to individual social or economic activity. They will include, for instance, contacts with family and friends, work opportunities, and the way people shop and travel. In so doing they may help support independence in the wider sense of participation, engagement and inclusion. But there are associated fears that use of such technologies may result in a reduction of social contact or be used to substitute more personal forms of care and support (Gott, 1995, pp 12, 128; Dick and Pomfret, 1996, p 4; Tetley et al, 2000, p 243). Wylde and Valins (1996, p 17) have warned of the danger of creating "societies of high-tech hermits".

That such a reduction in contact with support staff may not be a bad thing has been noted by Marshall (1995, p 14). She pointed out that technologies could free staff from some routine tasks and people with dementia in care homes, she argued, "... might prefer surveillance technology in the shape of [an] alarm to having staff constantly walking in their bedrooms at all hours of the night". The author of this book has argued in relation to a wider range of older people that such technologies can "liberate people from ageist and oppressive regimes of the sort that have, for too long, characterised many housing and care services" (Fisk, 1999, p 26; see also Chapter Two).

Smart technologies are, therefore, of potentially great importance to the position that individuals have in wider society, their interrelationship with others, their participation in economic and social life, and the extent of their disempowerment through inappropriate support and care frameworks. They are particularly relevant to older people and, depending on the way they are configured, can play a part in counterbalancing the forces of ageism and social exclusion.

There is, therefore, an aspect of smart technologies that demands careful consideration within social theory as endeavours are made to combat the structured dependency and oppression that underpins many current service frameworks (Braye and Preston-Shoot, 1995, p 107; Phillipson, 1998, p 18). This is particularly the case in view of their communications capacity, the development of which is expected to be the key feature of future generations of systems (Doughty et al, 1996, p 73; Tang and Venables, 2000, pp 11-12).

The origins of smart homes

The origins of smart homes are to be found in intelligent, or smart, buildings. They began to appear in the 1970s and 80s and were lauded as offering the potential means of improving energy efficiency, ventilation and the control of working environments. An intelligent building, according to Atkin (1988, p 2) contained a building automation system, an office automation system, and advanced telecommunications via a central computer system. The working environment within the building would be automatically controlled and, it was considered, could ensure the greater comfort of its occupants, with potential gains in energy efficiency and productivity.

Consideration of the potential for smart homes as opposed to buildings emerged in the 1980s. This came about as a result of the reducing cost of the technologies and the dramatically increased power of microprocessors to receive, handle, analyse and distribute information around the systems concerned. Costs have continued to reduce while the power of the microprocessors increases, these factors being seen as key elements in the development of markets for such smart technologies (Pragnell et al, 2000, pp 5, 25).

The growth in the attention given to smart homes has also reflected increasing awareness of their potential to incorporate: (a) assistive technologies for people with mobility problems and/or sensory impairments; and (b) specialised communications technologies that offered the means of obtaining help in necessitous circumstances and of monitoring physiological well-being.

Assistive technologies, as noted in Chapter One, have developed in range and number with some such devices becoming every day items of wide benefit, for instance, the electronic can opener and the television remote control. That assistive technologies represent an important backdrop to accommodation and support services for older people was recognised in Great Britain in work for the Royal Commission on Long Term Care (see Cowan and Turner-Smith, 1999).

With regard to monitoring well-being, it must be noted that the capability of social alarms has now dramatically increased and links to PIRs and other sensors can now offer the means of activity and lifestyle monitoring. This means that as well as smart homes beginning to consider more fully the role of communications technologies, social alarms are themselves starting to manifest features that are integral to the former, with steps being made towards incorporating the capacity to be proactive in recognising abnormalities in behaviour or environmental risk situations (see, for instance, Doughty and Williams, 2002, p 15); hence the technologies might be able to react immediately to an event such as a fall, seizure or heart attack. They may, furthermore, obviate the need for users to carry or wear the kind of radio trigger device, normally a pendant or on the wrist, that is associated with established social alarm devices.

There are several early examples of smart technologies having been developed in the context of pilot projects in Europe, North America and Japan (Fisk, 2001, pp 104-5). These initiatives have tended to concentrate on home automation but included a number of features seen as of specific relevance to older people, among them controlled or automatic lighting and a social alarm facility. Some attention has been given to the interface with users but ethical issues relating to the intrusiveness of technologies, the limits to surveillance, and the treatment of personal information, have rarely been touched upon.

Issues for debate

Moran (1993) was one of the first to pose crucial questions about the social impact of smart technologies. She stated (p 1) that:

> The introduction of advanced technology into the home has the potential to change qualitative and quantitative aspects of relationships between household members, as well as the role and function of the home and its relationship with the wider environment. Such technologies consequently have important implications for our health and quality of life.

She noted that the early initiatives were "largely the result of technology push" with "a clear conceptual paradigm" having not emerged to underpin their development.

The impetus of that technological push was, however, mitigated by commercial constraints. Vlaskamp et al (1994, p 57) noted in relation to various continental

European initiatives, that "integrated systems are only feasible when the manufacturers of system components agree upon a common standard". Doughty and Williams (2001, p 36) stated that the absence of common standards for smart homes had hampered take-up more than any other technological problem. Cowan and Turner-Smith (1999, p 333) noted that "builders do not want to commit to any new design so economies of scale [for smart homes] are not available". They added that "the future domestic market is likely to be led by entertainment rather than necessity". For North America Watzke and Birch (1994, p 168) observed that owing to the absence of protocols the three systems being then marketed had a "limited range of products to link to them".

The same difficulties encountered in the earlier period of smart home developments were still being encountered more recently and were problematic for the initiative in Great Britain supported by the Joseph Rowntree Foundation. Gann et al (1999, p 51) lamented that "attempts to develop standards have been painfully slow and generally resulted in cumbersome documents with little general agreement on the way forward".

Evaluation of the Joseph Rowntree initiative (see Chapter Thirteen) indicated that at least some of the signalling difficulties were being overcome with the opportunities relating to communication outside the dwelling being more fully explored (Gann et al, 1999, p 51). The extent of penetration of interactive cable networks in Great Britain and the rapidity by which users are gaining access to the Internet has given further impetus to this shift, the latter being noted by Pragnell et al (2000, p 5) as important to the development of the smart homes market.

Gann et al (1999, p 12) suggested that two forms of smart home were emerging, one more rooted in home automation, the other involving interactive communications within and outside the home. But perhaps better to help in the conceptualisation of smart homes is the distinction that was made by Vlaskamp et al (1994, p 58). They pointed to three technical environments for smart technologies: the direct environment where devices are worn or carried by the user; the fixed environment of the home itself; and the distant environment linking to remote consultation partners (see Table 11.1). Smart technologies with the potential to benefit older people through telecare services are considered to relate to all three. That element concerned with communications is particularly concerned with the distant environment even though that distance might, for someone with a physical or sensory impairment, be to an adjoining dwelling, a local shop or service provider.

Regardless of the extent to which particular smart systems relate to the three environments, fundamental questions must be posed. What, precisely, can a smart home usefully do? In the context of this book the supplementary questions to be asked are: what can they usefully do to benefit older people? and how can they help support independent living?

Current and recent initiatives in Great Britain begin to provide some of the answers. They respond not to technology push factors but to a desire to test the merits of smart technologies in relation to the needs of particular users.

Table 11.1: Environments for smart home technologies

Direct environment	Fixed environment	Distant environment
Equipment worn or carried by the user	Devices and sensors fixed within or close to the dwelling (using telephony and radio)	Networks operating in the wider community
Devices implanted within the user	Cabling linking such devices	Automated or personal services operating via such media
Devices attached to prostheses of the user (including wheelchairs)	Central processing and control unit	

Source: Based on Vlaskamp et al (1994, pp 58-9)

These have increasingly focused on the communications aspect of smart homes and importantly some have given attention to the support needs and independence of older people.

What should a smart home do?

The current lack of homes with installed smart technologies, the fact of their responding to different agendas according to the needs of residents or the predilections of their promoters, and the lack of systematic evaluations of their impact, mean that there is some scepticism regarding their merits. Such scepticism is healthy insofar as it helps to ensure that the minds of those involved in the further development and application of smart technologies are more likely to be focused on ensuring progress towards relevant outcomes that might meet with wider public acceptance.

But there is a danger that while the credentials of organisations that are undertaking or promoting the smart home initiatives may be sound, technologies could be used in ways (reflecting earlier concerns about call systems, see Chapter Four) that underpin or consolidate ageist and disempowering service frameworks. By so doing they may promote *dependence* rather than support *independence*. Any failure to adequately consider the social context in which such technologies are placed might therefore result in the reinforcement of medical models of older age and service provision.

Negative views and stereotypes of older people are not helped by some studies that conclude, without further thought, the reluctance of older people to embrace such technologies. Pragnell et al (2000, p 12) concluded, for instance, that "older people were most likely to express concern about new technology" since just 41 per cent of people aged 55 or over, in their overall sample of over 1,000 people aged 15 or over, said they would "welcome new technology in their home if it would save them time and effort". This contrasted with 76 per cent of the 15-24 age group. On the basis of such figures, Pragnell et al claimed (p 19) that "older people ... have fairly negative attitudes towards technology", without seeking to explain this in terms of income, familiarity with technologies or other factors.

By way of contrast is a Canadian study (Watzke and Birch, 1994, p 177) that exposed 25 people aged over 60 to smart home systems. It observed that "It is interesting that by the end of the study ... there were only four participants who said they would prefer human help over technical help compared with 18 who said so initially" and concluded (p 176) that "once exposed to the environmental technology the participants tended to display a positive response to the devices".

The devices in question included TVs, microwave ovens, telephones, door entry systems and social alarms (p 176). The idea that there may be a propensity for older people to reject technologies as they age was also countered by Collins et al (1992, p 281) who, in reporting on a postal survey of 2,500 older people in the United Kingdom, stated "we have found no evidence in this study for a positive relationship between age and technophobia". Furthermore, a survey for the Technology for Living Forum concluded from 500 telephone interviews with people aged over 55 in Great Britain, that "older people are using and value a wide range of technology" with a third regularly using computers, albeit that there was a relatively low level of interest (less than one in five) in curtain, lighting, heating and door opening/closure control.[1]

A survey of attitudes to a range of social alarm and smart technology functions was undertaken by the author of this book in 1998. This involved personal interviews with 50 sheltered housing tenants in schemes managed by the Liverpool Housing Trust. The survey sought to reveal the extent to which certain functions, generally associated with smart homes, were likely to be acceptable. It also questioned tenants about their attitudes to carrying, wearing or being implanted with certain physiological sensors. The latter relates to agendas concerned with healthcare and lifestyle monitoring discussed in Chapters Twelve and Thirteen. With regard to the functions associated with smart homes the percentages of respondents saying that these were a good idea are set out in Table 11.2.

Table 11.2: Smart home functions that are a good idea (%)

• Intruder alarm	57.1
• Activity monitoring	54.8
• Medical monitoring	38.1
• Measuring room temperature	38.1
• Automatic heating control	28.6
• Measurement of gas/electricity usage	23.8

Note: From work by the author.

Similar work was undertaken in an interview survey of 160 households in a sheltered housing scheme in Birmingham. This found (Brownsell et al, 2000, pp 200-1) that 68 per cent were interested in lifestyle monitoring; 57 per cent in a device for self-administered medical monitoring; and 46 per cent in video-telephone links with the warden and their neighbours. A higher percentage (77 per cent) were interested in a device that would automatically detect falls, though nine of those surveyed who had fallen in the previous year rejected such a device, an outcome that Brownsell et al (p 200) referred to as "surprising".

But while there are some promising signs regarding the interest of older people in some of the technologies associated with smart homes and their willingness to use them, there is a long way to go before these might be a key feature in the decentralisation, from institutions to the home, of care or support services and in their helping to achieve objectives concerned not just with independent living but also with individual empowerment, engagement and inclusion.

What is clear here, however, is that some older people do express negative views about new technologies where they are unfamiliar with them or cannot see their practical application. For many such technologies, being marketed with younger consumers in mind, the feeling of older people that these might not be relevant to them is, therefore, understandable. What is more, as pointed out by Östlund (1999, p 47), "Elderly people run the risk of being excluded mainly because of the high speed of development and the fact that they do not appear in the arena where there are opportunities to gain technical competence and training, i.e. in working life". The Watzke and Birch 1994 study, as noted above, showed how views about technologies can change after familiarisation.

The same issues of relevance have been noted for other technologies and point to a broad range of factors that needed to be considered. Karlsson (1995, p 81), for instance, stated that technology acceptance by older people implied the "acceptance of a change of routines, triggered by the technology's perceived usefulness which is, in turn, influenced by information and motivation". Karlsson's work with older people was concerned with their attitudes towards computers/home shopping and fax machines. She concluded (p 81) that "acceptability and adoption is a multi-dimensional problem extending beyond the narrow user-technology interface" with the benefit perceived by the older person being the most important factor. The importance of functionality to acceptance by older people has also been noted by van Berlo (1998, p 392).

Such views were echoed by Peeters (1997, p 14) who stated that "the elderly are attracted by products that improve their ability to live alone, to remain integrated and to live a normal life". A component of normal life, it is claimed here, is concerned with independence. For the smart technologies with which this book is more specifically concerned Pragnell et al (2000, p 4) noted that their acceptance might be helped because of older people's familiarity with at least some of the household appliances to which the systems would be linked.

An empowering and inclusive perspective regarding the liberation technologies as put forward and discussed in Chapter Two, is relevant here.

This offers a framework whereby smart technologies might be harnessed in ways that ensure that both they and the services accessed through them are in the control of the user. Such a liberation perspective is considered as useful, if not essential, to underpin any smart system, including those aspects concerned with telecare, especially where the needs and aspirations of older people are seen as being covered.

With regard to system functionality within smart homes, the possibilities are continually fluctuating and expanding. A welcome discussion of ideas such as the use of robots for lifting; guidance for wheelchair movement around the dwelling; and refrigerators that incorporate stock control facilities was offered by Gann et al (1999, p 89). Another possibility relates to the monitoring of medicines and user compliance with prescribed courses of treatment. Moran (1993, p 17), however, lamented that it would be a long time before smart technologies were able to do domestic work such as ironing, vacuum cleaning, cooking, bed-making and shoe-polishing!

A further idea that has been explored is the smart or health toilet. This may be the subject of some amusement among service providers and users alike but is considered to warrant serious attention insofar as there is a real and shorter-term possibility that such sanitary technology could play a role in healthcare monitoring. There is, after all, a potential for a smart toilet to monitor food consumption, a range of medical conditions and the success or otherwise of medical interventions, through the automated analysis of urine and faecal matter. The smart toilet can also be a means of checking body weight (Tamura et al, 1998, p 282; Gann et al, 2000, p 89).

Core functions of smart homes

With regard to generic smart systems there appears to be broad agreement on a core range of functions (see Table 11.3) – not that the full range of functions, sensors and actuators would necessarily be present, active or used in all installations. Indeed, a basic and now widely accepted parameter for systems is that they should be modular with the ability to add functionality as needs arise or in the course of dwelling refurbishment. For Great Britain and Ireland the latter is particularly pertinent in view of the age and variety of the housing

Table 11.3: Core functions of generic smart home systems

• Control of system	• Cooker safety
• Emergency help	• Water temperature control
• Temperature monitoring	• Window, blind and/or curtain control
• Water and energy use monitoring	• Property security
• Automatic lighting	• Safety and accident prevention
• Door surveillance	• On-line links

Note: Based on work by the author.

stock. However, Doughty and Costa (1997, p 23) pointed to the potential of smart technologies being installed in almost any kind of dwelling. They envisaged homes being fitted with a variety of sensors for monitoring, and with computer programmes being able to build up activity profiles so that changes in the habits of occupants could be identified. Their vision was one, therefore, that saw the potential of such technologies to include lifestyle monitoring. Added to these can be certain other functions that might be considered as particularly relevant to some older people (see Table 11.4).

The absence of user views about the merits of such functions, in view of the relatively limited experience of smart homes, has been noted. Gann et al (1999, p 80), however, reported that visitors to the Joseph Rowntree Foundation smart homes, when asked about their preferences among the range of functions, gave their highest rankings for gas detection, security alarm, social alarm and entry phones.

Detailed consideration of the manner of operation of smart technologies in relation to each of the functions is outside the remit of this chapter, but they are integral to the further development of system specifications discussed elsewhere (see Gann et al, 1999). Such work has sought to determine:

• the manner of control and operation of systems, that is from fixed or portable devices and via remote telephones; and the provision of a central locking security facility;
• the extent of discretion given to users to set or change timers and or system operational parameters, determining the degree of user control over system operation and any personal information collected by the system;
• the feedback provided to the user via displays or other means, that is in relation to the status of appliances, windows, doors; energy and water usage; visitors at the front door and so on; and
• the framework for the monitoring of activity and/or lifestyles, for instance regarding the appropriate range of sensors and the manner in which data is handled.

The different perspectives arising from such work may determine the types of smart home that will be encountered in the future. One of these, according to Doughty and Williams (2001, p 35) will be what they call a "health home" that will support hospital at home initiatives. Phippen (2000, pp 10-11) put forward

Table 11.4: Additional functions of smart home systems associated with provision for older people

• Memory joggers and diary facility
• Lifestyle monitoring
• Medical monitoring
• Dementia care

Note: Based on work by the author.

a similar idea in his description of the "well house" which, in addition to providing accommodation, would enable health monitoring and assessments to be undertaken. The range of potential on-line communication links to an assortment of services from the local library to home banking that could be added to smart homes have been explored elsewhere (Cullen and Robinson, 1997, p 39; Quigley and Tweed, 1999, p 1).

In addition, and with a keener eye on the commercial potential of such systems, more attention is being given to their user interface. User interfaces are, of course, as with functionality, crucial to the acceptance and use of smart technologies (Karlsson, 1995, pp 80-1; Cullen and Robinson, 1997, pp 233-5; Fisk, 1998, pp 82-3).

Recent initiatives

There are now several smart homes initiatives within Great Britain and other parts of the European Union (Clatworthy and Bjørneby, 1997; Gann et al, 1999; Curry, 2001). In addition, a small number of smart systems with limited functionality are being marketed. As yet, no system comes close to being able to offer the full range of core or additional functions noted above. Gann et al (1999, p 88) correctly summed the position up in saying that:

> In Britain, smart home markets, technologies and supply industries are immature. Customers are ignorant or sceptical about potential benefits; technologies are difficult to integrate for interoperability; the industry is fragmented and there are no one-stop-shop suppliers providing a full range of bundled products and services.

Notable within Great Britain is the Integer (intelligent and green) house initiative. This smart house development emerged from origins concerned with design, automation and energy efficiency. It did not, in other words, give special attention to the needs of older people or to people with physical disabilities or sensory impairments.

More relevant to this appraisal, therefore, is an array of smart home initiatives where telecare technologies have been focal to the attention of their designers and promoters. Such initiatives can be said to be proliferating in Great Britain as the potential for fitting smart technologies in existing dwellings is beginning to be realised.

Notable among these initiatives are those of the Joseph Rowntree Foundation in York and Edinburgh (Smart Home and Aid House); and agencies in Portsmouth (Smart Home); and in Greenwich (Millennium Homes). These are summarised below and, with Integer House, in Table 11.5. With the exception of Integer House and the Portsmouth initiative they were developed with what were seen as the specific needs of older people in mind. In Edinburgh, particular consideration was given to the needs of people with dementia.

Other initiatives more closely focused on developing the potential of social alarm technologies with some, as with those listed above, giving attention to the needs of people with dementia. These have taken place within Great Britain at Birmingham, Durham, Ealing, Glasgow, Gloucester, Guildford, Northampton and West Lothian; and within Northern Ireland at Derry. In addition to these is the Anchor Trust/British Telecom initiative that was completed in 2000 and focused on exploring the merits of using smart technologies for lifestyle monitoring. Some of these other initiatives are summarised and discussed in Chapters Twelve and Thirteen.

These are the main smart home initiatives that need to be considered at this point. They indicate the likelihood of greater numbers of new build smart homes being marketed in coming years and the availability of more flexible arrays of smart home technologies for fitting in existing dwellings.

It is necessary, however, to give closer attention to those elements of smart homes that relate most closely to social alarms. Hence the attention given where the smart homes initiatives noted above have addressed issues relating to older age or disability. In Chapters Twelve and Thirteen this discussion is widened in order to focus on matters that are important to this book. Table 11.5 is complemented by Table 13.1 (see Chapter Thirteen), which summarises

INTEGER HOUSE

The first Integer house was built in 1996, in Garston, Watford, at the site of the Building Research Establishment. The genesis of the Integer house lay in the work of designers and consultants whose primary focus was on lifestyle and energy issues. Related to these was the attention that was given to communications systems that responded, among other things, to security needs and the requirements of home workers. Kell and Thompson (2000, p 13) stated that "Integer is not just about new build. It seeks to create technology neighbourhoods and facilitates sustainable communities". Five pilot projects ensued that involved the construction of 60 houses and flats in the West Midlands, Wiltshire and the Home Counties. The intention was to "use this experience as a launching pad for the full commercial exploitation of the Integer approach to building homes" (p 9).

The costs of building such houses were claimed to be "marginally greater than for traditionally built housing" but with benefits that included reduced running costs, a shorter construction time and a higher standard of living for dwelling occupants (Pooley, 2000, p 46). Later, Integer developments were promoted by a consortium of over 150 companies that operated throughout the United Kingdom (Curry, 2001, p 18).

What enabled the Integer homes to be differentiated from other smart home initiatives was the lack of attention to agendas that specifically related to the needs of older people or people with physical disabilities and/or sensory impairments. The initiative was, therefore, firmly oriented towards the exploration and exploitation of smart solutions for the main housing market. There is no evidence that issues to do with independent living were closely addressed.

Table 11.5: Smart home initiatives: primary aims

Integer House

- Energy efficiency
- Technology neighbourhoods
- Higher living standards
- Automation and communication with the external environment

York and Edinburgh (Smart House and Aid House)

- Standardisation in signalling protocols
- Meeting the needs of an ageing population
- Responding to user needs for automation, communication and security
- Ability to install in new build and refurbished properties

Portsmouth (Smart Home)

- Energy efficiency
- Meeting the needs of severely physically disabled people
- Automation and user control
- Sensor integration

Greenwich (Millennium Home)

- Lifestyle monitoring
- Automation and communication with the external environment

the primary aims and key functions of those initiatives in Great Britain that are particularly focused on telecare, lifestyle monitoring and the needs of older people with dementia.

There are a growing number of initiatives characterised by similar functionality in other parts of the European Union.

YORK AND EDINBURGH (SMART HOME AND AID HOUSE)

The York and Edinburgh initiatives have been evaluated by Gann et al (1999). The former, developed within a newly built property, enabled technical details to be set out to help in determining future specifications for smart technologies (p 108ff). In considering the future application of such technologies Gann et al (p 30) noted the possibility of "using smart home systems for continuous monitoring of people's health and well-being" and of "diagnosing changes in health status, automatically triggering an appropriate response".

PORTSMOUTH (SMART HOME)[2]

The initiative in Portsmouth was initiated by John Grooms Housing Association in collaboration with Portsmouth City Council and the University of Portsmouth. A sizeable part of the funding was provided by the Housing Corporation. The focus was and remains on the needs of people with severe disabilities and followed consultations with some 70 people who were members of disability groups in Hampshire. It comprises installations in newly built homes that meet wheelchair and lifetime home standards.

Several of the smart functions incorporated in the Portsmouth initiative have depended on the successful integration of sensors into a multifunctional ceiling rose. This monitors movement, room temperature, lighting levels, smoke and gas and incorporates emergency lighting and an audible warning signal. Sensors elsewhere monitor energy usage, water flow and external weather conditions. Attention has also been given to door and window automation, these responding to the particular needs of users. Control of the system is planned via simple remote and/or wall mounted units.

GREENWICH (MILLENNIUM HOMES)

The Millennium Homes initiative was concerned both with automation and care. Indeed, according to Wolff[3] these were to be what he called "caring houses" and "different from smart houses which use technology to allow you to control them by drawing curtains, operating lights, etc. Caring houses will look after you, prevent you from doing something which may be injurious to yourself and ultimately able to call for help". Local authorities in the South East were invited to become partners in the enterprise, their payments then helping to support system development.

The benefits of and difficulties relating to smart homes

Overall, it is considered that smart homes can bring a range of benefits to older people and improve their quality of life. This is particularly the case now that the technologies are characterised by increasing communications capacity and are being applied in lifetime home contexts. And while all the components of what might be the ideal smart home are not yet in place, consideration can begin to be given to their benefits in terms of supporting independent living in both its narrower and wider senses. Facilitation of independent living in the wider sense, however, derives not from the smart technologies themselves but from the fact that older people can have control of the technologies and access to a range of on-line services.

Several difficulties have to be overcome in order to achieve such objectives. The barrier to technological advances, because of the lack of agreement in signalling protocols, has already been noted. The technology push as a result has been less effective than it might have been otherwise. Briefly mentioned, furthermore, was the fact that many older people have limited disposable incomes and would in many cases not be able to afford such technologies. The promotion of smart technologies by statutory agencies (with public sector funding) would be an essential prerequisite to supporting independent living, engagement and social inclusion of many older people who are already disadvantaged by virtue of physical or sensory impairment and their limited wealth (Fisk, 1999, pp 25–8). Tinker et al (2000, p 118) noted of assistive technologies that "without a major policy initiative, their distribution will be highly unequal, dependent on levels of wealth; large sections of the very old population may have no access to them".

A further and fundamental barrier to the development of smart homes relates to the absence of ethical frameworks to underpin them. This is especially the case as lifestyle monitoring develops (see Chapter Thirteen) and because of the danger that the associated technologies may be promoted according to medical models of older age and service provision. Users might, in other words, be regarded as dependants and/or patients. And while there might be clinical and practical benefits in terms of their increased compliance with regimes of treatment, there might be fewer gains in terms of engagement, social inclusion and wider notions of independence.

Smart technologies also have implications for dwelling designs. Through their communication capacity they offer the prospect of more people of all ages working from home and/or being active virtual participants in economic, social and family networks. Such activity would be likely to require additional workspace in at least one room and the need for siting terminal equipment in one or more other locations. With the increase in on-line activity comes the likelihood of more people shopping remotely, a phenomenon that Mills (1999, p 42) noted would reduce pressures on support workers. A design implication of this noted by Moran (1993, p 58) and Gann et al (1999, p 20) is the need for hatches or boxes to permit the delivery and the temporary safe storage of goods.

The association of smart homes with the support of people with severe physical or sensory impairments and, increasingly, a wide range of medical conditions points to the need for larger dwellings. These might usefully incorporate a spare room or rooms that, as well as accommodating one or more computer and/or video-telephony terminals, could provide for a spouse, partner or carer.

Finally, and following the foregoing discussion, it can be concluded that it is the potential gains in terms of supporting independent living and facilitating engagement in economic and social life that makes smart homes so relevant to debates about the needs of older people. Smart homes may, through home automation, have promised increased physical independence, but now, by harnessing their communication capacity, they will absorb traditional social alarms and have the potential to deliver so much more.

Notes

[1] Report of conference held to launch the Technology for Living Forum, Help the Aged, London (1999).

[2] Correspondence with Kevin McCartney (University of Portsmouth) and Judi Gray (John Grooms Housing Association).

[3] Wolff, H. (1999) in paper to launch the Technology for Living Forum, Help the Aged, London.

TWELVE

Social alarms, telemedicine and telecare

Introduction

An integral element of smart homes is the transmission and interpretation of data and information about the dwellings and the environment within which they are installed. The act of transmission reflects, of course, the ability to communicate. The act of interpretation, however, means that for systems to be smart they must have intelligence. And as seen in Chapter Eleven, such intelligence can be used in a variety of ways to assist and empower dwelling occupants.

It is the increased capacity for communication and the power of microprocessors that offer the ability for transmission and interpretation of data and information about people as well as the home environment. This ability, building on the experience of social alarms, has brought us telecare – care provided remotely. The link with smart homes is clear; Tang and Venables (2000, p 8) having referred to smart homes and telecare as "natural companions".

The origin of the term telecare is unclear. It was used with increasing frequency during the 1990s to describe medical services provided at a distance, albeit generally within hospital and clinical environments. It has also been used for some telephone mediated counselling and advice services. And with the development of medical services within people's own homes, as associated with hospital-at-home and early discharge schemes, the word telecare has been encountered with increasing frequency, although the meanings ascribed to care, as noted in Chapter Ten, are varied.

Curry and Norris (1997) reviewed telecare activity in the United Kingdom for the Department of Health, ascribing a somewhat medically oriented position to it. But they recognised that the use of communications systems could offer a means of redressing some of the power imbalances that are normally found with medical services in that they noted the opportunity (p 14) for patients to benefit from on-line information as well as for medical practitioners to remotely check on a patient's healthcare status. Of note in relation to this book, however, is the fact that Curry and Norris (1997, p 18) saw the "opportunity to develop rapidly the healthcare side of telecare using the existing community alarm infrastructure".

The first and broadest perspectives on telecare are those that see it as close to, or an integral part of, telemedicine.

Telemedicine

The origins of telemedicine are ascribed to Willem Einthoven of the University of Leyden in the Netherlands. Around 1905 he developed a technique of sending electrocardiograph records over the 1.5km distance between his laboratory and a local hospital (Snellen, 1977, p 7). Telemedicine experiments also took place in Sweden between 1910 and 1920 (European Commission, 2001, p 297). The term telemedicine was, according to Stanberry (1998, p 1), coined in the 1970s.

The simplest definition of telemedicine, of many, is "the practice of medicine at a distance" (Stanberry, 1998, p 1). The European Commission definition is "the use of remote medical expertise at the point of need" (p 304). An appropriate addition to such definitions must, however, make reference to the role of communications technologies to facilitate this. Stanberry (p 2) noted the overlap of telemedicine with the terms telehealth and telecare.

Despite the prevalence of technologies within various medical specialisms, by the late 1990s Stanberry noted that there were very few telemedicine services (p 6). Subsequently, however, there has been clear evidence of their rapid development as the quality of communications networks has improved. This has made it possible not only to transmit large amounts of data very quickly but also visual images. Clough et al (1998, p 10), for instance, noted the rapid development of telemedicine services in relation to radiology and imaging (enabling the transmission of X-rays and CAT scans) and in dermatology. They also noted (p 12) applications concerned with cardiology where hand-held devices could be used by patients to record and transmit ECG readings and for hospital-at-home applications (see below).[1] Particular maturity in telemedicine applications has been claimed for technically advanced countries such as Australia and Finland where medical outreach services provide for the needs of patients in rural and remote areas (European Commission, 2001, pp 23, 126).

Given the prime concern of this book, it is those telemedicine services that use communications networks to meet the needs of service users in the community that require closest consideration. Particularly relevant are hospital-at-home services since these explicitly acknowledge that clinical settings have a number of disadvantages, at least for certain kinds of patients or medical conditions. They also acknowledge, at least implicitly, a role in supporting independence.

Hospital-at-home services

The psychological and practical benefits of hospital-at-home services for the patient or service user have been recognised as requiring a "change of outlook and patterns of work on the part of medical practitioners" (Fisk, 1986, pp 176-7). Interest in the hospital-at-home concept has re-emerged more recently and is being driven by recognition of the possibilities of cost savings and reductions in the risks associated with hospital-acquired infections (Iliffe and Gould, 1995a, pp 663-4). Clough et al (1998, p 12) noted, in addition, the benefit of home-based services in providing "much higher quality data" and reducing the risk of "over-diagnosis and over-treatment".

An example is the hospital-at-home scheme in Waltham Forest, north London, which aimed to avoid admissions of people following falls and of people with acute illnesses that were suitable for intensive home nursing (Illiffe and Gould, 1995b, p 810). In the initial nine months of the scheme (up to mid-1995) about two thirds of users were aged 80 or over. Falls were the reason for referral for 36 per cent of scheme users (p 811), and there was a clear pattern of reducing service levels for the vast majority of users. During the period, 87 of the 102 users examined were able to stay living in their homes after being discharged from the scheme. By this means independent living in its most basic sense was being assisted. Shared objectives with social alarms were clearly evident.

A variant on hospital-at-home is a home health monitoring service that used video-telephony and was piloted in Hays, Kansas (see hmc.odys.net/tele.html).[2] With the benefit of medical equipment in the home, a visiting nurse or medical practitioner was able to record and transmit medical data to a designated health agency. The service was considered particularly appropriate in view of the substantial rural hinterland being served by the centre. In this scheme the data was sent via a cable TV system rather than the telephone. The standard equipment in the home included glucose and bloodpressure monitors.

Given sufficient resources, appropriate technologies and suitable dwellings, there are few limits to the extent of medical care that can be provided in the home. Alongside hospital-at-home schemes with high levels of direct nursing provision, therefore, note must be taken of schemes that provide medical equipment in the home as a means of reducing the extent to which nursing staff need to be present and by virtue of which the service user can take some responsibility for monitoring his/her own health. A presupposition is that in the event of changes in the person's medical condition appropriate action can be taken, where necessary, to effect treatment at home or speedy hospital admission.

Ruggiero et al (1999, p 11) outlined the typical framework for such a service involving the provision of medical equipment in users' homes. The equipment included sensor arrays, a monitoring unit and a transmission device. At the same time a receiving unit had to be available at a remote location for use by "a specialist, general practitioner or other caregiver". The service configuration Ruggiero et al described was in essence, the same as that which is beginning to be used for lifestyle monitoring (discussed in Chapter Thirteen).

Echoing the argument of Clough et al (1998, p 12) noted above, Ruggiero et al (p 12) saw one reason for introducing medical monitoring into the home as obtaining better physiological measures. This reflected their understanding that such measures taken in a clinical environment often gave false readings and made diagnosis more difficult. Bloodpressure and cardiovascular measures were noted as particularly liable to error. Ruggiero et al (p 12) also pointed to the ability to add different kinds of technologies in the home, thereby increasing potential applications and the monitoring capability of the service.

Various studies have noted the potential for cost savings for both the provider and user in such applications (Kaye, 1997, pp 244-5; Ruggiero et al, 1999, p 12). Of particular note, in addition, is that Ruggiero et al (p 12) saw the integration of telemedicine-at-home services with the new generation of social alarms associated with lifestyle monitoring.

Telecare

A perspective on telecare that sees it closely linked with telemedicine has been offered above. However, in considering the link between telecare and social alarms in the context of people's own homes, a telemedicine orientation is inappropriate.

This follows because for those concerned with medical matters and the clinical outcomes of medical interventions, care was, and largely remains, associated with patients, with treatment and medication proffered by doctors, nurses and pharmacists. For those concerned with housing and related support services including the use of social alarms care was, and largely remains, associated with service users and neighbourly and/or practical support proffered by home carers, wardens and support workers. Again, therefore, different understandings of the word care are evident and following from this, it is suggested, there are different understandings of telecare. Caution is therefore advised when reading or debating issues about service provision where this label is encountered.

More recently a clearer differentiation in terminology is beginning to emerge. This differentiation is supported in this book and sees the term telecare as including only support services, including medical interventions, which take place in people's own homes. Indeed, Clough et al (1998, p 6) overlooked use of the term in medical contexts and solely attributed the term telecare to the field of social care. The term telemedicine by contrast is, and it is considered should remain, more consistently used for services provided in medical settings. Adoption of this perspective means that the use of the word care, within telecare, may be regarded as location specific rather than relating to the nature of the care provided.

Regardless of the foregoing there will, however, be further cause for confusion by virtue of the term telecare being encountered in clinical settings. Demiris et al (2000) and Ruggiero et al (1999) for instance, used the term in such contexts. Some further terminological confusion may take place where the term telehealth is used to describe aspects of services that would otherwise be known as telemedicine or telecare. But telehealth is a relevant and useful term insofar as it signals an endorsement of the need for more holistic approaches to medical care through including preventative interventions (Gott, 1995, p 11). Telehealth, where applying to people's own homes, could therefore be seen as part of telecare. A variant on the telehealth theme is e-health (healthcare that uses interactive communications networks), which Della Mea (2001, p e22) has suggested as heralding the death of telemedicine.

That those concerned with social alarms are seeking to tackle some medical agendas is evident in the work of Tunstall Telecom through their involvement in a European Union funded initiative under the name SAFE 21 (Social Alarms for the 21st Century). A more recent initiative is that being undertaken at Guildford.

SAFE 21

The SAFE 21 project involved Tunstall Telecom in partnership with companies in different parts of the European Union. An early explicit aim was to "further develop social alarm products and services using the existing social alarm infrastructure".[3] More ambitiously, aims later included the "integration of medical technology into the community alarm monitoring system" together with demonstrating "the feasibility of delivering a telemonitoring service that is acceptable to patients, health-care professionals and the providers of the service" (McIntosh and Thie, 2001, p 69). The project was concerned (p 2) to develop a "new speech alarm trigger, a mobile social alarm, an information system, a model control centre sharing facilities with other local organisations, telemonitoring and a social alarm for the deaf".

The mobile social alarm that was devised used a global positioning system (GPS), this information being claimed to be able to locate callers within 5 metres.[4] Those who attended user group meetings regarding this technological application, however, pointed to the greatest potential being more likely not to relate to older people since they were seen as less likely to leave home or travel alone. Practical problems with such mobile devices were akin to those evident with mobile telephones, that is with difficulties in transmission and reception in some locations and the need for the mobile device to be periodically recharged.

SAFE 21 was also concerned to facilitate the communication, via normal telephone lines, of medical information gathered in people's own homes to remote monitoring and response centres. The focus was on measuring and communicating information relating to heartbeat, pulse, blood pressure, body temperature, breathing rate and breathing amplitude (McIntosh and Thie, 2001, p 70). The equipment sought to give the user the option of sending information on what McIntosh and Thie (p 70) termed a "snapshot" basis or in relation to longer monitoring periods, for instance, when the user was sleeping.

They described (p 70) operation of the equipment as follows:

> The telemedicine server receives incoming measurement data from patient monitors, checks them and places the information in the patient's electronic record. The patient's doctor or nurse can log on remotely at any time and view the results in graphical form. If the doctor or nurse has specified measurement limits or compliance requirements to be checked, the telemedicine server will test the incoming data against the patient's monitoring plan. An alert is raised for the centre operator if limits are exceeded or if non-compliance is detected.

Trials of the SAFE 21 telemonitoring equipment took place in Newcastle upon Tyne in 1998-99 using the City Council's Community Care Alarm Service. Other trials took place in Spain and the Netherlands. A high level of satisfaction (at 86 per cent) among users, who were volunteer patients with muscular dystrophy from the Newcastle Muscle Centre, was found in the Newcastle trials. The greatest benefit was seen as the avoidance of hospital care (McIntosh and Thie, 2001, p 71). A similar level of satisfaction was evident in a subsequent trial involving patients of the nearby Dryburn Hospital. This, in terms that echo the objectives of hospital-at-home services, aimed to replace "patient care on the ward with homecare" (p 70). Typically, use of the telemonitoring equipment lasted one week.

SAFE 21 is now being marketed by Tunstall Telecom as a community telemedicine system that operates with social alarms. One example of where such a joint application has taken place is at the West Yorkshire Metropolitan Ambulance Service NHS Trust (WYMAS) in Bradford. WYMAS handles calls for both and also deals with enquiries for the NHS Direct advisory service.

THE GUILDFORD INITIATIVE[5]

A further telecare project focused on support at home has been developed in Guildford. A particular focus has been on falls, a topic discussed in Chapter Thirteen. The project is a partnership between the local authority and a range of agencies representing medical and broader social welfare interests. Key aims include establishing the acceptability of the technologies to users; assessing their impact, if any, in reducing the need for hospital admission; and establishing the extent to which users are able to regain prior levels of independence after a fall.

The evaluative framework involves 20 users and a further 20 in a control group (that is older people assessed according to the same needs criteria but for whom just basic social alarm equipment has been provided). All are linked to the Guildford Borough Council monitoring and response centre.

Those among the main user group are provided with a social alarm device, a pendant trigger, fall detector, bed occupancy monitor and a key safe by the front door to facilitate access by a responder.

The above initiatives are fairly broad in their medical objectives and present, therefore, particular challenges when attempting to build on to social alarm technologies. There is, however, a medical service that is more narrowly framed in terms of functionality but which is particularly well developed in terms of the number of users and its international area of operation. The service is that of Shahal, established in Israel, which monitors cardiac readings of its users. It is therefore primarily concerned with facilitating speedy medical interventions rather than any broader objective relating to user independence. Other services have followed Shahal's example (see Zhang et al, 1997, pp 67-8).

SHAHAL (ISRAEL)

Shahal Medical Services operate from Tel Aviv, Israel. The service originated in 1987 "to provide efficient pre-hospital medical care to its subscribers" and had grown by 1997 to serve over 40,000 users (Roth et al, 1997, p 58;Yatim, 1997, p 28). It operates by providing users with a cardio bleeper device by which they can take their own cardiac readings and transmit them directly to one of the company's medical monitoring centres. There is an operational base in Hatfield, England, managed via the Nestor Healthcare Group. Yatim (p 28) described the task undertaken by the staff at the Tel Aviv centre as follows:

After comparing the subscriber's symptoms and ECG with their medical history, the medical professional makes a decision either to advise and reassure the subscriber or to dispatch one of the company's physician-staffed Mobile Intensive Care Units (MICUs).

The MICUs operate throughout Israel. Yatim noted (p 29) that only one in seven (14 per cent) of calls needed the mobile response and that just half of these resulted in a transfer to hospital, this process enabling Shahal to achieve its goal of reducing the time it took for treatment to be obtained. A further outcome was the positive affect on the users' self-confidence and their peace of mind. Roth et al (1997, p 59) noted that "while many calls to Shahal are made by individuals who do not require a medical intervention, an important goal of the system is to educate subscribers to sound an alert early, facilitating the prevention of attacks rather than only providing intervention after the fact".

Alongside the cardiac service, Shahal also offer equipment to enable subscribers to do tests on their respiration, this being aimed at asthmatics and those with other pulmonary conditions or high blood pressure (http://www.matimop.org.il/newrdinf/company/c1814.htm). They also offer an interactive video system and a conventional social alarm service (Roth et al, 1997, p 59)

Tele-emergency services in Israel of the kind offered by Shahal have been claimed to "prevent 95 per cent of unnecessary admissions to emergency rooms in hospitals" and to effect substantial reductions in in-patient days for users suffering congestive heart disease (European Commission, 2001, p 185).

Different ethical perspectives

The discussion above illustrates some of the variety of initiatives and services that can be considered within the umbrella term of telecare but which have objectives that are focused on the achievement of essentially clinical outcomes. The essential component of all of them is the provision of care in people's own homes and, though not always pointed to as such, there is a contribution towards supporting independent living.

The definition of telecare adopted here, therefore, is one that complements that noted earlier for telemedicine. It affirms that telecare is care at a distance, which takes place in people's own homes and is achieved with the assistance of communications technologies. It includes such services within all forms of ordinary housing, as opposed to institutions, and smart homes.

As indicated earlier one of the most obvious signs of difference in the ethical frameworks that underpin telemedicine and telecare services is in the terms used, with the former almost exclusively using the term patient for their service users. And though greater emphasis is being made within the medical profession on the rights of the patient, further change is considered necessary. Clark has stated, regarding a wide range of medical technologies, that "the technical aspect of medical authority must give way to a value authority held by the patient" (1996, p 750). In relation to the same Bursztajn et al (1984, p 180) suggested that "the question to be resolved is no longer should the patient be involved but how can the patient be involved and finally how do both the patient and the doctor stay involved rather than surrender the decision to purely technical considerations?"

The context is one where the medical imperative to cure or at least (per the Hippocratic oath) "do no harm", requires acknowledgement of the judgement of medical practitioners as experts and compliance by the patient with prescribed courses of treatment. Recognition of expertise among medical practitioners is, of course, easily afforded in view of the extent of their knowledge and training, this rendering them best placed, subject to examination of the patient and an understanding of their symptoms, to make appropriate clinical diagnoses. Gott (1995, p 11), however, argued that telemedicine is reductionist; and Nohr (2000, p 173) noted the tendency of medical practitioners to treat "cases rather than patients" with telemedicine tending to "split the patient up into different pieces, each treated by a separate, specialised, technical solution".

The possession of medical knowledge and command of relevant technologies ensures that there will almost always be a power imbalance between practitioner and patient. This results in decisions being made that reflect clinical objectives but which may have not adequately taken account of the views of the patient. At worst, as argued by Clark (1996, p 754), "the context within which older persons make health care decisions is coercive". He argued (p 762) that the perspective must change to one that is oriented towards broader goals rather than simply treating problems. Importantly, he argued that, "health must ultimately be defined by each individual" the goals relating to which "can best be determined through a dialogue involving the individual and his or her health care provider(s)".

With regard to medical care in the home, Tweed and Quigley (2000, p 9) warned of the potential of telecare to simply transfer dependence from the "institution to technology in the home". That this may be partly true regarding the use of social alarms is already recognised in view of indications that some older people do not use them in situations where they feel that they may be coerced into going to hospital and may be the subject of poking, prodding and testing, resulting in the discovery of conditions that result in their admission.

Information, privacy and confidentiality

There are also concerns about the privacy and confidentiality of information that can be gathered by medical equipment in the home. Demiris et al (2000, p 281), for instance, in a sample of 32 older people in a supported housing scheme and a church community in Minnesota, found nearly a third (32 per cent) were concerned about the potential of technologies in the home to violate their privacy.

In Great Britain, Stanberry (1998, p 13) considered that the issue of confidentiality raised by telemedicine services could be resolved through existing medical law. He acknowledged, however, that the "exact nature and extent of this duty is unclear" observing that "in the past, the concept of confidentiality meant that health records were kept secret from patients themselves"!

It should be noted that the issue of patient or service user involvement is not just an ethical one but also a legal one in the sense that inalienable rights are at risk of being infringed if treatments or services are provided against the will of the individual. The guidance given by the General Medical Council in Great Britain supports this and seeks to ensure that patients are aware of their rights. Indeed, the Access to Health Records Act of 1990 gives the service user the right to access their health records. However, Stanberry (p 26) has noted that:

> Legally speaking the concepts of ownership and control of a patient's medical records in the UK are somewhat underdeveloped. For while confidential details given to a teleconsulting doctor by their patient remain, in one fundamental sense, the property of the patient, control over the record rests largely with the doctor.

The increasing acceptance of approaches to medical services in which information is shared with service users points to what Bursztajn et al (1984, p 180) referred to as a shift from a model of medical decision making characterised by paternalism to one of consumer preference. However, Birch et al (2000, p 114) lamented telemedicine's general "lack of evidence of good governance controls" and (p 115) "a disturbing lack of evidence concerning patient and societal, behavioural and organizational effects". Clark (1996, p 762) argued that "final decisions about health goal priorities, and the amount of effort expended in their achievement, must reside with the individual" although he saw little indication that this perspective had been properly considered by most medical practitioners.

The housing context

The housing context is, of course, the one within which social alarms have emerged in Great Britain. The position and status of residents within such a context is one that sees them both as independent and involved in day-to-day transactions that are part and parcel of being customers and service users. The providers of services have, in general, afforded recognition to their views, wishes and aspirations. Indeed such perspectives are not only part of the dynamics associated with private sector service provision but within Great Britain are also increasingly central to endeavours to improve public sector service quality standards. Older people, and the services that they receive, are no exception, with greater attention having been given to the need for reform in service frameworks and, importantly, staff attitudes (see Audit Commission, 1998). The author of this book has, among others, affirmed the need for older people to be accorded the status that is offered more generally to service recipients and for that status not to be inappropriately eroded through, for example, deference to relatives who might consider that they know best, or by continued adherence to ageist or patronising service frameworks (Fisk, 1999, pp 23-5).

Paradoxically, it can be argued that the inappropriate location of many social alarm services in Great Britain, that is on account of most being managed by housing authorities, may have helped to ensure that greater attention has been given to responding to older people as customers than would otherwise have been the case. This reflects the fact that service frameworks around housing, and even sheltered housing, are arguably more flexible than those around the residential care or homecare services that are the responsibility of their social welfare counterparts. Furthermore, the funding reforms that demand that support services are more closely tailored to individual needs, rather than being determined by the type of accommodation lived in, are serving to assist the necessary changes in perspective.

What this means is that, while there are pressures to increase medical care in the home through the use of technologies, the perspectives being taken by service providers are strongly influenced by what has been determined through social alarms. The scenario, however, is one where separate services, set up by hospitals, health or ambulance trusts, are likely to increase in number. The example offered by the West Yorkshire Metropolitan Ambulance Service NHS Trust may, in other words, be replicated.

What is worrying is the extent to which some such new services may operate in ways that reflect clinical perspectives and perpetuate power imbalances by which all, but often especially older, people will be disadvantaged. Meanwhile, social alarm services that attempt to continue to operate without attention to the medical agenda are increasingly likely to be left on the sidelines. Hence Fisk's call for social alarm service providers to engage in dialogues with their counterparts who are more directly concerned with the pursuit of health and medical objectives (Fisk, 1995, pp 152-3). He observed elsewhere, however, that many existing services were ill prepared for the changes (Doughty and Fisk, 2001, p 5).

The view that social alarm services represent a ready-made network on which more medically oriented services might be based, at least in the shorter term, has been expressed, as noted earlier, by Curry and Norris (1997, p 18) and also by Doughty and Williams (2001, p 38). More broadly Clough et al (1998, p 13) have stated that "in practical terms there is no distinction between the social and health applications and there would appear to be a very good case for linking them so that the same facilities can be shared". Hawley (2003, p 68) pointed to the possibility of mergers between such different types of service or, in any case, for the "possible re-routing of calls between them".

This, of course, presupposes important changes in operational frameworks and has considerable significance with regard to the attitudes, skills and expertise of the staff of monitoring and response centres. It is essential, however, for social alarm services to address such issues lest centralised medical response services develop which operate according to an inappropriate service ethos and lest the objectives that they adopt which relate to independent living are too narrowly framed.

Conclusion

Given the overlap in the use of the terms telemedicine and telecare and the context where the services in question are put into operation, it was necessary that they be considered together. In fact, this chapter has shown that not only are there overlaps but that there are real benefits that stand to be realised by bringing together aspects of each kind of service. Clough et al (1998, p 19) noted that one barrier to change lay in professional interests. Relating to this are the differences in professional outlooks and differences in the extent to which there is a willingness to embrace agendas concerned with user choice and empowerment.

That there will be changes in service frameworks is certain. In addition, there can be no doubt that the expansion of home-based services concerned with medical care represent a threat to traditional social alarm services and, if allowed to develop without appropriate service objectives being in place and the resolution of key ethical issues, will set back objectives concerned with supporting and promoting engagement and social inclusion, as well as independent living.

As the healthcare as well as social needs of users of social alarm services become more apparent, therefore, it is absolutely essential that dialogues take place to ensure that medical expertise is brought on board in ethically appropriate ways. Much may be learnt from the few current initiatives at this interface. In the words of Clough et al (1998, p 24):

> Telemedicine and telecare are primarily new ways of delivering care and not new methods of treatment. The best ways of gaining benefit from these technologies will only be discovered as managers and clinicians begin to explore how their use can help in meeting the problems they face of providing healthcare, as efficiently as possible, in ways that are best suited to the needs and wishes of patients.

This view is endorsed here and a call is added for holistic and collaborative approaches. In any case, the threat of what Gott (1995, p 11) referred to as the "reductionist" effects of telemedicine must be averted.

Notes

[1] CAT stands for computed axial tomography, that is, multiple x-rays from different angles. Electrocardiograms record the electrical activity of the heart.

[2] Correspondence with Kathy Rupp (Hays Medical Center).

[3] Vlaskamp, F.J.M. and Price, S. (1999) in paper to conference on smart homes, Eindhoven.

[4] As above.

[5] Correspondence with David Thew (Guildford Borough Council).

THIRTEEN

Falls, lifestyle monitoring and dementia care

Introduction

One powerful reason for the use of social alarms is a concern about the consequences of falls experienced by older people. Indeed, as noted in Chapter One, the image of someone who had fallen and was unable to call for help became, as noted in Chapter Ten, an icon for social alarms and featured frequently in the advertising of both manufacturers and service providers.

The inappropriateness of the iconography was noted. It is undeniable, however, that social alarms have a role to play in enabling older people to call for help after they have fallen or, as noted in Chapter Three and as strongly affirmed in the work of Thornton and Mountain (1992), when they are stuck. More than this, one of the main benefits and possibly the main benefit of social alarms has been repeatedly affirmed as facilitating speedy interventions and thereby avoiding the adverse consequences of lying unaided for sustained periods.

The long-standing focus on the benefits of social alarms in relation to falls was a reflection of the fact that, while most services were located within housing departments, there was considerable relevance to social welfare and healthcare agendas. That such relevance was recognised by some was noted in Chapter Four. But the small scale of such recognition in Great Britain was instrumental in marginalising social alarms and arguably held them back from realising a greater potential.

The technological changes associated with smart homes, telemedicine and telecare, discussed in Chapters Eleven and Twelve, and the gradual awakening of social welfare and healthcare practitioners and policy makers to the potential of social alarms means, however, that a greater potential stands to be realised. The dangers associated with this relate to that potential being realised in ways that are narrowly focused on clinical objectives and which would be likely to treat older people as patients as opposed to service users. Chapter Twelve was clear about this and about some of the ethical issues that need to be addressed. Closely relating to this are the dilemmas associated with what has become known as lifestyle monitoring.

Lifestyle monitoring is a direct descendant of passive and activity monitoring. A proposed definition of lifestyle monitoring is the monitoring of environmental conditions, activity and physiology in order to identify situations or circumstances that reflect adverse changes in or threats to the personal well-being of dwelling occupants. The key difference from passive and activity monitoring is its focus on the person *and* their living environment as opposed to the person alone. While the monitoring of an individual's physiology is not, as yet, generally facilitated, sensors linked to intelligent processors can provide an increasing wealth of data that attest to their well-being. The data for example provide the potential means of identifying a change in normal patterns of activity because of illness, accident or the presence of intruders, or where the living environment is threatened, by flood, fire, low temperatures, or the gas being left on.

Doughty and Williams (2002, p 13) have pushed the agenda forward on such matters by defining certain situations of concern and incorporating provision for their monitoring or for automated responses within a proprietary system now being piloted by Tunstall Telecom. These situations arise when time limits determined for such matters as bed occupancy, bathroom usage or dwelling temperature are exceeded and other alternatives, such as the person being active in another room or sleeping in a chair, are ruled out.

It is important to recognise that a key feature of such systems is automation. In other words, as with activity monitoring, there is no need for the older person to press a button or pull a cord in order for a signal to be passed to a third party. Ethical dilemmas relating to this are discussed below. The present configuration of systems is, however, accompanied by the functionality normally associated with social alarms. Both active and passive elements are, therefore, present.

And as is noted later in this chapter, consideration is being given by those concerned with system development and service provision to the role of such technologies in relation to older people with dementia. Insofar as activity patterns can be established and any propensity for wandering can be monitored, the potential appeal of technologies in this context is understandable. Older people with dementia pose particular challenges for service providers. The means by which better justice can be done to their engagement and inclusion and independence are only just beginning to be explored (see, for instance, Goldsmith, 1996; Allan, 2001; and Killick and Allan, 2001).

Falls, lifestyle monitoring and dementia represent key areas that relate to the technologies and services that will characterise the future and may be key features of tomorrow's smart homes. In addressing these issues, therefore, this chapter attempts to shape some of the debate that must take place as new technologies and new service configurations emerge. That it will, in part, fail in its mission is inevitable. This was noted by Tweed and Quigley (2000, p 8) when affirming that Fisk's advice concerning the need for recognition of user perspectives in relation to the configuration of telecare services had come "too late in the process of technological intervention" with key decisions having already been made to adopt technological solutions to multifaceted problems.

Falls

The interest in falls among older people is long-standing, a review by Askham et al (1990, p 4) summarising the reasons for such interest as including the disproportionately greater prominence of falls among older people in home accidents; the increase in the incidence of falls with age; the adverse consequences to individuals and the cost to statutory services; and the fact that falls "may be an indication of undetected and/or unmet medical need". For England, based on research in the period up to 1990, they noted (p 7), that "approximately one third of people aged 65 years and over fall at least once per annum". The operation of fall detectors alongside social alarms has only been apparent since the 1990s.

The problem of falls is greater for women than for men. Alarmingly, Sowden et al (1996, p 2) reported that "falls are the leading cause of death from injury among people aged over 77" and that "over 85 per cent of all fatal falls in the home in England and Wales are in people aged over 65". With such matters in mind, and considering the cost implications for health services associated with the treatment and rehabilitation of those who experience falls, it is unsurprising that falls are one of the British government's foci within the National Service Framework for Older People (Department of Health, 2001, p 76ff).

With regard to the causes of falls, consideration needs to be given to both intrinsic and extrinsic factors. Intrinsic factors are those that relate to the person themself, their physiology, gait, strength, skills, sensory acuity and mental state. Linking to these Askham et al (1990, pp 21-2) noted that a number of medical factors including heart conditions, disorders of the brain and joint disease, all more commonplace in older people, were "by their very nature likely to precipitate a fall". And to these they added (p 28) the effects of medication, sleeping tablets and alcohol.

Extrinsic factors are those that relate to the environment and the extent of risk presented through such things as steps and stairs, loose carpets and wet floors. However, it is not necessarily the apparent risk presented by such environmental features that is the crucial factor but also the awareness of them among those who use them. Topper et al (1993, p 485), in examining the risk posed by steps, pointed to the fact that one available remedy, that of reducing step height, might not bring the desired parallel reduction in risk. They argued that such interventions "may be less important than the failure to attend to, perceive and/or avoid obstacles and hazardous ground conditions".

It is recognised as important to focus on both intrinsic and extrinsic factors when developing and implementing programmes aimed at preventing or reducing the incidence of falls (Askham et al, 1990, p 17). In the context of the former, increasing emphasis is being given to the inclusion within such prevention programmes of measures to increase individual fitness and strength. Sowden et al (1996, p 6) stated that "older people should be offered access to exercise classes or home exercise routines which include, for example, balance training such as Tai Chi" and noted (p 3) that a trial exercise programme in the United States appeared to result in a 10 per cent reduction in the risk of falling. They also suggested (p 6) the potential benefit of older people taking Vitamin D supplements to help maintain bone mass, thereby reducing the risk of fractures.

In certain contexts it has been suggested that greater emphasis should be placed on the wearing of hip protector pads (Sowden et al, 1996, p 6), the provision of soft floor coverings or even what have been termed dual stiffness floors that give way on impact, with each of these reducing the chances of hip fractures (Casalena et al, 1994; and Badre-Alam et al, 1994).

Finally, increasing attention is being given to psychological issues associated with the experience of falling. Tinetti et al (1994, p M140) noted, for instance, that "fear is a fall-related consequence that may limit function beyond what might be expected from the effects of injury or underlying physical ability alone". Based on a study of over 1,400 people aged over 72 in New Haven, Connecticut in the United States, they found (p M146) that "the level of confidence in performing certain self-care tasks without falling is a major correlate of the actual performance of those and related physical and social tasks". Askham et al (1990, p 43) noted that "the fear of falling often causes the elderly person to lose confidence, resulting in limited mobility and possibly becoming house-bound". Doughty et al (2000, p 150) reported that "fear of falling ... may lead to adverse lifestyle changes".

Significantly Tinetti et al (1994, p M146) also noted that the level of confidence expressed by the older people they studied was not just influenced by their own experience but also be the experience of others. They argued, therefore, (p M146) that:

> The most successful approach to prevention, rehabilitation ... and management may combine simultaneous attempts to improve both efficacy (i.e. people's perceptions of their own capabilities) and physical skills.

Long lies and social alarms

A further factor relating to falls, although less often considered, is the effect of a long lie after a fall has taken place. The essential point here is that any delay in medical treatment that is needed as a result of a fall, for instance because the person who fell was unable to obtain assistance, can lead to medical complications. Recovery from injury will be slower than would otherwise be the case thereby compromising mobility and increasing the risk of dying.

At the same time there are concerns that the psychological effect of experiencing a fall may have an impact on the rate of recovery. This point was made by McKee (1998, p 11). McKee then went on to discuss the relationship between the physical and social self. He argued (p 12) that falls represented "a sudden and catastrophic failing of the physical self that ... has immediate and significant implications for the social self, and ultimately recovery from the event". He speculated that:

> If an individual perceives the event as an indication of his or her failing body, a drop in its capacity to function adequately, then their perceived control over recovery and the avoidance of future similar events can be anticipated to be low.

The need for speedy responses in the event of falls and an awareness of risks associated with a long lie led Askham et al (1990, p 51ff) to recommend the wider provision of social alarms. The relevance of social alarms was seen by them both as part of strategies for prevention and for avoiding long lies. Their overview called (p 56) for research into the effectiveness of social alarms in this context in view of the evidence at that time which pointed to the fact that "some people did not receive all the help they wanted [from alarms]; nor could all recipients reach the alarm in an emergency" affirming that "this points to the need for alarms which people can carry on their bodies".

A contextual point is the apparent increased propensity for older people to be more likely to seek or accept the offer of a social alarm device after having experienced a fall or other difficulty (Thornton and Mountain, 1992, p 19). Herein may lie one important reason why social alarms should be utilised, not just to bring about speedy responses in the event of falls or other urgent situations but to help give people a greater sense of control at a time of recovery and/or coming to terms with some loss of control over their physical selves and, perhaps, redefining their view of independence.

Following from the above, no consideration of social alarms can be complete without some acknowledgement of their role in relation to falls. Such a role is certain to increase as a higher degree of frailty among older people who are users of such systems and services becomes evident and has already been clear in the evolution of systems and services in Great Britain (see Chapters Four, Five and Six).

But facilitating responses to falls can no longer be seen as the main reason for social alarms. Though considerations of falls may have been a key justification for the establishment and nurturing of social alarm services in the 1970s and 1980s, evidence about their use and their benefits in a much wider range of circumstances and in the more general supporting of independence has accumulated. And with the use of a wider range of sensors linked to social alarms and in the context of lifestyle monitoring, responding to falls will be increasingly seen as just one, albeit important, aspect of services that will come to characterise such systems and services in the first decades of the 21st century.

Lifestyle monitoring

As noted above, lifestyle monitoring has its origins in passive and activity monitoring. A noteworthy predecessor, therefore, is Clark's EMMA system configured over 20 years ago (Clark, 1979, p 214; and noted in Chapter Four). EMMA (Environmental Monitor/Movement Alarm) incorporated sensors that monitored movement, including getting out of bed, and dwelling temperature. The ideals put forward by Clark for an activity monitoring system are still relevant and appropriate in the context of more recent developments. These were (p 214) that the ideal device should:

> be reliable, detect a range of emergencies, require no positive action on the part of the user, not need the user to remember to activate it, to detect a variety of hazards, have low running and installation costs and not be so obtrusive that it causes anxiety to its user.

While it has taken some time for Clark's vision to be realised, activity monitoring (as noted in Chapter Four) was a feature of some social alarm systems. Similar principles now underpin the use of activity monitoring, although the use of pressure pads has been supplemented or replaced by PIRs (passive infra-red sensors). Glasgow City Council (1993, p 18), for instance, use PIRs that link to hard-wired social alarm systems to both monitor for activity and provide a means of intruder detection.

Justification for having an activity monitoring facility has been made by various researchers (Miskelly, 2001, p 455; Doughty and Williams, 2002, p 6). Fisk (1986, p 121), when appraising the merits of social alarms, put forward three reasons to support the use of activity monitoring. These reasons are amended and extended below and take on, it is suggested, new relevance as their usefulness is being reappraised in the context of the greater amount of data that can now be collected and its use in the context of lifestyle monitoring. Some such benefits are anticipatory in the sense that they will only be realised as and when more intelligent social alarm systems, that utilise some of the latest sensor technologies, are introduced.

1) Activity and lifestyle monitoring can ensure that help is obtained in the event of an emergency where someone remains: (a) unconscious; (b) out of reach of a pull cord or radio trigger; or (c) dies.

The need to respond as speedily as possible in these circumstances is obvious and the possibility of alerts being made immediately is heralded as sensor technologies to monitor physiological well-being, including respiration and heartbeat, become more widely utilised. By this means valuable time could be saved in responding to emergencies or other necessitous circumstances. This suggests positive benefits in terms of reducing anxiety among users, with swifter interventions taking place in relation to medical needs, which will reduce the need for hospital admissions.

2) Activity and lifestyle monitoring can add to the reassurance of some social alarm users. This is likely to be especially true for people who have certain

medical conditions and/or are intensive users of social alarm services. This would include the terminally ill, and those likely to experience seizures, fits, blackouts and/or frequent falls.

3) Activity and lifestyle monitoring could change the problem of what have been known as false alarms. Such a change arises through potentially obviating the need for users to carry or wear radio triggers, the consequence of which has been frequent or occasional accidental activation. Higher numbers of false alarms will, however, arise when agreed parameters regarding activity patterns are exceeded but with such alarms being necessary as a prelude to precautionary checks on the user's circumstances.

The extent to which people do not wear pendant transmitter devices has been noted in several studies (Duncan and Thwaites, 1987, p 48; Fisk, 1989, p 115; Gott, 1995, p 83; Peeters, 1997, p 15; van Berlo, 1998, p 390).

4) Activity and lifestyle monitoring can assist in identifying and understanding the reason for calls. This is particularly the case for lifestyle monitoring where intelligent devices are incorporated that can monitor longer-term physiological well-being and environmental measures. Responses might in such circumstances be better tailored to the nature of any need. Fires, medical emergencies or death would, of course, require immediate responses. Other alerts, relating for example to low dwelling temperatures on a cold winter night, would result in subsequent monitoring, but not necessarily an immediate response and/or intervention.

5) Activity and lifestyle monitoring may have a particular role to play for people with dementia. This potential is discussed later in this chapter. It signals an extension in the role and scope of social alarms since confused older people have often been excluded from both sheltered housing schemes and from among those considered as potential beneficiaries of carephones.

While there are, therefore, several benefits to activity and lifestyle monitoring it must be borne in mind that the manner in which they operate can result in help being obtained, perhaps in response to what might be deemed false alarms, when it is not wanted. In certain other circumstances some users will not wish an intervention to be made either because they fear the consequences of medical treatment, hospitalisation, or they want to die. Such wishes should be respected and carefully considered when establishing procedures relating both to the way that such technologies should operate and the ways in which calls or alerts are handled.

Two projects in Great Britain are worthy of special consideration by virtue of their offering or having offered some form of lifestyle monitoring. The first is the British Telecom/Anchor Trust initiative, which involved installation of prototype smart systems in 22 households in Newcastle upon Tyne, Ipswich, Knowsley and Nottingham. It was evaluated by Sixsmith (2000) and reported on by Porteus and Brownsell (2000). The second relates to a range of installations for local authorities in Durham. The differences between these signal the fact that lifestyle monitoring, as with smart homes (see Chapter Eleven), can relate to many configurations of sensors, social alarm devices and processing equipment.

Antecedents for such initiatives took place in Australia. The work, undertaken by Celler, was concerned to monitor the interaction of older people and their environments.[1] Key features included, in addition to the detection of movement using PIRs, electricity and switch usage and the measurement of sound. A primary concern was to detect changing patterns of behaviour that might indicate parallel changes in a person's health status. British Telecom (1996, p 144), reporting on Celler's work, affirmed the purpose as to "permit people who are frail to continue living independent lives to the greatest possible extent. Only if behaviour patterns change significantly do carers need to intervene". However, while this work was important in pointing to options for gathering data, it appears not to have adequately developed the means of processing these.[2]

Summary information about these initiatives together with others concerned with telecare (described in Chapter Twelve) and those concerned with the needs of people with dementia (summarised later in this chapter) is presented in Table 13.1.

Types of activity and lifestyle monitoring

Doughty suggested four types of sensor configurations associated with activity and lifestyle monitoring. These are as follows.[3] The first two are concerned with activity monitoring only.

1) Single fixed sensor approach.

This approach is characterised by use of a single pressure mat or by a single PIR. A timer is also present so that movement or non-movement can be recorded against predetermined time periods. The benefits of the single sensor approach are related to enabling the identification of non-movement in occupied dwellings, normally in the morning, before an agreed time, or the identification of movement in unoccupied dwellings.

2) Single body worn sensor approach.

This approach requires the user to wear a sensor device to monitor their movement or non-movement. It might also be used to gather certain physiological information. A variant of this approach would use implanted devices. Characteristically the body worn sensor would be on the wrist and enable monitoring of the extent of movement. As with the single fixed sensor approach, information is normally only sent to a third party on a periodic basis. Speedy responses to what may be urgent and/or necessitous situations may not, therefore, be readily facilitated.

Other body worn devices, notably fall detectors worn on the belt, are able to recognise impacts and/or changes in orientation. The advantages of such sensors in such circumstances are that calls may immediately be transmitted to a third party and help obtained.

Table 13.1: Initiatives relating to telecare, lifestyle monitoring and dementia care

	Primary aim(s)
SAFE 21	
(Development of product to facilitate monitoring at home with off-site data transfer. Initiative completed. Derivative product on market)	• Further development of social alarms • Medical and healthcare monitoring at home • Physiological data transfer to monitoring and response centre • Mobile social alarm device able to be carried by user
THE GUILDFORD INITIATIVE	
(Inter-agency service development and evaluation using fall detectors and other sensors with social alarms)	• Medical and healthcare monitoring at home • Responding to user needs • Inter-agency collaboration • Development of social alarm service
BRITISH TELECOM / ANCHOR TRUST INITIATIVE	
(Trial social alarm installations with sensors in homes of 22 users. Initiative completed)	• Lifestyle monitoring in users' homes • Detection of deviations from normal behaviour patterns • Integration of sensors with social alarm device
THE DURHAM PROJECT	
(Prototype smart systems installed in dwellings within sheltered housing schemes)	• Integration of sensors with call systems • Lifestyle monitoring in users' homes • Development of behavioural algorithms and predictive indices
THE GLOUCESTER INITIATIVE	
(Trial installation in 3-bedroomed house)	• Technologies to serve needs of people with dementia • Development of appropriate lifestyle monitoring framework • Automation to facilitate cut-offs and safety interventions • Development of appropriate user interfaces
SEVEN OAKS, DERRY	
(Installations in 35 dwellings. Reablement bungalow for people newly discharged from hospital)	• Technologies to serve needs of people with dementia • Development of appropriate lifestyle monitoring framework • Automation to facilitate cut-offs and safety interventions • Establishing the implications of technologies for packages of care

3) Multiple sensors with no local intelligence.

The use of multiple sensors, although more costly, increases the amount of data that can be gathered. At the same time, however, new problems of interpretation are created. Again there are problems that arise because of information only being sent to or collected periodically by a third party. Urgent or necessitous situations may not, therefore, be responded to quickly. The lifestyle monitoring pilot involving British Telecom and Anchor Trust discussed below falls within this category.

4) Multiple sensors with local intelligence.

In contrast to lifestyle monitoring systems where the information must be gathered and interpreted by a third party at a remote location, the provision of local intelligence provides opportunities for parameters to be set that reflect a greater understanding of the data. Importantly such parameters might be able to be agreed and modified in consultation with the user in the light of experience and/or changing needs. As noted by Brownsell et al (1999, p 143) the inclusion of local intelligence "ensures that only information relevant to well-being is transferred outside the home".

Because of the local intelligence, such systems are more expensive. They pose a number of important questions, furthermore, which are only beginning to be addressed. These are concerned with interpretations of the meaning of data collected and ethical issues regarding the intrusiveness of the systems and data ownership.

In either case where multiple sensors could be used, the scope for those concerned to gather physiological information is being increasingly explored. This follows from the technological developments associated with telemedicine, noted in Chapter Twelve, and will draw greater attention to the potential of implanted devices. Such devices were called for by Brownsell et al (1999, p 146) when they affirmed that "what is required ... is a range of sensors in a form capable of being implanted in a manner similar to a pacemaker". They added that:

> An individual could have a series of devices implanted to record their electro-cardiogram, blood sugar concentrations and blood pressure, all of which would report to a local node worn by the patient. The local node might incorporate a mobile phone which would be responsible for onward transmission of the data.

A particular question that arises is concerned with the minimum number and type of sensor devices that is commensurate with service objectives associated with the well-being of different kinds of service users. The ideal number of sensors and their roles remains a matter for debate. Doughty and Williams (2001, p 40) considered that three or four would be too few because they would provide incomplete data, offering a poor potential for analysis. They suggested, however, that too many sensors would be unnecessarily intrusive and would create "data smog".

Only time and careful consideration of the variety of initiatives in this field will enable such questions to be answered. Peeters (1997, p 16) gave some pointers when suggesting the "most sensitive parameters for distinguishing changes in health and physiological status" relate to such matters as sleeping patterns, bath and toilet usage, cooking own meals and general mobility. This, he noted (p 19) required a lifestyle monitoring system to detect signs of human life, generate an alarm in the case of an emergency and transmit that alarm to a predetermined point. He saw (p 25) fall detectors and bed-use sensors as necessary to facilitate this.

Two initiatives concerned with lifestyle monitoring are discussed below.

THE BRITISH TELECOM/ANCHOR TRUST PROJECT

The British Telecom/Anchor Trust initiative involved the installation of what they termed "lifestyle monitoring telecare" systems. The primary aim was to "harness the application of new technology in a non-intrusive way to service the needs and wishes of older or vulnerable people, central to which is that of maintaining independence and choice" (Porteus and Brownsell, 2000, p 25). The system was developed by British Telecom but appears to have replicated another initiative in France (see Chan et al, 1998) and followed work in Australia noted earlier in this chapter.[4] In looking for deviations in normal patterns of behaviour, Porteus and Brownsell (2000, p 13) argued that "detecting situations as they occur will enable people to be treated before the situation worsens and consequently we move from a reactive to a preventative system that should result in a reduction in healthcare costs per head".

The patterns of daily living of residents were recorded using PIRs in every room and magnetic switches on the entrance and refrigerator doors. Dwelling temperatures were also monitored using sensors in the living room. The devices in question were linked in most cases by radio to the system control box and the information gathered was forwarded or collected via the telephone network to or by the British Telecom laboratories in Ipswich. Each home had a total of between nine and 12 sensors installed (Sixsmith, 2000, p 64).

As noted by Sixsmith and Sixsmith (2000, p 190) the system developed in the British Telecom/Anchor Trust initiative was "designed to work in parallel with social alarm systems in order to provide a more comprehensive service". People did not need to carry or wear any kind of device and, if they wished, they could turn off the system by dialling a designated telephone number.

The importance of this cannot be overstated in view of the fact that it gathered more than 5,000 days of lifestyle data and provided valuable pointers to their potential for use in identifying what were described as alert situations, that is where there was significant deviation from the normal pattern of activity. Five types of alert situations were described by Sixsmith (2000, p 65). These were:

- lack of expected activity;
- person not arisen from bed;
- lack of use of refrigerator;
- low room temperature; and
- unusual pattern of activity.

The first four alert situations were identified in relation to time periods agreed with users. Identification of any unusual pattern of activity was, however, more difficult. Porteus and Brownsell (2000, p 35) acknowledged that "finding the balance between detecting what is a deviation from the normal ... and what is not was particularly difficult to solve".

In all, 60 alert situations, one per household in every 80 monitored days, were identified (Porteus and Brownsell, 2000, p 38). These generated automatic calls from the British Telecom laboratories to the dwelling so that the user could key in '1' to indicate that all was well. If the user keyed in '2' or did not respond to the call, nominated contacts would then be automatically telephoned in turn until one indicated that they could attend. While this was not part of the initiative, in the event of no nominated contact being available, it was intended that a telephone link would be made to a social alarm service.

Sixsmith and Sixsmith (2000, p 191) were clearer about the issues. They affirmed that:

the data generated were very unspecific, making data interpretation and the identification of alerts a highly complex task. The algorithms developed to identify alert situations focused on patterns of inactivity or unusual activity. While these may indicate a problem, the likelihood was that this was not the case, so the majority of alerts identified by the system were false positives.

False positives are what would be generally understood in relation to social alarms as false alarms. Sixsmith and Sixsmith (2000, p 191) added that "in order to make the system acceptable to users the number of false positives had to be minimised, decreasing the sensitivity of the system".

Here lies the crucial problem with the system in that Sixsmith and Sixsmith pointed to expectations of service users not being fulfilled. For users, they affirmed (p 191) "the key criterion for assessing the value of the system was its capacity to generate reliable alert calls immediately or soon after a problem occurred, preferably with no false positive alert calls". Clearly these preferences were not met. Neither was the value of the system in really urgent or necessitous situations tested.

Sixsmith (2000, p 70) also noted that users had a number of misapprehensions about the technologies. Some believed, for instance, that continuous monitoring was taking place, others thought that specific situations such as lying on the floor would be recognised, and most "did not fully appreciate that the system generated alerts by looking for variations outside normal activity patterns". Views about the system expressed by users, noted below, therefore, need to be considered with some caution.

Focus groups involving those who used the system and their carers revealed that over three quarters of both groups were satisfied or very satisfied with the system; 86 per cent of users thought the new technology was a good thing. Carers were even more in favour (93 per cent) (Porteus and Brownsell, 2000, p 43). But it needs to be borne in mind that, as Porteus and Brownsell reported (p 36), the initiative had "some difficulties in recruiting volunteers", suggesting the possibility that those who agreed to be part of the trial were likely to be more favourably predisposed to the technologies in question. In addition, Sixsmith (2000, p 7) noted that the confidence of users "was undermined when the system did not work in the way ... expected". This was notably so because users felt too many alert calls were generated. The unavoidable conclusion to be inferred is that user satisfaction with the technologies may have diminished had the trials continued for a longer period.

The potential benefits (Porteus and Brownsell, 2000, p 38) were recognised by users as:

- reducing anxieties for them and their families;
- facilitating earlier discharges from hospital; and, in respect of temperature monitoring
- providing a safeguard for people who might be frugal with heating.

Nearly half (47 per cent) responded positively to the statement "it helps me stay living at home" but this was quite strongly counterbalanced by the 36 per cent who disagreed (Sixsmith, 2000, p 67). Reservations were expressed (Porteus and Brownsell, 2000, p 38) by users relating to:

- the potential loss of privacy and feelings of being watched;
- the potential for service providers to reduce personal care provision and/or warden services; and
- the possible predisposition of service providers to focus on the cost savings that might be brought about by use of the technologies rather than enhancing service levels.

While, as indicated, the Porteus and Brownsell evaluation is of undoubted interest, some of its conclusions appear unsupported by the evidence. Examples are the affirmations that the "only disadvantages discovered centred on the possibility that technology could ultimately reduce or remove human contact" whereas a range of concerns regarding the initiative have been noted above; and the claim that lifestyle monitoring is proven as "an effective tool in automatically recognising alert conditions" (pp 60-1). A claim (p 59), furthermore, that the Royal Commission on Long Term Care suggested a requirement to have some form of monitoring in the home, is erroneous.

More cautionary conclusions would, it is considered, have been expected in view of the relatively small number of households included in the trial, the manner of their selection and the limited period over which the trial took place. This meant that there was almost no experience of real alerts. There were, in fact, two emergency situations that arose during the trial period. In both cases the user had fallen and had activated their alarm device by pushing the button on their portable transmitter device (Sixsmith, 2000, p 68). They had, in other words, used the system in the way associated with social alarms. This meant that there was insufficient time for information to be gathered by sensors and sent to a third party by which some abnormality in activity might have been identified.

Significantly, Sixsmith remarked (p 69) that for a substantial minority of users there were concerns about "the response time and sensitivity with respect to the generation of alerts" and that there was a "common feeling that only continuous analysis of the monitoring data was acceptable" (p 70). Put bluntly he asserted (p 70) that the criteria for assessing the performance of the system were first, "its immediacy, that is, its ability to generate an alert immediately or soon after the problem had occurred"; and second, "its infallibility, so that it would generate an alert on all occasions when a problem occurred".

Added to this could be the need for minimisation of false alerts though Porteus and Brownsell (2000, p 12) stated that "when the LMS [lifestyle monitoring system] did raise an alert and participants were not in need, they were very tolerant of it, appreciating the protection and care the system was affording them". But, as others, this statement appears unsupported. Furthermore, the limitations of the monitoring period were clearly such that a full assessment against Sixsmith's criteria could not be made. Sixsmith's conclusions therefore stand in contrast to the observations of Porteus and Brownsell.

Much of importance is, however, discussed in Porteus and Brownsell's work and there is a welcome call for longitudinal research into the effectiveness of such technologies in fulfilling some of the claims made (p 61). Sixsmith (2000, p 71), in addition, called for larger scale and more rigorous field trials with more attention given to ensuring clarity of understanding among users. Significantly, however, his final cautionary note casts doubt on just how far lifestyle monitoring might go when affirming that, within such systems, "the data generated ... [are] very non-specific and difficult to interpret and, in practice, it may be difficult to achieve a speed of response that is in line with clients' expectations".

THE DURHAM PROJECT

Prototype lifestyle monitoring systems were installed in sheltered homes managed by various authorities in County Durham. The initiatives have been undertaken in collaboration with the County Council and are seen as potentially underpinning the delivery of community support services. The systems were installed following a comprehensive review of relevant technologies that were available in the United Kingdom (Mills, 1999).

Doughty has affirmed the potential merits of the systems concerned in the context of sheltered housing and attested to their ability to operate with a wide range of sensors.[5] Such sensors reflect the focus of this initiative on the needs of older people and herald the possibility, with the aid of lifestyle monitoring and smart technologies, of further steps being taken to realise objectives associated with care in the community and the decentralisation of healthcare. The various sensors and devices tested have included:

- fall and collapse detectors;
- high and low temperature sensors;
- night-time monitoring devices to identify when a user is out of bed for an extended period;
- video systems to offer images of visitors at the front door; and
- video recording to transmit facial images of visitors for storage, to a monitoring and response centre.

The Durham systems are concerned to provide technologies that can detect emergencies but also monitor environmental factors and patterns of activity that may indicate developing problems or support needs. In other words, both patterns of behaviour that deviate from the norm (as in the British Telecom/Anchor Trust initiative) and longer-term changes, perhaps over many months, can be identified. The latter could, it was surmised, help in the identification of deteriorating mobility and such things as longer-term changes in patterns of sleeping, eating and bathing. Of interest, in addition, is the proposal for predictive indices to be developed, based on lifestyles, that can help signal the risk of falls and identify behaviour that is consistent with the early stages of dementia (Doughty et al, 2000, p 152). Already the Durham initiative has identified, through recording video images of visitors, the fact that some users, in having very few or no visitors, appear to be very socially isolated.[6]

User perspectives

With such lifestyle monitoring initiatives a concern must be expressed regarding the extent to which users' views are being properly taken into account. That there were methodological shortcomings in the evaluation of the British Telecom/Anchor Trust initiative has been noted. But inevitably there are difficulties in evaluating initiatives that involve the application of new technologies, especially where the benefits are uncertain and service objectives may be vague. Certainly, given the importance of such systems in monitoring for urgent or necessitous circumstances that occur only infrequently, it can be argued that no evaluation has been sufficiently thorough or lengthy to make judgements on their overall merits. Despite the claims of Porteus and Brownsell (2000, pp 60-1), the jury on lifestyle monitoring must stay out.

However, symptomatic of the potential for use of such systems in health or medical care is the experimentation, in Durham and elsewhere, with fall detectors that are carried or worn by the user; bed movement detectors to determine the need for turning in order to guard against bedsores; and incontinence detectors to effect action in the event of beds being wet or soiled. Crucially, however, it is not only reactive interventions to such events that can put things right after the event, but the planning of proactive interventions. To illustrate the point in the three cases indicated, the respective responses might be as set out in Table 13.2.

Both the British Telecom/Anchor Trust and Durham initiatives point to the possibility of facilitating proactive interventions, with envisaged health gains, through monitoring some aspects of people's daily and nocturnal routines. Associated with health gains is also a potential for cost savings, which research in Birmingham, when extrapolated to the United Kingdom as a whole, pointed to as £58 million a year through the use of lifestyle monitoring as opposed to conventional social alarms (Porteus and Brownsell, 2000, p 62).

Table 13.2: Reactive and proactive interventions

Nature of event	Reactive intervention	Proactive intervention
Occasional or regular falls	Check for injury; obtain medical assistance if appropriate; arrange for hospital visit, X-rays, etc.	Reduce danger of falling due to external causes; promote personal exercise regime to improve strength; check personal health for any adverse effects of medication.
Regular bed-wetting or soiling at night-time	Wash person; provide clean night-clothes; change bedding as necessary.	Check personal health; promote exercises to improve control of body functions; arrange for toileting at appropriate intervals before likely times of bed-wetting or soiling.
Problem of bedsores due to long periods of immobility when sleeping	Treat bedsores; apply dressings; provide special mattress.	Arrange for turning at appropriate intervals and/or within maximum period of immobility deemed advisable; reduce sedative effects of medication.

Finally, some further attention must be given to users' views on lifestyle monitoring. Some responses have already been indicated in the evaluation of the British Telecom/Anchor Trust initiative; other work helps to develop a clearer focus. In 1998, for instance, and as noted in Chapter Eleven, personal interviews took place with 50 older people in six sheltered housing schemes in Liverpool. In this, the opportunity was taken to establish views regarding the wearing, carrying or implantation of sensor and trigger devices. Examples of the devices were carried by the interviewer and shown to respondents. This found (Table 13.3, Plates 13.1 and 13.2) that there was considerable discomfort among respondents with anything other than the more familiar pendant or wristwatch-type trigger devices associated with social alarms. For all devices, three in 10 or more were uncertain. Very few respondents were comfortable with the idea of underwear with sensors embedded in the material.

Attitudes expressed in this survey clearly related to the extent to which the technologies were seen as familiar and/or intrusive. They may also have related to the extent to which respondents felt that they would be in control of them. Brownsell et al (1999, p 147) affirmed, for instance, in relation to a wide range of technologies that could be used to improve healthcare, that older people "dislike the thought that the technology is in control of them, rather than the other way round".

A study by Brownsell et al (2000, p 199) of older people in 160 households of a large sheltered housing scheme in Birmingham sought views on technical enhancements to the social alarm system and services with which they were already familiar. This found (p 200) that 77 per cent were interested in the automatic detection of falls and 68 per cent were interested in lifestyle monitoring. A concern regarding control is, however, implicit in the fact (p 200) that 21 per cent of older people who had fallen in the year prior to the interview rejected the offer of a fall detection device "because they felt that the [device] would contact the warden or control centre unnecessarily and that they would rather manage on their own".

Table 13.3: Comfort of older people with the idea of wearing, carrying or having implanted devices

	Comfortable (%)	Don't know (%)
Pendant trigger	52.1	31.3
Wristwatch device	46.8	36.2
Implanted device	10.4	31.3
Sensory vest	10.4	37.5
Sensory shorts	0.0	47.8

Note: Those uncomfortable are excluded.

Plate 13.1: Portable triggers and implant

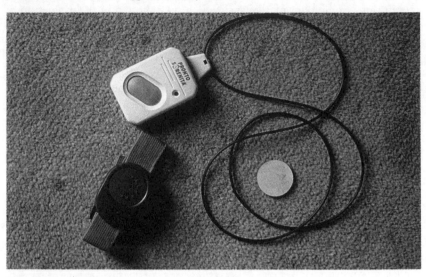

Source: Author's photograph

Plate 13.2: *Sensors in underclothes*

Source: Author's photograph

The debates and discussions around lifestyle monitoring are destined to continue over the next decade. It is too early to indicate the standard configuration of systems that might emerge, this being dependent on a range of factors that have been signalled in this chapter. In the first instance, greater clarity is needed about the purpose of lifestyle monitoring albeit that this might affirm an all-embracing role that will include the one traditionally ascribed to social alarms.

Certainly one of the concerns is that lifestyle monitoring systems, or at least the trial systems in place, simply do not respond speedily enough to necessitous or urgent circumstances. The vision of an older person lying helpless for hours, that old icon of social alarms, may be resurrected as justification for retaining, or at least including, the old technologies regardless of their limitations. More likely is that, while lifestyle monitoring increases in sophistication and greater understanding is developed as to how to deal with data that arise from such systems, active devices will operate in parallel. Idealistic notions of being able to dispense with radio triggers that are worn or carried will have to be set aside, at least in the shorter term.

Finally the potential longer-term role of lifestyle monitoring systems in providing the capability of identifying changes in activity rates or patterns as pointers to illness or to deterioration or improvement in physiological functioning must not be overlooked. Such possibilities place lifestyle monitoring at least partly in the arena of healthcare and can be linked directly to issues concerned with prevention and monitoring progress following operations or other medical interventions. The need for social alarm services to consider their position in relation to such agendas, as noted in Chapter Twelve, is therefore reaffirmed.

At one extreme in relation to healthcare lies the needs of older people with dementia. Interventions that can carry the labels explored by this book, that is telemedicine, telecare, smart homes and lifestyle monitoring, have all given at least some consideration to such needs. It is to this challenge that this appraisal now turns.

Dementia

The consideration being given to the use of technologies in the context of older people with dementia is growing. This both reflects views about the capacity of the technologies in such contexts and the attention being given to the empowerment and inclusion of older people with dementia, despite their long-standing position at the periphery of social welfare services. With regard to the latter, the work of Goldsmith (1996), Allan (2001) and Killick and Allan (2001) is notable. Of relevance with regard to the use of technologies to assist people with dementia is the work of the ASTRID project (Marshall, 2000). The context is one, however, where as noted by Leikas et al (1998, p 402) there are only a "few experiences of using technology in the care of demented persons".

Goldsmith argued that it was fundamental to recognise that people with dementia were mostly "ordinary people endeavouring to get on with their lives and make the most of the increasingly bewildering world in which they find themselves" (Goldsmith, 1996, p 9). He recognised, however, that the empowerment and inclusion of older people with dementia presupposes an ability to communicate with others and interact with their environments in meaningful ways. The onus for this he placed on others (pp 14–15) when affirming that:

> Great numbers of people with dementia, even in advanced states, who are not thought able to communicate, actually have a great desire to do so. It is for others to acquire the skills which enable them to understand and interpret the experiences and views of those who struggle to make themselves heard.

He added (p 48) that such communication "can be a difficult and a slow process, requiring time, patience, skill and commitment".

Allan has built on the work of Goldsmith. She pointed to "a small but convincing body of evidence that people with dementia want to be involved in decisions about their daily lives" and set about to show how this could be achieved (Allan, 2001, p 15). In trying different ways of communication to establish, for instance, the views of older people with dementia about the services that they received, she concluded (p 103) that:

> The chances of direct and specific probes linking in sufficiently to the individual's perspective in order to generate a full exchange are low ... for most this is likely to be too crude an instrument. It appears ... that providing the types of starting point which enable the person to pursue their own interpretation of material, and to have the maximum control over what they say or otherwise express, are the most likely to be successful.

Communication is, therefore, possible in ways that are more than simply verbal and an understanding is beginning to emerge regarding the ways in which this can take place. Some of the mysteries around the behaviour of older people with dementia are also beginning to be unwrapped and an understanding is arising that much of the behaviour reflects the desire to communicate and establish meaningful, perhaps normal, relationships within what was noted above as a bewildering world. Goldsmith noted (p 126) that most wandering leads to logical destinations and that what might often seem to be jumbled and meaningless words often carried clear meanings which the older person with dementia was unable to communicate in a way that others understood.

There is a need to recognise, in addition, that many older people with dementia retain varied skills and abilities that can be nurtured. Goldsmith noted that the ability to read aloud often remained "to a relatively late stage" (p 73). Marshall (1995, p 13) observed that two people with dementia had written books on word processors after apparently having lost the skill of writing. She had warned us elsewhere (Marshall, 1997, p 2), not to assume that people with dementia cannot operate equipment, noting that "it does seem that some people with dementia can work with touch screens if there are pictures".

In the context of social alarms, smart homes, telecare and related new technologies, therefore, questions arise as to their relevance or appropriateness for older people with dementia. The question is an important one insofar as many older people with dementia live in sheltered housing schemes with social alarm devices fitted and where there are issues to be addressed regarding any extended role of wardens or support staff in relation to particular needs that might arise. It is also important for people with dementia in the wider community, though a precondition for using technologies might be the need for their home to be what Marshall (2001, p 139) called "dementia friendly".

Marshall (2000, p 8) set out in the ASTRID Guide some of the opportunities that such technologies might offer. These included:

• assistance with memory functions and cognitive capabilities;
• adding to safety and security;
• assistance with leisure activities and meaningful occupation; and
• providing support to family carers.

That such older people can be supported in sheltered housing was borne testimony to by Kitwood et al (1995). They found an average of two older people with dementia in each of the 51 sheltered housing schemes that they studied, with wardens expressing the view that more than nine out of 10 (92 per cent) of them would be likely to remain living in sheltered housing for the ensuing six months without any major problem (Kitwood et al, 1995, p 46). Kitwood et al (p 67) concluded that "sheltered housing has been found to be a successful environment in which those with dementia can live with well-being". The question then arises as to how older people with dementia interact with the technologies provided in their living environments and what potential there might be for their further development to facilitate empowerment, inclusion or to underpin relevant support services.

An early experiment based on social alarms, undertaken in Central Region, Scotland, (and profiled in Chapter Six), noted four main areas of risk for people with dementia as (Macnaughtan, 1997, p 5):

• the risk of fire from household appliances or smoking;
• the risk of hypothermia from inadequate heating;
• the risk of suffocation from gas from household and heating appliances; and
• the risk of injury as a result of wandering from the home.

In addressing two of these areas of risk, installations of pressure mats next to beds, smoke detectors, and door switches were made for two service users, the former to facilitate a form of lifestyle monitoring (Macnaughtan, 1997, p 6). Among the lessons learned was the need to hide the equipment because it was damaged or tampered with by those it was intended to benefit (p 7). The

Central Region and its successor service in Falkirk went on to include many more people with dementia. Hence, in 2001, 60 people with dementia were included who "would otherwise be in institutional care" (Marshall, 2000, p 31; and 2001, p 134).

Leikas et al (1998) noted that carephones on their own for people with dementia were of little help since they "require the user to be conscious of the need for help" (p 402). Pilot installations in the homes of a small sample of people with dementia in Finland, however, added various sensors. Hence benefits were found (p 403) in having a front door detector but "the safety wristband was useless for the test persons" since "they didn't know how to use [it] or understand the meaning of it" (p 404). But the overall conclusion was that "with the help of the safety alarm system ... it was possible to increase the safety of demented persons and to postpone institutionalisation" (p 405).

A relatively long-standing initiative in Norway that involved the installation of smart technologies for people with dementia has been widely reported on and offers useful lessons for others (Fisk, 1997a, p 1058). Importantly this initiative was concerned not just with the technologies themselves but also with:

a) the ethical frameworks that should underpin the way that they are configured and used; and
b) the extent of intrusiveness of the technologies and the nature of the user interface (Denman, 1996, pp 30-1).

Denman (pp 28-9) summarised the work in Norway, which involved working with eight people in the early stages of dementia who moved into a group home in Tønsberg, near Lillehammer. The smart technologies included some automated features, for instance automatic cut-offs of the cooker when overheating or left on, and dimmed lights coming on when someone got up in the night. Full-time staff monitored residents' activities through use of the various technologies and were alerted, therefore, in the event of people getting up at night-time. This would not, however, necessarily be a cause for concern unless sensors reported them opening an outside door. Marshall (2000, p 32) noted, for the same initiative, that:

> Through the use of this technology, the municipalities saved the entire cost of the smart house installation in one year. This is an economic benefit in addition to the social benefits for the person with dementia and their carers.

An evaluation of this initiative pointed to cost savings over and above the additional £2,500 per dwelling spent on the technologies (Fisk, 1997a, p 1058).

Types of technologies

Technologies have been used over several decades in the context of service provision for older people with dementia, essentially concerned with their containment and management and normally applied in institutions. In all, three types of device can now be recognised:

- door alarms;
- tracking devices or tags; and
- activity and lifestyle monitoring systems.

Such devices have been considered, in the wider context of restraint, by Clarke and Bright (2002).

Door alarms involve the use of electronic contacts, which alert a staff member when the door is opened. Tracking devices are tags, worn by the individual as a wristwatch device or attached to clothing and which are detected by sensors mounted at key locations, usually at exit doors. These can be used in ways that affect the automatic locking of doors as they are approached by the wearer or simply to alert staff members, as with door alarms. As discussed earlier in this chapter, activity and lifestyle monitoring systems are generally associated with monitoring movement and are sometimes associated with automatic safeguards (as within smart homes) which, for instance, cut off gas appliances or turn off taps, as well as providing alerts to staff.

Claims that even simple tagging technologies can save money for service providers are long-standing (see Ball, 1982, p 101). To date, however, there is no information on the extent of their use. Door alarms, however, are used in Great Britain within NHS hospitals (Counsel and Care, 1993, pp 1-2).

The notion of tagging is fraught with potentially negative associations. The mere wearing of a tag can be seen as a restriction on freedom and therefore at odds with rights and choices (see Clarke and Bright, 2002, p 5). But Parkin (1995, p 441) argued that "tagging alone does not produce restraint but acts as a trigger for restraint to be exercised". He added that attaching a tag "may technically be an assault unless otherwise justified, for example by the defence of necessity".

Initiatives of note that are exploring the use of technologies for older people with dementia are taking place in Gloucester, Northampton and Derry.

THE GLOUCESTER INITIATIVE

In Gloucester an ordinary three-bedroom house has been converted into a demonstration environment suitable for a person with dementia. It is being tested by people with dementia and their carers with a view to such technologies being made available to them in their own homes (see www.bath.ac.uk/Centres/BIME/projects/smart/smart.htm).

The property is owned by Housing 21 and is linked to a local sheltered housing scheme. The project also involves Dementia Voice, a dementia services development centre serving the southwest of England, and the Bath Institute of Medical Engineering, which is part of the University of Bath.

A wide range of automated features is incorporated. These include the use of water level monitors for the bath whereby an initial alert is given to the user and, if they do not respond, the tap is turned off; automatic lights fading up and fading down to signal the path to and from the toilet or bathroom and the bedroom; and the automatic switching off of cooker knobs where dangers are identified through gas, smoke or pan heat temperature sensors. Some key features include verbal reminders and messaging together with a locator facility for lost items, these emitting a tone when the user presses a call button. A smart tap has been developed that responds to the danger of overflows through an automated cut-off facility but can then be reopened in a normal manner.

Of particular interest is the parallel study that is investigating the most suitable ways of communicating with the users to convey messages or reminders. Among the avenues being investigated that use verbal communication the project is "exploring whether the user (may) be happier" with the voice of a person close to them, or a caring professional, or an anonymous voice, or even their own voice". Literature about the initiative reveals that the alternatives to voice messaging being explored include animated TV and the use of message panels.

SAFE AT HOME PROJECT, NORTHAMPTON

The Safe at Home initiative has been promoted by Northamptonshire County Council in partnership with the Northampton City Council, the Northamptonshire NHS Healthcare Trust and the Alzheimer's Society (Woolham et al, 2002; Woolham and Frisby, 2002). The objective has been to "reduce carer stress" and explore "whether technology can delay admission into residential care" (Woolham and Frisby, 2002, p 2).

A demonstration house enabled the testing of different technologies. It also helped staff, carers and potential users to familiarise themselves with them and the manner of their operation (Woolham et al, 2002, p 3). Importantly, however, different technologies, determined by careful assessment of individual needs, were tested with 18 users in their own homes. Seven users were provided with social alarms linked as appropriate to such devices as fall and smoke detectors, gas detectors and shut-off devices. How the user group fared was compared with that of a well-matched 'comparator' (or control) group of 18 others (p 13). They concluded that the technologies "did play a part in helping to *maintain* the independence of service users" [their emphasis], as a result of which considerable cost savings were made (p ii, p 43).

Having said this, the researchers noted that any success in the use of technologies for people with dementia presupposed their operation in the manner specified (something that they lamented was not always the case), their appropriateness to the needs of the user and the compliance of carers (p ii).

SEVEN OAKS, DERRY

Fold Housing Association has developed accommodation and day care facilities in Derry for older people with dementia. As well as 30 flats, the development comprises five bungalows for couples, one of whom would have dementia, and offices for the local Alzheimer's Society and the dementia team of the Foyle Health and Social Services Trust. One of the bungalows is designated for reablement.

A specific feature of the development is the inclusion of smart sensor technologies by which, with appropriate consents and safeguards, the well-being of tenants is being monitored and support frameworks adjusted and reconfigured in relation to them. The normal facilities associated with social alarms are also incorporated.

For each tenant, sensors are used to monitor movement, wandering, falls and bed moisture; with environmental sensors monitoring heat extremes. Such devices link to a central computer which affects automatic responses where required and maintains a record of lifestyles and events.

Key elements of the evaluation of this initiative are examining the impact of the technologies and new service frameworks on the personal well-being of older people with dementia and the extent of any reduction in risk. More generally, account is being taken of the extent of and nature of interpersonal contact between tenants, the extent of and nature of interpersonal contact between tenants and staff, and the operation of care and support services.

Discussion

Exploring the role of social alarms and related technologies in the context of older people with dementia perhaps represents the greatest of all the challenges. With differences of view existing between healthcare and social welfare practitioners, as indicated in Chapter Twelve, and with little attention, to date, having been given to the ethical frameworks within which such technologies should operate, it is in the arena of dementia care that some of the dilemmas may be first resolved.

The ASTRID Guide (Marshall, 2000) is useful here in raising a number of ethical issues and juxtaposing them with some of the opportunities to be realised. Importantly it noted the way in which people's needs change with a commensurate requirement, therefore, that the technologies should be configured flexibly (Marshall, 2000, p 26). Some of the very same messages were, therefore, given as are clear from other sections of this book, notably in relation to the potential (see Chapter Two) for technologies to liberate their users.

Most relevant, perhaps, and echoing the concerns in this book about the potential for technologies to be used and configured in ways that reflect medical models of older age, the ASTRID Guide (Marshall, 2000, p 40) noted that:

Traditional approaches to dementia care have tended to focus on the problems posed by dementia in terms of risk to the person with the dementia and/or disruption for the carers. As a result, they have often emphasised institutional, pharmaceutical and custodial solutions.

Seeking the means of effectively communicating with people with dementia and using technologies in ways that could help maximise the extent of their social inclusion would clearly not be facilitated by such approaches.

Conclusion

Of note in this chapter has been the exploration of the role of lifestyle monitoring in a context where health needs are increasing. The latter are, of course, reflected in the growing numbers of vulnerable people served by social alarm services and for whom there are greater risks of falling, and a greater frequency in the need to deal with the aftermath of falls; and where, in addition, the potential of the technologies is being explored for people with dementia.

If for a while there had been some doubts about the movement of social alarms towards a clearer social welfare and healthcare role, these must now have been dispelled. More than this, it is possible to claim that the threshold for realising claims for social alarm technologies and their second-generation derivatives has been reached. This means that they may now be poised to develop in ways that not only help to improve service provision but may also help to facilitate the inclusion of some older people who would otherwise be in institutional care.

That there are dilemmas to be addressed, ethical frameworks to establish and further lessons to be learned has been made clear. The context is one, however, of rapid change and there remain a number of unknowns and a number of threats. Among the unknowns is the question of the full extent of technological possibilities and of how they might be applied. Greater unknowns apply when the needs of older people with dementia are considered and where the lessons relating to technologies may be learned simultaneously as the very means of better interpersonal communication are being developed. The greatest unknown relates to the extent to which it will be possible to ensure that the application of the technologies takes place in accordance with the pursuit of objectives concerned with promoting engagement, social inclusion and the support of independent living.

Notes

[1] Celler, B. (1994) in paper to health informatics conference, Gold Coast, Australia.

[2] Correspondence with Dr Andrew Sixsmith (University of Liverpool).

[3] Correspondence with Dr Kevin Doughty (Technology in Healthcare).

[4] Celler, B. (1994) as above.

[5] Doughty, K. (2000) in paper to symposium at City University, London.

[6] Correspondence with Dr Kevin Doughty (Technology in Healthcare).

FOURTEEN

Conclusions

Introduction

The objectives of this book were stated in Chapter One as:

- To establish the position regarding social alarms in Great Britain and Ireland, to explore their evolution and the services provided, and to consider their place within social policy frameworks.
- To establish in broad terms the position regarding social alarms in other parts of the world, the services provided, and to make comparisons where possible between them and with Great Britain and Ireland.
- To consider the role and effectiveness of social alarms in supporting independent living.
- To explore the implications for social alarm services of current technological developments associated with smart homes, certain aspects of telemedicine, and lifestyle monitoring.

The hypothesis that affirmed that social alarms and the services associated with them help to support independent living was also to be tested.

The intellectual context in which the work has been undertaken was set out in Chapters One to Three This pointed to the fact that there was a paucity of literature on the subject of social alarms and that there had been no prior attempt to position such technologies within any social theoretical framework.

The material gathered in this book that is pertinent to social alarms has served to confirm that social alarms are peripheral to the housing, social welfare and health services within which they have been used. That such a position on the periphery is no longer appropriate is, it is considered, borne out by its findings.

However, social alarms have not been considered in isolation. They have been placed in the context that relates to the interface between older people and technologies. The book has also considered technological developments that will lead to social alarms becoming part of broader arrays of technologies that underpin smart homes, telecare and lifestyle monitoring services.

Making the links with social theories

Chapter Two bore testimony to some of the range of social theories to which social alarms could be related. Further ideas were added that were concerned with the potential for communications technologies to liberate their users from what could otherwise be oppressive and inappropriate service frameworks. It was pointed out that there was no single social theory or group of theories that appeared directly to apply to social alarms. More than this it was noted that social theories relating to older people were, in any case, undergoing changes with it being only recently that a critical gerontology, which has some relevance in this context, is beginning to emerge.

Despite those changes and the lack of a clearly focal social theoretic framework it is worthwhile to consider some of the research identified in relation to some of the social theories in question and to consider, in light of this exercise, how future research into social alarms, telecare and lifestyle monitoring might usefully move forward.

In the first instance it is clear that the focal hypothesis put forward was rooted in a view of older people that was concerned to reject the adoption of service frameworks that were ageist, disempowering, fostered the social exclusion of older people or promoted their dependence. In so doing, the author shares a position with other social scientists who find some aspects of the theories purveyed by Cumming and Henry (1961) inadequate. The author acknowledges, therefore, that if and when the disengagement of older people takes place this is at least in part a consequence of the structures and institutions of our society that force this to come about. The pernicious effects of enforcing a statutory retirement age were pointed to in Chapter Two as an example of these.

Instead, it is considered that greater credence must be given to theories that point to older people making choices about their lifestyles either freely or in response to circumstances that relate to their ageing. An important point that older people see themselves as little different to their younger selves in their tastes, aspirations, views and beliefs was made. The wider acknowledgement of the place of older people as consumers, as strongly espoused by Riseborough (1998), was considered as relevant here in signalling the need for service providers to facilitate the exercising of such choices by older people.

The broader context, however, has been one where for Great Britain and Ireland the frameworks of housing and social welfare services have tended to separate and foster the disengagement of older people rather than to facilitate their exercising of active choices. The parallel development of social alarm services, being driven essentially by housing and social welfare agendas, was therefore trapped within this relatively narrow perspective. It seems, furthermore, that Christian notions of caring may have helped to tie such services within inappropriate frameworks.

Chapter Two also touched on an alternative set of theories that were more concerned with the use of technologies but had generally not been configured with older people or social alarms in mind. The exception is the author's liberation theory, which began with a vision that derived from a detailed knowledge of social alarms and of how services might change by harnessing the potential deriving from technological advances.

Also of note, when considering different theories, are the notions more generally concerned, first, with the risk society in which Beck (1994) saw us as living and, second, with the idea of social emergency (Soulet, 1999). The latter may be seen as a subordinate part of the former in that it is the risk society that impels interventions to reduce or avert such risks.

The relevance of social emergency to social alarms is clear. This book bears testimony to the fact that the primary rationale for most social alarm services has been to provide the means of help in the event of an emergency. As noted in Chapter One, in the United States such technologies, in earlier years, were sometimes described as Personal Emergency Response Systems (PERS). In Great Britain and Ireland several services carry the word emergency in their titles and some are managed within those departments of local authorities that are concerned for emergency services.

Dealing with emergencies remains a focal purpose of social alarm services today and will maintain its focal position in view of the increasing numbers of vulnerable people who are service users. This is despite the recognition that is being given to the role of social alarm services in providing reassurance and, perhaps, affording a degree of prevention.

It is very important to consider the nature of that imperative to intervene to help others. It derives, arguably, from our sociability and our empathy with our fellow human beings. It may also derive from a belief in reciprocity whereby we can expect others to intervene on our behalves when we have a particular need. However, our increasingly complex world with its array of technological possibilities means that, where the opportunities are afforded to us, we can now intervene earlier and earlier.

The temptation to stray onto issues arising from knowledge gained regarding the human genome, and the potential to identify susceptibility to certain medical conditions and even to treat them before they arise, is resisted here. Some of the dilemmas can be seen, however, as essentially the same as those that apply to social alarms and, more particularly, to lifestyle monitoring. Indeed, claims are beginning to be made about the ability of lifestyle monitoring to indicate medical conditions of which the user may be unaware. These relate to the symptoms of colds, coughs or influenza through a diminution of physical activity, or of a dementia condition through unnecessarily repeated activity patterns.

Surveillance and video communication

There is a big question that relates to the extent to which it is legitimate to gather the range of information considered necessary to facilitate the interventions that might be deemed appropriate. The issue of legitimacy is, of course, one that must be decided by older people themselves, though within many service frameworks this right may be denied. As discussed in Chapter Eleven there is a presupposition that the technologies and related services should be configured in ways that facilitate the exercising of choices. But there is a further question, not known to have been addressed in the context of such technologies and services, as to the extent of surveillance that is legitimate and appropriate.

Chapter Two touched on the issue of surveillance and acknowledged the generally accepted place of what is considered to be benign surveillance. But when surveillance develops in a way that gathers personal information relating to physical activity within the home, with the potential to know when someone takes a bath or shower, goes to bed, receives visitors, cooks a meal and so on, there can be no alternative but to acknowledge that legitimacy can only be won through full and informed consent of the older person. Such a perspective acknowledges that personal information about any person must not be collected without due regard to their privacy.

The need for a clear stance on this becomes all the more apparent because of the occasional discussions that are arising about the use of cameras. For some, the use of cameras is being considered simply in the context of video-telephony. In this context, only one camera is normally in place and the user has control over its use. Clough et al (1998) envisaged "video conferencing with patients about their state of health, medication, etc." and noted that video visits can both supplement and reduce home visits by nursing or medical practitioners.

For others, however, the wider use of cameras has been considered. Schoone et al (1998) examined video technologies in relation to the support needs of a small sample of older and disabled people in the Netherlands. They affirmed (p 25) that "the benefit of video monitoring to support personal social alarms is limited until such time as a large part of a person's residence has been fitted out with cameras, although for participants with speech difficulties a visual image was found helpful". They did, however, point to the need for ultimate user control of video communications when arguing:

> From a privacy point of view it is very important that the client is empowered to break off or prevent connections and [that] agreements to that end are made ... client side operation should be based on technology that the client is familiar with, such as telephone, TV and social alarm pendant.

Like Clough et al (1998), Schoone et al noted the potential for what they described as expensive visits to be replaced, in part, by video monitoring.

In relation to the SAFE 21 initiative (see Chapter Twelve) Vlaskamp and Price suggested that "video-nursing and video-consulting would be a very interesting extension for the future".[1] Miskelly (2001, p 458) went further by suggesting the use of video for scanning dwellings. Others have even explored the idea of a virtual presence by a doctor or nurse through the projection of "the image of the person or object into free-standing space ... providing the illusion of actual presence" (Satava and Jones, 1996, p 196).

An important, and often overlooked, point that adds justification for video telephones was made by Cullen and Robinson (1997, p 90) in affirming their use for those who "use sign language or who lip-read". For them, "video-telephones may be considered the equivalent of voice telephones" (p 90).

Debates about the use of cameras have particular potency in the context of lifestyle monitoring and especially where the purported beneficiaries are older people with dementia. Here some have suggested that more than one camera could be in place. Robinson et al (1995) argued that:

> A significant potential advantage of advanced alarm applications is that the additional information provided by being able to see the client can speed up and increase the accuracy of the diagnosis of the emergency situation ... the patient can communicate more effectively than with audio alone, especially where stress or other factors cause speech comprehensibility to drop.

In the context of lifestyle monitoring it is suggested that the use of cameras, other than for video-telephony from a fixed point should, for reasons of privacy, not normally be countenanced.

Meeting the objectives

This book has, it is considered, succeeded in establishing and documenting the position of social alarms in Great Britain and Ireland. It has done so, in particular, by:

a) debating their evolution and role in relation to the housing and social welfare agendas that have been extant over the three decades; and
b) examining the likely future evolutionary path by reference to developments associated with smart homes, telecare and lifestyle monitoring.

Differences in perspective between the position in England and Wales (considered together in Chapter Five), Scotland (Chapter Six) and Ireland (Chapter Seven) were noted, these generally being rooted in their different histories, government agendas and/or service funding frameworks. Broader differences were noted with services in the rest of the world, these differences having persisted in part, as noted in Chapter Ten, because of mutual ignorance. The beginnings of a divergence from these different perspectives in Great Britain has only been apparent in the gradual adjustments that are taking place in response to more recent legislation and other initiatives concerned with services used by older people.

The position in other countries can be noted as sometimes showing parallels with Great Britain and Ireland. In general, however, there has been less emphasis on municipal service provision, with social alarm development frequently responding to market needs and increasingly recognising the importance of the older person as a customer. The latter has particularly been the case in North America.

The position of social alarms in the rest of the world has also been documented with particular attention having been given to their evolution in North America.

Comparisons with the position in Great Britain and Ireland have been made with the anomalies relating to both the latter having been noted.

An immense variety of contexts and applications have been identified in which social alarm developments often took place in isolation. The common reference points in service development were noted, therefore, as relating as much, if not more, to the agendas set by, and marketing messages of, manufacturers and suppliers rather than any shared consideration of the role of social alarms by governments or other agencies concerned for social welfare and related services.

The position of social alarms that has been documented is fascinating in its complexity. But certain key themes have been found throughout. The most ubiquitous of these are concerned with the role of social alarms in:

• enabling responses to be made in an emergency;
• providing reassurance; and
• supporting independent living.

It has been pointed to that the last two have gradually been afforded greater recognition as the role of social alarms has become better understood and their potential more widely debated. The role that relates to supporting independence is discussed further below.

Perhaps the most conspicuous finding regarding the position of social alarms is the extent to which national or regional governments have generally ignored them or, at best, have demonstrated only sporadic interest. The exceptions would include Australia, Finland, Ireland and the Netherlands, although in the case of Ireland (see Chapter Seven) this is not to say that the attention given has led to the most appropriate outcomes in terms of service configurations.

Supporting independent living

Chapter One discussed the meaning of independent living. Central to this was that not only did different people have different ideas as to what independence was but also that it changed over time in response to personal circumstances and life events. Supporting independent living was considered as taking place at two levels, the first being concerned with staying at home (and, therefore, in ordinary accommodation of the person's choosing), the second with engagement and involvement in the economic, social and family life of the community. Both levels of independence were considered as being served by social alarms if the claims made for them could be substantiated. The main claims, as noted in Chapter One, had been concerned with outcomes associated with speedier interventions in medical or other emergencies.

One focus of this book has been on the role of social alarms in enabling interventions that relate to medical rather than other emergency circumstances, although dealing with problems of immobility, for instance being stuck in the bath, has been included. The crucial question arises, therefore, as to the extent to which the evidence gathered from what are indubitably disparate sources is sufficient to justify the claims that are made for social alarms regarding supporting independent living.

In answering this question it must be reaffirmed that this appraisal has to some extent been disadvantaged by the lack of in-depth research on the topic of social alarms. The subjectivity associated with the notion of independence or independent living also has created a difficulty. But it is clear that wider notions of independence concerned with engagement and involvement were generally not considered in the material identified. However, the more readily measured concern about older people being able to stay living at home had. Indeed, the focus of much of the research identified in this book has related to the built environments in which older people live. The ordinary home, in other words, has been repeatedly pitched against the hospital or the care home with the success or otherwise of social alarms being measured in accordance with the extent of their ability to enable an older person to stay put in the former.

The claims made in early studies from the United States were mainly concerned with the role played by social alarms in enabling people to stay at home; minimising the time, if any, spent in hospital; and delaying or obviating moves to care homes. The first of what was a relatively small number of studies, that of Sherwood and Morris (1981) was, perhaps, the most important in that it signalled findings that were to be repeatedly endorsed in the outcomes of further work. More than this, as noted in Chapter Eight, it did so on the basis of reasonably sizeable matched samples of users and non-users of social alarms. The finding by Sherwood and Morris (1981, pp 14-16) of cost savings, at least for some types of user, through the "reduced use of institutional and community based resources" (p 15) was, however, the one that others were keenest to test and which manufacturers and suppliers, unsurprisingly, were keenest to replicate. This led to subsequent studies in both the United States and Canada that pointed to cost savings through decreased hospital admissions and in-patient days (Cain, 1987, p 26; Roush et al, 1995, p 919; Roush and Teesdale, 1997, pp 360-1); and reductions in home support (Dixon, 1987, p 2; Chumbler et al, 1998, p 209).

Outside North America only three studies have looked at the potential for cost savings. The first, by Tamborini et al (1996, p 134ff) in Italy, found, as noted in Chapter Nine, that the use of social alarms had enabled cost savings to be made through a reduced need for residential care. The second, by Brownsell et al (1999), pointed to the same. The third, by Farquhar et al (1992, p 6), was unable to state whether social alarms were or were not cost effective.

That there are some matters that must be considered as qualifying the statements about cost savings should not be overlooked. Sherwood and Morris themselves stated that though there were overall cost savings, this was attributable only to those older people who were severely functionally impaired and not socially isolated (Sherwood and Morris, 1981, p 15). For others the effect was neutral or negative. In addition, it should be borne in mind that social alarms were seen in one study to have led to an initial increase in hospitalisation among social alarm users (Koch, 1984, p 31); and that no significant differences were found in hospital admission rates or in-patient days in a study quoted by Roush et al (1995, p 922).

Having said this, and despite the absence of what would be the desired range of in-depth studies on this topic, there is an immense amount of practice experience and evidence from small research studies and service evaluations. These almost invariably point to objectives of social alarms concerned with supporting independent living having been met and, ipso facto, costs that might have been associated with moves to alternative accommodation or prolonged hospital stays having been averted. Much of the work of the author has been concerned with such service evaluations and support this conclusion. Key outcomes of four such surveys undertaken by the author as part of three studies of users with carephones, are noted below.

In the first of these, the parallel personal interview surveys, in 1994, found among social alarm users in Oldham and Ottawa, that 100 per cent (of 17 respondents) and 90 per cent (of 20 respondents) respectively felt that having such a device and being linked to a service meant that they were or would be able to live at home longer (see Chapters Five and Eight; Fisk, 1995, p 150). In the second and third of these studies, personal interview surveys in 2000 undertaken in Shropshire on behalf of Wrekin Link, and in the border counties of Ireland on behalf of CallCare (Ireland), found that 82 per cent (of 28 respondents) and 52 per cent (of 33 respondents) respectively considered that having a social alarm had enabled them or would enable them to stay put in their present home for longer than would otherwise be the case (see Chapters Five and Seven).

What might be regarded as an anomalously low figure, albeit still a majority, for the Irish study could, it is considered, be ascribed to the way in which the users generally received their social alarm devices. This, as noted in Chapter Seven, in most cases related to the activities of voluntary groups operating in a context where anyone aged 65 or over and who lived alone was eligible. Overall, however, the findings point to social alarms as being effective in supporting independent living. Of note is that the endorsement of social alarms in the above surveys is greater than that found in the British Telecom/Anchor Trust lifestyle monitoring pilot where, as noted in Chapter Thirteen, 47 per cent stated that the system helped them to stay living at home (Sixsmith, 2000, p 67).

There are a number of other reports that have testified to the views of users about social alarms enabling them to stay put (Löckenhoff, 1988 , p 41; Östlund, 1994, p 51) and from the opinions of service providers on the issue (Zoche, 1994, p 64; Department of Human Services, 1998, p 23). Interestingly, the Department of Human Services quoted Australian research that suggested that the key factor in staying put might be the felt ability to cope rather than the older person's actual physical capabilities.

Pointers regarding the ability of social alarms to help to support independent living are also provided by their increasing sponsorship by healthcare insurers and through government healthcare programmes. Examples of the former have been noted in various countries from Slovenia to the Netherlands. An example of the latter is Medicaid's funding now being available to eligible social alarm users in most of the United States.

The implications of technological developments

The key technological developments affecting social alarms have been explored in Chapters Eleven, Twelve and Thirteen. Broadly speaking these related to smart homes, telecare and lifestyle monitoring and showed how they linked to, or were influencing, the development of social alarms. The much wider context of technological change was, however, noted and was important to the discussion of social theories, the setting out of a liberation theory, and to the understanding of the potential of the second generation of social alarms that has been heralded.

The position of social alarms at the interface between social welfare and health has made consideration of technological developments more difficult. This difficulty does not, however, arise from the intrinsic capabilities of the technologies. It relates to the ways in which they are configured and used. This gives great importance to social and political contexts and makes the attitudes of professionals towards older people absolutely crucial.

For the most part, therefore, what has been demonstrated is the way in which technologies are being explored with a view to supporting independent living in a practical sense. What has generally not been demonstrated in current or recent initiatives is how the technologies can help the empowerment and inclusion of older people by enabling them to take greater control over their lives. Nor have there been more than the smallest demonstrations of interactive capability of such technologies in ways that indicate the opportunity for links to information, new service frameworks, virtual communities and the like.

Hence there is clearly some way to go before the best technological frameworks that can support independent living are identified and utilised. The finding is that smart home initiatives, the first main reference point for social alarms explored in Chapter Eleven, are generally narrow in their view of the potential of the technologies which they could use. Some, furthermore, are at risk of adopting approaches that are too closely associated with medical, and disempowering, models of older age.

The second main reference point, that of telemedicine and telecare, appears even more restricted in its perspective and has, to date, given little consideration to the implications other than cost and related staffing needs of devolving more medical and healthcare services to people's own homes. It appears that few who are concerned with medical and healthcare agendas have considered the fact that the communications revolution signals the potential to dismantle the institutional frameworks and attitudes that are fossilised within dated and inappropriate practices. This is despite several researchers having suggested the wider use of technologies to facilitate health and medical care at home (Karinch, 1994, p 9; Wylde and Valins, 1996, p 22; Doughty and Williams, 2001, p 31).

Regarding this matter the author has argued that, aside from some specialist institutions, hospitals might "give way to locally based resource and response centres that support a wide array of medical and social needs" (Fisk, 1997a, p 1059). Valins and Salter (1996, p 4) went further in arguing that the hospital as the focus for acute medical care may be "no more than an uninvited detour to satisfy a set of circumstances that may no longer apply".

Converging paths

That the two sets of technologies, smart homes and telemedicine/telecare, are on a convergent path has been suggested. This means that telecare will become a key feature of smart homes. And one area where such a convergence is beginning to become apparent is with developments concerned with lifestyle monitoring.

That this should be a point of convergence was, in some respects, inevitable. Setting aside the issue of differentials in affordability and access, social alarm services were destined to be increasingly used by or provided for those considered most vulnerable in terms of medical and healthcare needs and, therefore, with the greatest need for the same. The long-term role of social alarms as a means of obtaining help in emergencies, and often as a consequence of falls or being stuck, is, therefore, to find a place within new technological configurations.

Such configurations owe much to medical models of older age and could, as discussed in Chapters Twelve and Thirteen, work against objectives concerned with promoting engagement, social inclusion and independent living. Narrow perspectives will serve only to nurture and sustain established ageist attitudes and service frameworks, with new telecare services being found to support independent living only in physical terms. In such situations any broader potential will not be realised. The debate that needs to take place with regard to lifestyle monitoring must bring such issues to the fore. And with it, given the capabilities of the growing range of technologies, issues relating to their use for people with dementia will, in addition, need to be considered.

Few answers to the questions that will be raised in that debate are given in this book, though important issues concerned with the rights of older people as service users have been signalled. Central questions relating to the ongoing debate have been noted as being concerned with surveillance, privacy and the ownership of personal information.

The British and Irish anomalies

Worthy of some final consideration is the extent to which the anomalies identified regarding the position of social alarms in Great Britain and Ireland have persisted. More accurately, as noted in Chapters Five and Seven, the anomalies pertain to England and Wales, and to the Republic of Ireland. This means that despite the way in which social alarms in other parts of the world have developed, distinctive features have remained apparent.

Two factors explain this phenomenon. First, for England and Wales there is the historical happenstance of social alarms that emerged in the context of sheltered housing. This was comprehensively discussed in Chapter Four. The persistence of the housing orientation, or in Fisk's words the property rather than person-based perspectives (Fisk, 1989, p 3) has been despite claims about their social welfare role; despite the stimulus of the Research Institute for Consumer Affairs (1986) report; and despite the growing pressures faced by housing authorities because of the increasing support needs of many older people linked to their services.

The battle between housing and social services authorities in England and Wales has been noted. But the movement of social alarm services away from housing authorities in recognition of their social welfare role has been slow. It is arguable that some opportunities for service developments in ways that could do greater justice to social welfare needs have been lost.

In the Republic of Ireland the anomaly is a different one by virtue of the emphasis on social alarms as a means of offering greater security for older people. The main mechanism of service development, furthermore, the Scheme of Support for Older People has been criticised for inadequacies in its targeting of social alarm provision (Fitzpatrick Associates, 1999, p 16). Calls for statutory authorities in Ireland to consider the use of social alarms in a more clearly social welfare context have, as shown in Chapter Seven, met with a poor response (Brenner and Shelley, 1998, p 64).

The second factor that explains the persistence of the anomalies in England and Wales and the Republic of Ireland is simply the general lack of knowledge about social alarms. Studies in Great Britain, with the exception of the early work by McWhirter (1984) and later work undertaken by Fisk (1989 and 1995), simply failed to find out and discuss how such technologies were being used in other countries. The one study of note in Ireland (O'Connor et al, 1986) was disadvantaged by just taking Great Britain as its reference point. Of some surprise is the fact that those concerned with service provision in England and Wales ignored the fact that social work authorities in Scotland had ensured that many providers in that country were pursuing a rather different agenda. That this different agenda resulted in the more substantial use of carephones and their more frequent use as part of broader packages of care was considered in Chapter Six.

That the anomalies will diminish is now signalled by the debates surrounding new technological developments. Telecare services and technologies concerned with smart homes are poised to replace social alarm services in the coming decades. And by this means social welfare and healthcare agendas relating to older people will be better served. Services throughout Great Britain and Ireland in this context will develop in ways that are closer to services in the rest of the world. And with common regulatory frameworks beginning to develop there may be particular closeness in the position and manner of operation of social alarm services and their successors to those in other parts of the European Union.

Concluding remarks

Social alarms and more recent technologies associated with smart homes, telecare and lifestyle monitoring cannot be ignored. Together they point to a substantial growth in the role of technologies in supporting independent living among older people.

Discussion of the issues includes potent reminders that technological developments will take place come what may. Their being harnessed in appropriate ways could assist in the engagement, inclusion and independent living of older people. The usage of technologies in inappropriate ways would represent a failure to grasp the opportunities available, and would serve to exacerbate social exclusion and the marginal position of many older people.

This is not to say, it must be added, that harnessing the technologies in appropriate ways would necessarily have a magical effect on the extent of change in the position of older people that might be considered desirable. Social alarms and their successor technologies are, after all, part of a much more complex framework of services each of which operate within particular contexts that have been shaped by decades or even centuries of social and demographic change, and economic and political development. That many elements of the frameworks that have evolved in Great Britain and Ireland can be regarded as ageist was noted in Chapter Two.

Appropriate changes in social alarm service frameworks are therefore predicated on parallel changes in attitudes. Changes in attitudes are likely to take place only slowly and require the successful undertaking of practical initiatives that may have to be brought about by government diktat. Having said this, changes are afoot. Older people are being afforded greater recognition, at least as consumers. As a consequence they are more evident within the general range of images associated with the advertising of goods and services. The same is true of social alarms, these having moved from an association with portrayals of older people as vulnerable and in need of support (see Plate 1.1) to ones of older people clearly in control of their lives or at least in control of the services they receive (see Plate 10.1). A sense of control, as noted by Tinker et al (2000, p 101), motivates people to stay at home and ipso facto is an issue associated with perceptions of their independence.

Such changes in the imagery associated with social alarms have come about through greater awareness among manufacturers and suppliers that negative images did not reflect the service ethos that has become increasingly central to the work of housing and social welfare practitioners. Those negative images certainly did not reflect the perspective of most older people.

Case proven?

This book has considered the position of social alarms within a range of social theoretical frameworks and has examined the ways in which they have been used in different countries worldwide. It has also considered the implications of new technological developments. It has done so with the assistance of an immense range of information obtained from multiple sources. It has also drawn on a substantial range of original published and unpublished work of the author. Insofar as there has been no previous work that has attempted to draw together such material it is hoped that this book makes an important contribution to discussions that must take place regarding technologies and their role in supporting the independent living of older people.

The case for social alarms as having made a contribution to supporting independent living, in terms of people staying put, is considered proven. The evidence for this that is set out in this book is considerable. And while the number of in-depth evaluative studies of such technologies and their applications is few, the general consistency of their outcomes and the supportive evidence from related research and practice in Great Britain, Ireland and the rest of the world is compelling.

Having said this, no claim is made that social alarms do, or their successor technologies will, help support independence without the formal and informal support of other people and services. As has been noted, social alarms, although often operating alone, must be seen as relevant components of broader packages of care. The same is true of the technologies associated with smart homes, telecare and lifestyle monitoring. In addition it must be reaffirmed that inappropriately designed, older housing and housing in poor condition can militate against objectives concerned with independent living, engagement and social inclusion. Social alarms and related technologies cannot remedy these, however smart they become.

With regard to the evolution of the technologies it is interesting to consider the extent to which their relatively consistent features and the manner of their current evolution may promote greater consistency in service frameworks internationally. The variety of ways in which social alarms have been viewed and service frameworks established has been a key feature of this book. Insofar as social alarm services are increasingly serving the needs of people with healthcare and medical needs, it can be argued that greater consistency becomes highly desirable. This will especially become the case as social alarms are absorbed into smart home, telecare and lifestyle monitoring systems.

Much will be determined by older people as service users. The customer ethos that is evolving and the potential for the technologies to liberate older people, as noted in Chapter Two, suggest that for many, albeit subject to suitable configurations, technology acceptance will take place. However, the increasing technological awareness and prowess of today's and tomorrow's older people has major implications for such configurations and will certainly require intrusion to be minimised and for control by the user to be facilitated.

The suggestion is that, if our society is to respond to the choices and wishes of older people and is truly committed to supporting their independent living and facilitating their engagement and social inclusion, then social alarm and their successor technologies will evolve in ways that reflect this. Ignoring the technologies or adopting a laissez faire approach to them will, by default, allow their development to take place in inappropriate ways, fostering marginalisation and social exclusion. An opportunity to strike a blow against ageism and help make our communities a better place for older people to live and participate in will, as a consequence, have been lost.

Recommendation

While this book fills a substantial gap in the knowledge of social alarms and related technologies there is still much to learn. The need for further knowledge becomes greater as technological advances take place and there are pressures to respond to demographic, social and political agendas that are concerned with such matters as cost savings and the decentralisation of healthcare and support services. That social alarms, smart homes, telecare and lifestyle monitoring will have a role in responding to those pressures is certain.

It is essential, therefore, that further work is undertaken that carefully examines for older people the way in which communications technologies are employed in responding to the agendas noted above; and the ways in which choice and control can be facilitated for their users.

In pursuit of this recommendation, recognition of the shortcomings in many current approaches, as detailed in this book, is essential. Notable among these is the predisposition of technologies to be used in ways that reflect medical models of older age and for them to be used in ways that indicate relatively narrow understandings of the meaning of independence. If nothing else, these predispositions reflect a long-standing failure of technologists and service providers to take proper account of the views and aspirations of older people. Attention to the outcomes of this appraisal will, it is to be hoped, help to correct this.

Note

[1] Paper presented to Smart Homes Foundation conference, Eindhoven.

A note on methodology

Uncharted waters

The role of social alarms has been very poorly researched, despite their increasing provenance and the variety of claims made about their benefits. Indeed, apart from within the communities of service providers and older people in Great Britain, the United States and a handful of other countries, social alarms are generally little known and only occasionally are they considered within broader service or social policy frameworks.

The reason that social alarms are poorly documented is because they have been seen as, at worst, irrelevant and, at best, as tools that are used as a means of helping fulfil objectives that relate to other services. Academics and practitioners who are concerned with housing, social welfare and healthcare have usually viewed social alarms as a kind of adjunct to their work, peripheral to the mainstream and, therefore, not worth much attention.

This book remedies this by bringing social alarms into focus. An approach was taken that, in the very first instance, was concerned to gather basic information from within Great Britain, Ireland and other countries. This information was then built upon through more focused work that was concerned with the operation of social alarm services; establishing user perspectives; exploring the extent to which claims made for social alarms had been, in reality, fulfilled; and considering the implications of recent technological developments.

The ways in which the methodology more specifically responded to the objectives of this book are noted below.

Establishing the position of social alarms in Great Britain, Ireland and internationally

Gathering information in relation to the first two objectives took place over many years. The objectives were, as noted in Chapter One, concerned with establishing the position of social alarms in Great Britain, Ireland and other parts of the world. In Great Britain, Ireland and to some extent the United States, this involved an exploration of their evolution and of the services provided, and consideration of their place within social policy frameworks. This work, when broadened to include other countries, then explored different themes and enabled the making of international comparisons.

A range of different approaches was taken to gathering information, this in several cases involving case study visits and original survey work with service users in Great Britain, Ireland and beyond.

Exploring the role and effectiveness of social alarms in supporting independent living

Addressing this objective required trawling the publications, reports and other information in order to identify where user perspectives had been explored. This was, however, often not the case. Nevertheless, an interesting variety of studies was successfully identified and drawn upon.

Within any individual country, studies on social alarms are few. In Great Britain, aside from some work by the author of this book, there are just two academic studies that have sought to offer a greater understanding of social alarms through, in part, the exploration of user perspectives. These were undertaken by Thornton and Mountain (1992) and Riseborough (1997a). Work relating to user perspectives that was undertaken by the author was documented in Fisk (1997a and 1997b).

Outside Great Britain some personal interview surveys are reported on that examined the needs and views of users of services in the United States (Sherwood and Morris, 1981; Gatz and Pearson, 1988); in Canada (Fisk, 1995); and in Germany (Löckenhoff, 1988). Personal interviews by or under the direction of the author were undertaken for a cross-border social alarm service serving the Republic of Ireland and Northern Ireland (see Chapter Seven) with the interview framework being closely matched to that undertaken by the author for Telford and Wrekin Council in England (see Chapter Five). Overall, however, such studies involving social alarm service users are rarely cross-referenced and the knowledge and information arising from them has generally not been shared in different countries.

While most such studies, in considering user perspectives, are implicit or explicit in their questioning of what have often been glib assumptions about the role of social alarms, few have considered the notion of independence in other than practical terms. This is particularly the case in the United States. Therefore, desired reference points for much work undertaken by the author of this book are largely absent. As a consequence information relating to independence has often had to be inferred or related to practical outcomes such as staying put.

The notion of independence was initially discussed in Chapter One. Given the subjective nature of independence and the link with often sensitive circumstances associated with ageing, disability and exclusion, the approach has normally been through personal interviews. Alternative options examining the perspectives of service providers were also pursued but it became clear, with some notable exceptions, that providers had not generally considered in any depth the role of social alarms from a service user point of view.

In addition to the paucity of user-focused research, the broader context was recognised as one where studies have often paid insufficient attention to some of the methodological questions that conspire to compromise good research involving older people. This means that there remains a clear risk that, as well as the benefits of social alarms being taken somewhat for granted by service providers, there are too few stimuli to ask the questions about those benefits. There may, for instance, have been too great a readiness to accept either the virtual absence of complaints or the readiness of many older people in disadvantaged positions to give 'Yes' answers to questions regarding satisfaction with their social alarm and associated services. Where personal interviews have been undertaken or directed by the author, attempts have been made to overcome such problems.

The approach taken in this book sought to address a range of issues (as noted by Abbott and Fisk, 1997, p 44). These included the negative self-image of many older people who may feel that they have little or nothing to say and who may harbour a fear that any criticisms, implicit or explicit, might be seen as biting the hand that feeds them. Other service users might have difficulties in communication that arise from a hearing impairment.

More specifically in relation to social alarms, the personal interview surveys by the author that have been reported in this book, often encountered people initially reluctant to take part because of fears of being assessed and, perhaps, found ineligible for the services in question. A fearful service user in Oldham, for instance, on being interviewed said "You're not going to take it off me, are you?" (Fisk, 1995, p 151).

Exploring the implications of current technological developments

The key technological developments that were identified as having greatest relevance to social alarms were those associated with smart homes, certain aspects of telemedicine, activity and lifestyle monitoring. Although not necessarily known by such terms their potential to influence, or usurp the role of, social alarms is substantial as has been noted in this book. In contrast with the methodology used for other objectives, however, the way in which the implications of technological developments have been addressed is different and less reliant on published sources.

The reason for the different emphasis follows from the fact that while material on social alarms, at least when viewed internationally, might appropriately be described as scarce, material relating to the technological change that relates to or acknowledges the existence of social alarms is rare in the extreme. Two key publications in Great Britain (Gann et al, 1999; Porteus and Brownsell, 2000) are exceptions, as are a few articles in the *Journal of Telemedicine and Telecare*.

Given the paucity of information, this book is, therefore, in part reliant on case study work. This is especially the case when it explores current technological developments. As is inevitable where rapidly developing technologies are considered no methodology can wholly counter what must remain as areas of uncertainty about the future direction of those technologies or the services that use them.

Moving the agenda forward

In many respects the personal interview surveys, case study work and other research reported on in this book, take the agenda relating to research on social alarms forward. The interviews that were undertaken with users reflected an enquiring approach that refused to take social alarms for granted. They recognised that the way that older people interacted with their social alarms and the services associated with them was important and had a bearing on their independence. Social alarms were relevant, therefore, to the position of older people in their communities in Great Britain, Ireland and elsewhere and to the way in which older people were seen by others. There were, in other words, dimensions of social alarms that had been generally overlooked and which personal interview surveys and case studies might throw some light upon.

The same is true of other information gathered. As with the personal interview surveys and case studies, these provided insights into that broader context and have helped this book escape from views associated with what are often narrow frameworks of service provision. Typically the areas addressed in the personal interview surveys, as well as gathering basic information about the service user, explored the user's familiarity with and use of the social alarm equipment; their confidence in the equipment and the associated service; the circumstances in which they used or did not use it; their overall satisfaction with it; and the extent to which it had helped them stay put.

In the survey undertaken by the author for the Liverpool Housing Trust the opportunity was taken to explore views relating to the extended roles of social alarm technologies and related social alarm services in the areas of home security, energy usage, dwelling heating and temperature control, and medical and activity monitoring. The personal interviews, in this instance, were aided by showing respondents prototype devices. Views were specifically sought in relation to sensors that would either be integrated with underclothes and, therefore, worn next to the skin, or implanted. The outcome of this survey is reported on in Chapter Twelve.

Other surveys have sought information about social alarm services themselves and were either more specifically concerned with the technologies employed (see Fisk, 1990) or the size and configuration of services (see Stafford and Dibner, 1984; and the telephone survey of services in the United States undertaken by the author and reported on in Chapter Eight).

Most such surveys were framed, therefore, either in ways that sought to establish baseline figures about services and their configuration or to explore the broader benefits of social alarms. The latter often touched on emerging debates regarding empowerment, engagement, social inclusion and changing meanings and understandings of independence and older age. Such matters and their relationship to social theories were discussed in Chapter Two.

Overall framework

The foregoing indicates that, dovetailed within the vast array of material gathered, this book is the product of much original work. It has involved the author in visits to or collaborative work with over 30 social alarm services in Great Britain and Ireland. In addition to these the author has undertaken study visits and/or consultancy work with social alarm service providers and equipment manufacturers in Canada, Italy and the United States. Visits were also made to smart home and related developments in Great Britain, Northern Ireland, Norway and the Netherlands.

Relevant outcomes from consultancy work involving surveys with service users and/or providers have in many cases been presented here for the first time. Unpublished work from a variety of other sources is frequently used. The overall context is one where the information gathered and the work undertaken facilitates the answering of key questions about social alarms and their role.

In summary, various methodologies have been included, taking in both original survey work that incorporates quantitative and qualitative approaches; case study work; secondary analysis of data and information from other studies; and the exploration and application of theoretical frameworks that relate to the context within which housing and social welfare services respond to the needs of older people.

References

AARP (American Association of Retired Persons) (1987) *Meeting the need for security and independence with personal emergency response systems (PERS)*, Washington, DC: AARP.

AARP (1992) 'Product report – PERS, personal emergency response systems', 2, 1, Washington, DC: AARP.

Abbott S. and Fisk M.J. (1997) *Maintaining independence and involvement – older people speaking*, St Albans: The Abbeyfield Society.

Abe M. (1992) 'Recent trends in ERS in Japan', in A.S. Dibner (ed) *Personal response systems: An international report of a new home care service*, Binghampton, IL: The Haworth Press, pp 81-100.

Adam C. (1995) 'Hausnotruf-Dienste in Nordrhein-Westfalen: Bestandsaufnahme Konzeptionen Empfehlungen an die Landesregierung', Köln: Ministerium für Arbeit, Gesundheit und Soziales des Landes Nordrhein-Westfalen.

Alaszewski A. (1995) *Health: The risk business*, Working Paper No 2, Hull: Institute of Health Studies, University of Hull.

Alaszewski A., Walsh M., Manthorpe J. and Harrison L. (1997) 'Managing risk in the city: The role of welfare professionals in managing risks arising from vulnerable individuals in crisis', *Health and Place*, vol 3, no1, pp 15-23.

Allan K. (2001) *Communication and consultation: Exploring ways for staff to involve people with dementia in developing services*, Bristol: The Policy Press.

Allen A., Cristoferi A., Campana S. and Grimaldi A. (1997) 'An italian telephone-mediated home monitoring service: TESAN personal emergency response system and teleservices', *Telemedicine Today*, December, pp 25, 33.

Askham J., Glucksman E., Owens P., Swift C., Tinker A. and Yu G. (1990) *A review of research on falls among elderly people*, London: Age Concern Institute of Gerontology, Kings College.

Atkin B.L. (1988) 'Progress Towards Intelligent Buildings', in B.L. Atkin (ed) *Intelligent buildings: Applications of IT and building automation to high technology construction projects*, London: Kogan Page.

Attenburrow J. (1976) *Grouped housing for the elderly: A review of local authority provision and practice with particular reference to alarm systems*, Cmm 48/76, Watford: Building Research Establishment.

Audit Commission (1992) *The quality exchange: Housing services report*, London: Audit Commission.

Audit Commission (1998) *Home alone: The role of housing in community care*, London: Audit Commission.

Badre-Alam A., Casalena J.A., Ovaert T.C., Streit D.A. and Cavanagh P.R. (1994) 'A dual stiffness floor for the reduction of fall injuries: testing and implementation', proceedings of Symposium Injury Prevention through Biomechanics, Wayne State University, May 5-6, pp 11-19.

Baker S. and Parry M. (1984) 'Review of dispersed alarm systems', *Housing*, vol 20, no 9, September, pp 25-34.

Ball M. (1982) 'An alarm system for wandering patients', *Geriatric Medicine*, March, pp 96-101.

Beck U. (1994) 'The reinvention of politics: towards a theory of reflexive modernisation', in U. Beck, A. Giddens and S. Lash (eds) *Reflexive modernisation: Politics, traditions and aesthetics in the modern social order*, Cambridge: Polity Press.

Beck U., Giddens A. and Lash S. (1994) *Reflexive modernisation: Politics, traditions and aesthetics in the modern social order*, Cambridge: Polity Press.

Benson W.F. (1992) 'Public financing for personal response systems: a federal viewpoint', in A.S. Dibner (ed) *Personal response systems: An international report of a new home care service*, Binghampton, IL: The Haworth Press.

Bernard M. and Phillips J. (2000) 'The challenge of ageing in tomorrow's Britain', *Ageing and Society*, vol 20, no1, pp 33-54.

Birch K., Rigby M. and Roberts R. (2000) 'Putting the tele into health-care effectively', *Journal of Telemedicine and Telecare*, vol 6, suppl 1, pp 113-15.

Birmingham City Council (1986) *A review of the dispersed alarm programme for elderly people*, Birmingham: Birmingham City Council.

Boal F. (1995) *Shaping a city: Belfast in the late twentieth century*, Belfast: Institute of Irish Studies, Queens University.

Board for Social Responsibility (1990) *Ageing*, London: Church House Publishing.

Borgia B. (1989) 'Case Study 3: Barnsley Metropolitan Borough Council', in M.J. Fisk (ed) *Alarm systems and elderly people*, Glasgow: The Planning Exchange, pp 88-94.

Bouma H. (1992) 'Gerontechnology: making technology relevant for the elderly', in H. Bouma and J.A.M. Graafmans (eds) *Gerontechnology*, Amsterdam: IOS Press, pp 1-5.

Braye S. and Preston-Shoot M. (1995) *Empowering practice in social care*, Buckingham: Open University Press.

Brenner H. and Shelley E. (1998) *Adding years to life, life to years: A health promotion strategy for older people*, Dublin: National Council on Ageing and Older People.

British Telecom (1996) *Putting disability on the agenda*, London: BT Age and Disability Unit.

Brownsell S.J., Bradley D.A., Bragg R., Catlin P. and Carlier J. (2000) 'Do community alarm users want telecare?', *Journal of Telemedicine and Telecare*, vol 6, no 4, pp 199-204.

Brownsell S.J., Williams G., Bradley D.A., Bragg R., Catlin P. and Carlier J. (1999) 'Future systems for remote health care', *Journal of Telemedicine and Telecare*, vol 5, no 3, pp 141-52.

Bureau for the Aged (1986) *Community initiatives for senior citizens: Report of the ministerial task force*, Perth: Bureau for the Aged.

Burrows R. and Nettleton S. (2000) 'Reflexive modernisation and the emergence of wired self-help', in R. Burrows and N. Pleace (eds) *Wired welfare: Essays in the rhetoric and the reality of e-social policy*, York: Centre for Housing Policy, University of York, pp 9-22.

Bursztajn H.J., Hamm R.M. and Guthiel T.G. (1984) 'The technological target: involving the patient in clinical choices', in S.J Reiser and M. Anbar (eds) *The machine at the bedside: Strategies for using technology in patient care*, Cambridge: Cambridge University Press, pp 177-91.

Butler A. (1981) 'Dispersed alarm systems for the elderly', *Social Work Service*, vol 25, pp 17-22.

Butler A. (1989) 'The growth and development of alarm systems in sheltered housing', in M.J. Fisk (ed) *Alarm systems and elderly people*, Glasgow: The Planning Exchange, pp 8-19.

Butler A. and Oldman C. (eds) (1981) *Alarm systems for the elderly: Report of a workshop held at the University of Leeds, September 1980*, Leeds: Department of Social Policy and Administration, University of Leeds.

Butler A., Oldman C. and Greve J. (1983) *Sheltered housing for the elderly: Policy, practice and the consumer*, Hemel Hempstead: George Allen and Unwin.

Butler A., Oldman C. and Wright R. (1979) *Sheltered housing for the elderly: A critical review*, Leeds: Department of Social Policy and Administration, University of Leeds.

Cabrero G.R. (1999) *Social protection for dependency in old age in Spain*, Leuven: Katholieke Universiteit.

Cahn D. (1992) 'Emergency response systems in Israel', in A.S. Dibner (ed) *Personal response systems: An international report of a new home care service*, Binghampton, IL: The Haworth Press.

Cain B.A. (1987) 'Effects of a lifeline program on hospitalization', thesis to the Department of Social Work, California State University, Long Beach.

Calling for Help Group (1993) *A guide to community alarms*, London: Research Institute for Consumer Affairs.

Calling for Help Group (1994) *Community alarm services: A national survey*, Oxford: Anchor Trust.

Callinicos A. (1999) *Social theory: A historical introduction*, Cambridge: Polity Press.

Cameron A. (1979) *Mobile emergency care service: Dossier*, Stirling: Central Regional Council.

Cameron A. (1981) 'Planning the implementation of a dispersed alarm system for the elderly', in A. Butler and C. Oldman (eds) *Alarm systems for the elderly: Report of a workshop held at the University of Leeds, September 1980*, Leeds: Department of Social Policy and Administration, University of Leeds, pp 59-68.

Cameron A. (1992) 'Community alarm systems in Scotland', in A.S. Dibner (ed) *Personal response systems: An international report of a new home care service*, Binghampton, IL: The Haworth Press, pp 149-58.

Casalena J.A., Badre-Alam A., Ovaert T.C., Cavanagh P.R. and Streit D.A. (1994) 'A dual stiffness floor for the reduction of fall injuries: finite element analysis and design', proceedings of symposium, Injury Prevention Through Biomechanics, Wayne State University, May 5-6, pp 21-5.

Cavan R.S., Burgess E.W., Havighurst R.J. and Goldhamer H. (1949) *Personal adjustment in old age*, Chicago, IL: Science Research Association.

Ceely M. and Loughlin M. (1991) 'Community alarms - supply and demand', in R. Walker (ed) *The future for community alarms*, London: National Housing and Town Planning Council, pp 5-8.

Chan M., Bocquet H., Campo E., Val T., Extève D. and Pous J. (1998) 'Multisensor system and artificial intelligence in housing for the elderly', in J. Graffmans, V. Taipale and N. Charness (eds) *Gerontechnology: A sustainable investment in the future*, Amsterdam: IOS Press, pp 145-9.

Chumbler N.R., Beverly C.J. and Beck C.K. (1997) 'Rural older adults likelihood of receiving a personal response system: the Arkansas Medicaid waiver program', *Evaluation and Program Planning*, vol 20, no 2, pp 117-27.

Chumbler N.R., Beverly C.J. and Beck C.K. (1998) 'Determinants of in-home health and support service utilization for rural older adults', *Research in the Sociology of Health Care*, vol 15, pp 205-27.

Clark A.K. (1979) 'EMMA: a comprehensive alarm system for the elderly and infirm and disabled who live alone', *Occupational Therapy*, September, p 214.

Clark H., Dyer S. and Horwood J. (1998) *'That bit of help': The high value of low level preventative services for older people*, Bristol/York: The Policy Press/Joseph Rowntree Foundation.

Clark P.G. (1996) 'Communication between provider and patient: values, biography, and empowerment in clinical practice', *Ageing and Society*, vol 16, pp 747-74.

Clark R.L. and Ogawa N. (1996) 'Public attitudes and concerns about population ageing in Japan', *Ageing and Society*, vol 16, pp 443-65.

Clarke A. and Bright L. (2002) *Showing restraint: Challenging the use of restraint in care homes*, London: Counsel and Care.

Clatworthy S. and Bjørneby S. (1997) 'Smart House installations in Tønsberg', in S. Bjørneby and A. van Berlo (eds) *Ethical issues in use of technology for dementia care*, Akon series, vol 13, Knegsel: Akontes Publishing, pp 67-72.

Clough K., Jardine I., Horswell M. and Wortham K. (1998) *Telemedicine and telecare: Impact on healthcare*, London: The Institute of Health Services Management.

Collins S.C., Bhatti J.Z., Dexter S.L. and Rabbitt P.M.A. (1992) 'Elderly people in a new world: attitudes to advanced communications technologies', in H. Bouma and J.A.M. Graafmans (eds) *Gerontechnology*, Amsterdam: IOS Press, pp 277-82.

Corp M. (1991) 'Looking forward', in R. Walker (ed) *The future for community alarms*, London: National Housing and Town Planning Council, pp 19-22.

Counsel and Care (1993) *People not parcels: A discussion document to explore the issues surrounding the use of electronic tagging on older people in residential care and nursing homes*, London: Counsel and Care.

Cowan D. and Turner-Smith A. (1999) 'The role of assistive technology in alternative models of care for older people', in S. Sutherland (Chair) *With respect to old age: Long term care – rights and responsibilities*, Royal Commission on Long Term Care, Research, volume 2, Cm 4192-II/2, London: The Stationery Office, pp 325-46.

Crosby G. (ed) (1993) *European directory of older age*, London: Centre for Policy on Ageing.

Cullen K. and Robinson S. (1997) *Telecommunications for older people and disabled people in Europe: Preparing for the information society*, Assistive Technology Research Series, Amsterdam: IOS Press.

Cumming E.M. and Henry W. (1961) *Growing old*, New York: Basic Books.

Curry R.G. (2001) *The use of information and communication technology (ICT) in assistive technology for older and disabled people: An overview of current UK activity*, report for Department of Health, R.G. Curry (rcurry@dialin.net).

Curry R.G. and Norris A.C. (1997) *A review and assessment of telecare activity in the UK and recommendations for development*, Southampton: New College, University of Southampton.

Daatland S.V. (1999) *Social protection for dependency in old age in Norway*, Leuven: Katholieke Universiteit.

Darroch H. (1987) 'Alarms keep community intact', *Voluntary Housing*, December, p 19.

Datlen B. (1988) *The need for emergency response systems for senior citizen public housing tenants in Ontario*, report for the Ontario Ministry of Housing, Toronto.

Davis M. (1979) 'Stand-in call service provides relief for the warden', *Housing*, August, pp 16-17.

Day J.B. (1979) 'Rescue service for the elderly', *Housing*, August, pp 12-13.

De Leo D., Carollo G. and Dello Buono M. (1995) 'Lower suicide rates associated with a tele-help/tele-check service for the elderly at home', *American Journal of Psychiatry*, vol 152, no 4, pp 632-34.

Della Mea V. (2001) 'What is e-health (2): the death of telemedicine?', *Journal of Medical Internet Research*, vol 3, no 2, p e22.

Demiris G., Speedie S. and Finkelstein S. (2000) 'A questionnaire for the assessment of patients impressions of the risks and benefits of home telecare', *Journal of Telemedicine and Telecare*, vol 6, no 5 pp 278-84.

Denman M. (1996) *Technology and prevention: Enhancement of capacities*, report from a Eurolink Age seminar in Brussels, London: Eurolink Age.

Denton M.A. and Davis C.K. (1986) *Patterns of support: The use of support services among senior citizen public housing tenants in Ontario*, Hamilton: Social Data Research Ltd.

Department of Health (2001) *National service framework for older people*, London: Department of Health.

Department of Human Services (1998) *The Victorian personal assistance call service – VICPACS – supporting independence*, Melbourne: Aged Care Branch.

Department of the Environment (1990) *Efficiency report and action plan: Training, education and performance in housing management*, London: Department of the Environment.

Devins T. (1984) *Hospital planning and program development in geriatrics and long term care – report 2: Personal emergency response systems*, Burlington, MA: Massachusetts Hospital Association.

Dibner A.S. (1990) 'Personal emergency response systems: Communication technology aids elderly and their families', *Journal of Applied Gerontology*, vol 9, no 4, pp 504-10.

Dibner A.S. (ed) (1992) *Personal response systems: An international report of a new home care service*, Binghampton, IL: The Haworth Press.

Dick S. and Pomfret D. (1996) 'Community alarm systems study', Edinburgh: Age Concern Scotland (unpublished).

Dixon L. (1987) *The city of New York human resources administration medical assistance program: Evaluation of electronic call device pilot project*, New York: Office of Program Design.

Doughty K. and Costa J. (1997) 'Continuous automated care of the elderly', *Journal of Telemedicine and Telecare*, vol 3, pp 23-5.

Doughty K. and Fisk M. (2001) 'Extending the scope of community alarm services', *Housing, Care and Support*, vol 4, no 2, pp 24-7.

Doughty K. and Williams G. (2001) 'Practical solutions for the integration of community alarms, assistive technologies and telecare', *Quality in Ageing*, vol 2, no 1, pp 31-47.

Doughty K. and Williams G. (2002) 'Towards a complete home monitoring system: safety by design', selected papers, Birmingham: Royal Society for the Prevention of Accidents.

Doughty K., Cameron K. and Garner P. (1996) 'Three generations of telecare of the elderly', *Journal of Telemedicine and Telecare*, vol 2, pp 71-80..

Doughty K., Lewis R. and McIntosh A. (2000) 'The design of a practical and reliable fall detector for community and institutional telecare', *Journal of Telemedicine and Telecare*, vol 6, suppl 1, pp 150-54.

Dowling H. and Enevoldson H. (1988) *The elderly at home project: Final report*, Liverpool: Merseyside Improved Houses.

Duncan T. (1988) (1993) *Community alarm services in Scotland*, information sheets, Glasgow: The Planning Exchange.

Duncan T. and Thwaites F. (1987) *Community alarms and housing associations*, Glasgow: The Planning Exchange.

EC (European Commission) (1996) *Telematics applications programme: Project summaries – disabled and elderly sector*, Brussels: EC.

EC (2001) *Telemedicine glossary: Glossary of standards, concepts, technologies and users*, 3rd edn, Version 3.10, Brussels: DG INFSO-B1.

ECRI (1986) 'Personal emergency response systems (PERS)', New Technology Briefs 5P.10, Plymouth Meeting, PA: ECRI.

ECRI (1998) 'Signalling devices, personal emergency: health care product information system', Plymouth Meeting, PA: ECRI.

Edward S. (1989) 'Case study 4: Angus District Council', in M.J. Fisk (ed) *Alarm systems and elderly people*, Glasgow: The Planning Exchange.

Epps B.M. (1981) 'A corporate approach to planning services for the elderly', in A. Butler and C. Oldman (eds) *Alarm systems for the elderly: Report of a workshop held at the University of Leeds, September 1980*, Leeds: Department of Social Policy and Administration, University of Leeds, pp 31-8.

Erkert T. (1998) 'Videotelephony-based services: the proven improvement of quality of life', in J. Graafmans, V. Taipale and N. Charness (eds) *Gerontechnology: A sustainable investment in the future*, Amsterdam: IOS Press, pp 182-6.

Ernst and Young (1994) *A national study of the provision of specialised housing for elderly people*, Housing Research Report 1, London: Department of the Environment.

Estes C.L. (1991) 'The new political economy of aging: introduction and critique', in M. Minkler and C. Estes (eds) *Critical perspectives on aging: The political and moral economy of growing old*, New York: Baywood Publishing, pp 19-36.

Estes C.L., Linkins K.W. and Binney E.A. (1996) 'The political economy of aging', in R. Binstock and L. George (eds) *Handbook of aging and the sciences*, New York: Academic Press, pp 346-61.

Farquhar D.L., Fonda C.L., Danek C.L. and Ryan A.M. (1992) 'A survey of personal emergency alarms for the frail elderly', *Australian Journal on Ageing*, vol 11, no 1, pp 3-7.

Feeney R.J., Galer M.D. and Gallagher M.M. (1974) *Alarm systems for elderly and disabled people*, Loughborough: Institute for Consumer Ergonomics Ltd, University of Technology.

Fennell G. (1989) 'Raising the alarm', in M.J. Fisk (ed) *Alarm systems and elderly people*, Glasgow: The Planning Exchange, pp 20-33.

Fisk M.J. (1984) 'Community alarm systems: a cause for concern', *Housing Review*, vol 33, no 1 Jan/Feb, pp 22-3.

Fisk M.J. (1985) 'Home alarms reduce anxiety', *Social Work Today*, May 27, pp 24-2.

Fisk M.J. (1986) *Independence and the elderly*, Beckenham: Croom Helm.

Fisk M.J. (ed) (1989) *Alarms systems and elderly people*, Glasgow: The Planning Exchange.

Fisk M.J. (1990) *Dispersed alarm systems in the United Kingdom: A listing of central controls and appraisal of current issues*, Glasgow: The Planning Exchange.

Fisk M.J. (1995) 'A comparison of personal response services in Canada and the United Kingdom', *Journal of Telemedicine and Telecare*, vol 1, no 3, pp 145-56.

Fisk M.J. (1997a) 'Telemedicine, new technologies and care management', *International Journal of Geriatric Psychiatry*, vol 12, pp 1057-59

Fisk M.J. (1997b) 'Telecare equipment in the home: issues of intrusiveness and control', *Journal of Telemedicine and Telecare*, vol 3, no1, suppl 1, pp 30-2.

Fisk M.J. (1998) 'Telecare at home: factors influencing technology choices and user acceptance', *Journal of Telemedicine and Telecare*, vol 4, no 2, pp 80-3.

Fisk M.J. (1999) *Our future home: The housing and inclusion of older people in 2025*, London: Help the Aged.

Fisk M.J. (2001) 'The implications of smart home technologies', in S. Peace and C. Holland (eds) *Inclusive housing in an ageing society*, Bristol: The Policy Press, pp 101-24.

Fisk M.J. and Phillips D. (2001) *New vistas for Abbeyfield: Housing and support services for older people*, St Albans: The Abbeyfield Society.

Fitzpatrick Associates (1999) *Review of the scheme of community support for older people*, report to the Minister for Social, Community and Family Affairs, Dublin: Department of Social, Community and Family Affairs.

Friediger H. (1992) 'Services for the Danish elderly: the role of technical aids', in A.S. Dibner (ed) *Personal response systems: An international report of a new home care service*, Binghampton, IL: The Haworth Press, pp 33-40.

Galvin J.C. (1997) 'Assistive technology: Federal policy and practise since 1982', *Technology and Disability*, vol 6, pp 3-15.

Gann D., Barlow J. and Venables T. (1999) *Digital futures: Making homes smarter*, Coventry: Chartered Institute of Housing.

Gann D., Burley R., Curry D., Phippen P., Porteus J., Wells O. and Williams M. (2000) *Healthcare and smart housing technologies: Report of a DTI international technology services mission to Japan*, Brighton: Pavilion Publishing.

Garavan R., Winder R. and McGee H.M. (2001) *Health and social services for older people (HeSSOP): Consulting older people on health and social services – a survey of service use, experiences and needs*, Dublin: National Council on Ageing and Older People.

Gatz M. and Pearson C. (1988) *Evaluation of an emergency alert response system from the point of view of subscribers and family members*, Los Angeles, CA: Department of Psychology, University of Southern California.

Giddens A. (1990) *The consequences of modernity*, Cambridge: Polity Press.

Giddens A. (1991) *Modernity and self identity: Self and society in late modern age*, Cambridge: Polity Press.

Glasgow City Council (1993) *Housing and elderly people in north west Glasgow: Results of a survey of housing alarm users and sheltered housing applicants*, Glasgow: Housing Department.

Glastonbury B. and LaMendola W. (1992) *The integrity of intelligence: A bill of rights for the information age*, Basingstoke: Macmillan Press.

Goddard E. and Savage D. (1994) *General household survey: people aged 65 and over*, London: Office of Population Censuses and Surveys.

Goldsmith M. (1996) *Hearing the voice of people with dementia: Opportunities and obstacles*, London: Jessica Kingsley Publishers.

Gott M. (1995) *Telematics for health: The role of telehealth and telemedicine in homes and communities*, Oxford: Radcliffe Medical Press.

Graafmans J. and Taipale V. (1998) 'Gerontechnology', in J. Graafmans, V. Taipale and N. Charness (eds) *Gerontechnology: A sustainable investment in the future*, Amsterdam: IOS Press, pp 3-6.

Hansen E.B. (1999) *Social protection for dependency in old age in Denmark*, Leuven: Katholieke Universiteit.

Hantrais L. (2000) *Social policy in the European Union*, Basingstoke: Macmillan Press.

Harding N. (1993) *Alarm systems in community care for elderly people*, Social Work Monograph No 123, Norwich: University of East Anglia.

Harris A.I. (1968) *Social welfare for the elderly: A survey in thirteen local authority areas in England, Wales and Scotland*, London: HMSO.

Harrison J.D. (1997) 'Housing for the ageing population of Singapore', in S. Brink (ed) *Housing older people: An international perspective*, New Brunswick, NJ: Transaction Publishers, pp 21-34.

Hawley M. (2003) 'Implications for health and social care', in J. Porteus (ed) *Assistive technology and telecare*, Bristol: The Policy Press, pp 67-72.

Henwood M. (1998) *Our turn next: A fresh look at home support services for older people*, Leeds: Nuffield Institute for Health.

Herman W.R. (1992) 'Mid-range technology: a New Zealand perspective', in A.S. Dibner (ed) *Personal response systems: An international report of a new home care service*, Binghampton, IL: The Haworth Press, pp 123-34.

Heumann L. and Boldy D. (1982) *Housing for the elderly: Planning and policy formulation in Western Europe and North America*, Beckenham: Croom Helm.

Heywood F., Oldman C. and Means R. (2002) *Housing and home in later life*, Buckingham: Open University Press.

Hielkema A. (2001) 'Quality standards for personal alarm service organisations: Upgrading of the GQ approval mark', in C. Marincek, C. Bühler, H. Knops and R. Andrich (eds) *Assistive technology – added value to the quality of life*, Amsterdam: IOS Press, pp 559-64.

Hobbs M.L. (1992) 'Product design and social implications in a personal response program', in A.S. Dibner (ed) *Personal response systems: An international report of a new home care service*, Binghampton, IL: The Haworth Press, pp 23-32.

Hojnik-Zupanc I. (1996) 'Autonomy of the elderly in Slovenia: a case study of Ljubljana', in H. Mollenkopf (ed) *Elderly people in industrialised societies: Social integration in old age by or despite technology*, Berlin: Sigma, pp 185-94.

Hojnik-Zupanc I., Hlebec V. and Licer N. (1998) 'Telecommunication technology for the elderly and other vulnerable groups in Slovenia', in J. Graafmans, V. Taipale and N. Charness (eds) *Gerontechnology: A sustainable investment in the future*, Amsterdam: IOS Press, pp 191-4.

Hunt A. (1978) *The elderly at home*, Office of Population Censuses and Surveys, London: HMSO.

Hunt J. (1985) *Housing and care for elderly people*, Cwmbran: Cwmbran Development Corporation and Torfaen Borough Council.

Iliffe S. and Gould M.M. (1995a) 'Hospital at home: a substitution technology that nobody wants?', *British Journal of Health Care Management*, vol 1, no 13, pp 663-5.

Iliffe S. and Gould M.M. (1995b) 'Hospital at home: a case study in service development', *British Journal of Health Care Management*, vol 1, no 16, pp 809-12.

Institute of Housing (1958) *A memorandum on housing the aged*, London: Institute of Housing.

Johnson D. (1987) 'Community alarm systems', *Housing and Planning Review*, Oct/Nov, pp 8-9.

Karinch M. (1994) *Telemedicine: What the future holds when you're ill*, Far Hills, NJ: New Horizon Press.

Karlsson M. (1995) 'Elderly and new technology: On the introduction of new technology in everyday life', in I. Placencia Porrero and R. Puig de la Bellcasa (eds) *The European context for assistive technology*, Amsterdam: IOS Press, pp 78-81.

Kasalová H. (1994) 'Status report from the Czech Republic', *Ageing International*, pp 26-30.

Kasalová H. and Mellanová A. (1998) 'Keeping the elderly at home', in J. Graafmans, V. Taipale and N. Charness (eds) *Gerontechnology: A sustainable investment in the future*, Amsterdam: IOS Press, pp 258-60.

Kaye L.W. (1997) 'Telemedicine: extension to home care?', *Telemedicine Journal*, vol 3, no 3, pp 244-46.

Kell A. and Thompson N. (2000) 'Integer: the story so far', *Building Homes*, May, pp 8-13.

Kelly M. (2001) 'Lifetime homes', in S. Peace and C. Holland (eds) *Inclusive housing in an ageing society*, Bristol: The Policy Press, pp 55-76.

Killick J. and Allan K. (2001) *Communication and the care of people with dementia*, Buckingham: Open University Press.

King A. (1993) 'Older people across the EC: similarities and differences', in G. Crosby (ed) *The European directory of older age*, London: Centre for Policy on Ageing, pp 10-16.

Kirschner A. (1994) 'Independent living of the elderly – how can safety alarms systems (SAS) support it? Function and services of SAS in Austria', in C. Wild and A. Kirschner (eds) *Technology for the elderly: Safety alarm systems, technical aids and smart homes*, Akon series Ageing in the Contemporary Society, vol 8, Knegsel: Akontes Publishing, pp 25-46.

Kitwood T., Buckland S. and Petre T. (1995) *Brighter futures: A report on research into provision for persons with dementia in residential homes, nursing homes and sheltered housing*, Oxford: Anchor Trust.

Koch W.J. (1984) 'Emergency response system assists in discharge planning', *Dimensions in Health Service*, vol 61, no 11, pp 30-1.

Kose S. (1997) 'Housing elderly people in Japan', in S. Brink (ed) *Housing older people: An international perspective*, New Brunswick, NJ: Transaction Publishers, pp 125-39.

Leeson G. (1992) 'General and specific aspects of emergency response systems in Denmark', in A.S. Dibner (ed) *Personal response systems: An international report of a new home care service*, Binghampton, IL: The Haworth Press, pp 41-56.

Leichsenring K. (1999) *Social protection for dependency in old age in Austria*, Leuven: Katholieke Universiteit.

Leikas J., Salo J. and Poramo R. (1998) 'Security alarm system supports independent living of demented persons', in J. Graafmans, V. Taipale and N. Charness (eds) *Gerontechnology: A sustainable investment in the future*, Amsterdam: IOS Press, pp 402-5.

Lenk K. (1982) 'Information technology and society', in G. Friedrichs and Schaff A. (eds) *Microelectronics and society: For better or for worse: A report to the Club of Rome*, Oxford: Pergammon Press, pp 273-310.

Lerner J.C. and Stevens R.B. (1986) *Personal emergency response systems*, Background Paper Series No 3, Baltimore, MD: Commission on Elderly People Living Alone.

Lewis R.J. (1979) 'Flying warden answers 80-year olds mayday call', *Modern Geriatrics*, March, pp 27-33.

Löckenhoff U. (1988) 'Nutzen und Soziale Auswirkungen des Haus-Nostruf-Dienstes', *Mitteilungen zur Altenhilfe*, vol 25, no 4, pp 38-47.

Lyon D. (1999) *Postmodernity: second edition*, Buckingham: Open University Press.

Lyon D. (2001) *Surveillance society: Monitoring everyday life*, Buckingham: Open University Press.

McCafferty P. (1994) *Living independently: A study of the housing needs of elderly and disabled people*, Department of the Environment, London: HMSO.

MacCreath B. (1980) 'Communication systems for protecting the elderly in their homes', *Housing Review*, July-August, pp 123-24.

McGarry M. (ed) (1983) *Community alarm systems for older people*, Edinburgh: Age Concern Scotland.

McGarry M. (ed) (1985) *Community alarm systems for older people*, 2nd edn, Edinburgh: Age Concern Scotland.

McIntosh A. and Thie J. (2001) 'The development of a new model for community telemedicine services', *Journal of Telemedicine and Telecare*, vol 7, suppl 1, pp 69-71.

McKee K.J. (1998) 'The body drop: a framework for understanding recovery from falls in older people', *Generations Review*, vol 8, no 4, pp 11-14.

MacLaren Plansearch (1988) *The study of emergency response systems for the elderly*, Ottawa: Canada Mortgage and Housing Corporation.

McLuckie I. (1984) 'Advanced communications for sheltered housing', *Electronics and Power*, May, pp 374-78.

McTavish J. (1989) 'Case study 5: Hyde Housing Association', in M.J. Fisk (ed) *Alarm systems and elderly people*, Glasgow: The Planning Exchange, pp 103-9.

McWhirter M. (1984) *An evaluation of the mobile emergency care service – a dispersed alarm service for the elderly and other persons at risk in central region*, Stirling: Forth Valley Health Board.

McWhirter M. (1987) 'A dispersed alarm system for the elderly and its relevance to local general practitioners', *Journal of the Royal College of General Practitioners*, June, pp 244-7.

Macnaughtan D. (1997) *The role of technology in the care of people with dementia in the community*, Stirling: Dementia Services Development Centre, University of Stirling.

Maginnis, I. (1991) *Brick by brick: A short history of the Northern Ireland Housing Executive 1971-1991*, Belfast: Northern Ireland Housing Executive.

Mandlestam M. (1997) *Equipment for older or disabled people and the law*, London: Jessica Kingsley Publishers.

Mann K. (2001) *Approaching retirement: Social divisions, welfare and exclusion*, Bristol: The Policy Press.

Marshall M. (1995) 'Technology is the shape of the future', *Journal of Dementia Care*, May/June, pp 12-14.

Marshall M. (1997) *Dementia and technology: A discussion of the practical and ethical issues surrounding the use of technology in helping people with dementia*, London: Counsel and Care.

Marshall M. (2000) *ASTRID, a social and technological response to meeting the needs of individuals with dementia and their carers: A guide to using technology within dementia care*, London: Hawker Publications.

Marshall M. (2001) 'Dementia and technology', in S. Peace and C. Holland (eds) *Inclusive housing in an ageing society*, Bristol: The Policy Press, pp 125-43.

Middleton L. (1982) 'Cause for alarm: a report on alarm usage in sheltered housing', *Voluntary Housing*, February, pp 27-9.

Mills P. (1999) *People at home and in touch: The use of technology to support older people in their own homes*, Durham: Durham County Council.

Ministry of Housing and Local Government (1968) *Grouped flatlets for old people: A sociological study*, London: HMSO.

Ministry of Social Affairs (1990) *Pensioner in Denmark: Main features of Danish old age policy and care for the old*, Copenhagen: Ministry of Social Affairs.

Ministry of Social Development (2001) *Positive ageing in New Zealand: Diversity, participation and change: Status report 2001*, Wellington: Ministry of Social Development.

Miskelly F. (2001) 'Assistive technology in elderly care', *Age and Ageing*, vol 30, pp 455-8.

Montgomery C. (1992) 'Personal response systems in the United States,' in A.S. Dibner (ed) *Personal response systems: An international report of a new home care service*, Binghampton, IL: The Haworth Press, pp 201-22.

Moran R. (1993) *The electronic home: Social and spatial aspects*, Dublin: European Foundation for the Improvement of Living and Working Conditions.

National Assembly for Wales (2001) *Welsh house condition survey 1998*, London: National Statistics.

National Council for the Aged (1985) *Housing of the elderly in Ireland*, Dun Laoghaire: National Council for the Aged.

National Old People's Welfare Council (1966) *Wardens and old people's dwellings: A memorandum*, London: National Council of Social Service.

Nettleton S., Pleace N., Burrows R., Muncer S. and Loader B. (2000) 'The reality of virtual social support', in R. Burrows and N. Pleace (eds) *Wired welfare: Essays in the rhetoric and the reality of e-social policy*, York: Centre for Housing Policy, University of York, pp 39-49.

Nohr L.E. (2000) 'Telemedicine and patients rights', *Journal of Telemedicine and Telecare*, vol 6, suppl 1, pp 173-4.

Northern Ireland Housing Executive/Northern Ireland Federation of Housing Associations (1993) *Housing services and community care*, Belfast: Northern Ireland Housing Executive.

O'Connor J., Ruddle H. and O'Gallagher M. (1989) *Sheltered housing in Ireland: Its role and contribution in the care of the elderly*, National Council for the Aged report No 20, Dublin: National Council for the Aged.

O'Connor J., Wren M., McQuade E., Burkley C., Hall T., Sorensen T. and Stephenson S. (1986) *Communications networks and the elderly*, Dublin: The Stationery Office.

Oldman C. (1989) 'The role of dispersed alarms in community care', in M.J. Fisk (ed) *Alarm systems and elderly people*, Glasgow: The Planning Exchange, pp 34-49.

Ontario Ministry of Community and Social Services (1986) *Evaluation of an emergency response system based at Rainycrest home for the aged*, Toronto: Program Technology Branch.

Ontario Ministry of Community and Social Services (1987) *Information on emergency response systems*, Toronto: Program Technology Branch.

Organisation for Economic Co-operation and Development (1996) *Caring for frail elderly people*, Social Policy Studies No 19, Paris: OECD.

Östlund B. (1994) 'Experiences with safety alarms for the elderly in Sweden', in C. Wild and A. Kirschner (eds) *Technology for the elderly: Safety alarm systems, technical aids and smart homes*, Akon series Ageing in the Contemporary Society, vol 8, Knegsel: Akontes Publishing, pp 47-58.

Östlund B. (1999) *Images, users, practices: Senior citizens entering the IT society*, Stockholm: KFB – Kommunikationsforsknings-beredningen.

Parker R.E. (1984) *Housing for the elderly: The handbook for managers*, Chicago, IL: Institute of Real Estate Management.

Parkin A. (1995) 'The care and control of elderly and incapacitated adults', *Journal of Social Welfare and Family Law*, vol 17, no 4, pp 431-44.

Parry I. and Thompson L. (1993) *Effective sheltered housing: A handbook*, Coventry: Institute of Housing.

Parsloe P. (1995) *Ethical issues in care in the community*, the Beckly Lecture, Bristol, 27 June, London: The Methodist Church Division of Social Responsibility.

Peeters P.H.F. (1997) *Living independently in a safe way: An innovation on safety alarm systems*, Eindhoven: Stan Ackermans Instituut, Technische Universiteit Eindhoven.

Pellow J. (1987) *Keeping watch: A study of caring for the elderly at home with the aid of electronics*, London: John Clare Books.

Phillipson C. (1982) *Capitalism and the construction of old age*, London: Macmillan Press.

Phillipson C. (1998) *Reconstructing old age: New agendas in social theory and practice*, London: Sage Publications.

Phippen P. (2000) *Building for longevity: The Abbeyfield Lecture 2000*, St Albans: The Abbeyfield Society.

Pooley D. (2000) 'How much did it cost to build?', *Building Homes*, May, pp 46-7.

Porteus J. and Brownsell A. (2000) *Using telecare: Exploring technologies for independent living for older people*, Oxford: Anchor Trust.

Power A. (1993) *Hovels to high rise: State housing in Europe since 1850*, London: Routledge.

Power B. (1979) *Old and alone in Ireland: A report on a survey of old people living alone*, Dublin: St Vincent de Paul Society.

Pragnell M., Spence L. and Moore R. (2000) *The market potential for smart homes*, York: Joseph Rowntree Foundation.

Prass J. (1992) 'Structure, aims and prospects of PRS in Germany', in A.S. Dibner (ed) *Personal response systems: An international report of a new home care service,* Binghampton, IL: The Haworth Press.

Premik M. and Rudel D. (1996) 'Community social alarm network in Slovenia', *Central European Journal of Public Health*, vol 4, no 4, pp 223-5.

Prophet H. (1998) *Fit for the future: The prevention of dependency in later life*, London: Continuing Care Conference.

Quigley G. and Tweed C. (1999) *Added-value services from the installation of assistive technologies for the elderly*, Research Report on EPSRC GR/MØ5171, Belfast: School of Architecture, Queens University.

Randall B. (1999) *Social housing for older people: Meeting the challenge in the EU*, Hilversum: CECODHAS.

Research Institute for Consumer Affairs (1986) *Dispersed alarms: A guide for organisations installing systems*, London: RICA.

Research Institute for Consumer Affairs (1987) *Calling for help: A guide to emergency alarm systems*, London: RICA.

Research Institute for Consumer Affairs (1997) *Guide to community alarms*, London: RICA.

Ricability (2000) *Calling for help: A guide to community alarm systems*, London: Ricability and The Housing Corporation.

Riseborough M. (1997a) *Community alarm services today and tomorrow*, Oxford: Anchor Trust.

Riseborough M. (1997b) *Community alarm: Who wants community alarm services today – area report 4 (Anchor call service)*, Birmingham: Centre for Urban and Regional Studies, University of Birmingham.

Riseborough M. (1998) *From consumerism to citizenship: New European perspectives on independent living in older age*, HOPE – Housing for Older People in Europe, Oxford: Anchor Trust.

Robinson S. (1992) 'Support for elderly people using video-telephony: the Frankfurt pilot', in H. Bouma and J.A.M. Graafmans (eds) *Gerontechnology*, Amsterdam: IOS Press, pp 305-16.

Robinson S., Kubitschke L., Cullen K. and Dolphin C. (1995) *Final report on telecommunications requirements of assistive technology applications*, Dublin: Work Research Centre.

Rodriguez L. (1992) 'Emergency response systems – the Canadian perspective', in A.S. Dibner (ed) *Personal response systems: An international report of a new home care service*, Binghampton, IL: The Haworth Press.

Rosenburg L. and Wang Y.P. (1992) *The tenants' views: Report of the 1991 Bield tenant survey*, Edinburgh: Bield Housing Association.

Roth A., Carthy Z. and Benedek M. (1997) 'Telemedicine in emergency home care – the Shahal experience', *Journal of Telemedicine and Telecare*, vol 3, no 1, supplement, pp 58-60.

Roush R.E. and Teesdale T.A. (1997) 'Reduced hospitalization rates of two sets of community residing older adults after use of a personal response system', *Journal of Applied Gerontology*, vol 16, no 3, pp 355-66.

Roush R.E., Teesdale T.A., Murphy J.N. and Kirk M.S. (1995) 'Impact of a personal emergency response system on hospital utilization by community-residing elders', *Southern Medical Journal*, vol 88, no 9, pp 917-22.

Ruchlin H.S. and Morris J.N. (1981) 'Cost benefit analysis of an emergency response system: a case study of a long-term care program', *Health Service Research*, vol 16, no 1, pp 65-80.

Ruddle H., Donoghue F. and Mulvihill R. (1998) *The years ahead report: A review of the implementation of its recommendations*, Dublin: National Council on Ageing and Older People.

Rudel D. and Fisk M. (2001) 'Can users of personal response systems in slovenia benefit from the 3rd generation technology?', in C. Marincek, C. Bühler, H. Knops and R. Andrich (eds) *Assistive technology – added value to the quality of life*, Amsterdam: IOS Press, pp 734-7.

Rudel D., Premik M. and Hojnik-Zupanc I. (1995) *Caring network based on community social alarm centres in Slovenia: A country in transition*, proceedings of the Eighth World Congress on Medical Informatics, Vancouver, pp 1503-5.

Rudel D., Premik M. and Licer N. (1999) 'The community social alarm service as a primary health care service', in P. Kokol, B. Zupan, J. Stare, M. Premik and R. Engelbrecht (eds) *Medical Informatics Europe 99*, Amsterdam: IOS Press, pp 203-6.

Ruggiero C., Sacile R. and Giacomini M. (1999) 'Home telecare', *Journal of Telemedicine and Telecare*, vol 5, no 1, pp 11-17.

Sand P. (1986) 'Communications and alarm systems for elderly and disabled people', *Housing and Planning Review*, conference issue, pp 26-7.

Satava R.M. and Jones S.B. (1996) 'Virtual reality and telemedicine: exploring advanced concepts', *Telemedicine Journal*, vol 2, no 3, pp 195-200.

Schantz B.J. (1992) 'ERS as a community outreach service from a nursing home', in A.S. Dibner (ed) *Personal response systems: An international report of a new home care service*, Binghampton, IL: The Haworth Press, pp 229-38.

Schoone M., Bos W. and Piël A. (1998) 'Monitoring Thuiszorg', Leiden: TNO Preventie en Gezondheid.

Scottish Local Authorities Special Housing Group (1980) *Warden communication systems*, Review Paper 2/80, Edinburgh: Scottish Local Amenities Special Housing Group.

Sewel J. and Wybrow P. (1985) 'Highland Helpcall – a case of a dispersed alarm system', in M. McGarry (ed) *Community alarm systems for older people*, Edinburgh: Age Concern Scotland, pp 16-30.

Shepherd J. (1985) 'Rotherham sounds the alarm bells for elderly residents', *Housing and Planning Review*, vol 40, no 4, August, pp 16-18.

Sherwood S. and Morris J.N. (1981) *A study of the effects of an emergency alarm and response system for the aged*, executive summary, Boston, MA: Department of Social Gerontological Research, Hebrew Rehabilitation Center for the Aged.

Siddell M. (1995) *Health in old age: Myth, mystery and management*, Buckingham: Open University Press.

Singlelenberg J. (2000) *Housing and care for older people in Denmark and the Netherlands*, HOPE – Housing for Older People in Europe, Oxford: Anchor Trust.

Sixsmith A. (1995) 'New technology and community care', *Health and Social Care*, vol 2, pp 367-78.

Sixsmith A. (2000) 'An evaluation of an intelligent home monitoring system', *Journal of Telemedicine and Telecare*, vol 6, no 2, pp 63-72.

Sixsmith A. and Sixsmith J. (2000) 'Smart care technologies: Meeting whose needs?', *Journal of Telemedicine and Telecare*, vol 6, suppl 1, pp 190-92.

Snellen H.A. (1977) *Selected papers on the electrocardiography of Willem Einthoven*, Leyden: Leyden University Press.

Soulet M.-H. (1999) 'Social emergency: between myth and reality', in D. Avramov (ed) *Coping with homelessness: Issues to be tackled and best practice in Europe*, Aldershot: Ashgate Publishing, pp 407-28.

Sowden A., Sheldon T., Pehl L., Eastwood A., Glenny E. and Long A. (1996) *Effective health care: Preventing falls and subsequent injury in older people*, York: NHS Centre for Reviews and Dissemination, University of York.

Stafford J.L. and Dibner A.S. (1984) *Lifeline programs in 1984: Stability and growth*, Watertown: Lifeline Systems Inc.

Stanberry B.A. (1998) *The legal and ethical aspects of telemedicine*, London: The Royal Society of Medicine Press.

Stenberg B. (1992) 'The Swedish model of social alarm systems for care of the elderly', in A.S. Dibner (ed) *Personal response systems: An international report of a new home care service*, Binghampton, IL: The Haworth Press, pp 135-48.

Széman Z. (1998) 'Ageing and technology: an innovative model in Hungary', in J. Graafmans, V. Taipale and N. Charness (eds) *Gerontechnology: A sustainable investment in the future*, Amsterdam: IOS Press, pp 455-8.

Tamborini R., Favotto F., Dose C. and Rebba V. (1996) *Analisi Economica del Servizio di Telesoccorso Telecontrollo*, Dipartimento di Scienze Economiche Marco Fanno, Universita di Padova.

Tamura T., Togawa T., Ogawa M. and Yamakoshi K. (1998) 'Fully automated health monitoring at home', in J. Graffmans, V. Taipale and N. Charness (eds) *Gerontechnology: A sustainable investment in the future*, Amsterdam: IOS Press, pp 280-4.

Tang P. and Venables P. (2000) 'Smart homes and telecare for independent living', *Journal of Telemedicine and Telecare*, vol 6, no 1, pp 8-14.

Task Force on Security for the Elderly (1996) *Report to the Minister for Social Welfare*, Pn2470, Dublin: Government Publications.

Tester S. (1996) *Community care for older people: A comparative perspective*, Basingstoke: Macmillan Press.

Tetley J., Hanson E. and Clarke A. (2000) 'Older people, telematics and care', in A.M. Warnes, L. Warren and M. Nolan (eds) *Care services for later life: Transformations and critiques*, London: Jessica Kingsley Publications, pp 243-58.

Thompson L. (1981) 'The role of the central control in dispersed alarm systems', in A. Butler and C. Oldman (eds) *Alarm systems for the elderly: Report of a workshop held at the University of Leeds, September 1980*, Leeds: Department of Social Policy and Administration, University of Leeds, pp 39-49.

Thornton P. (1993a) 'Developing community alarm services to meet community care needs: implications of some new research', Packages of Care for Elderly People – Ageing Update Conference Proceedings, 10 June 1992.

Thornton P. (1993b) 'Communication technology – empowerment or disempowerment?', *Disability, Handicap and Society*, vol 8, no 4, pp 339-49.

Thornton P. and Mountain G. (1992) *A positive response: Developing community alarm services for older people*, York: Joseph Rowntree Foundation.

Tinker A. (1984) *Staying at home: Helping elderly people*, Department of the Environment, London: HMSO.

Tinker A. (1995) 'Disembodied voices', *Community Care*, April 13-19, p 30.

Tinker A., Askham J., Hancock R., Mueller G. and Stuchbury R. (2000) *85 not out: A study of people aged 85 and over at home*, Oxford: Anchor Trust.

Tinetti M.E., Mendes de Leon C.F., Doucette J.T. and Baker D.I. (1994) 'Fear of falling and fall-related efficacy in relationship to functioning among community-living elders', *Journal of Gerontology*, vol 49, pp M140-M47.

Topper A.K., Maki B.E. and Holliday P.J. (1993) 'Are activity-based assessments of balance and gait in the elderly predictive of risk of falling and/or type of fall', *Journal of the American Geriatrics Society*, vol 41, pp 479-87.

Townsend P. (1962) *The last refuge: A study of residential institutions and homes for the aged in England and Wales*, London: Routledge and Kegan Paul.

Tout K. (1996) *Towards a golden age: The history of help the aged*, Bishop Auckland: Pentland Press.

Tweed C. and Quigley G. (2000) 'Some ethical considerations of dwelling-based telecare systems for the elderly', Working Paper, Belfast: School of Architecture, Queens University of Belfast.

Twigg J. (2000) 'The medical-social boundary and the location of personal care', in A.M. Warnes, L. Warren and M. Nolan (eds) *Care services for later life: Transformations and critiques*, London: Jessica Kingsley Publishers.

Tunstall Telecom (1997) *Home alone 97: Independence and isolation*, Whitley Bridge: Tunstall Telecom.

Vaarama M. and Kautto M. (1999) *Social protection for dependency in old age in Finland*, Leuven: Katholieke Universiteit.

Valins M.S. and Salter D. (1996) 'Looking back', in M.S. Valins and D. Salter (eds) *Futurecare: New directions in planning health and care environments*, Oxford: Blackwell Science, pp 1-5.

van Berlo A. (1998) 'How to enhance acceptance of safety alarm systems by elderly?', in J. Graafmans, V. Taipale and N. Charness (eds) *Gerontechnology: A sustainable investment in the future*, Amsterdam: IOS Press, pp 390-3.

van Berlo A., Vermijs P. and Hermans T. (1994) 'Experiences with safety alarms for the elderly in the Netherlands', in C. Wild and A. Kirschner (eds) *Technology for the elderly: Safety alarm systems, technical aids and smart homes*, Akon series Ageing in the Contemporary Society, vol 8, Knegsel: Akontes Publishing, pp 69-78.

van der Leeuw J.J. (2001) *Personenalarmering in Nederland*, Utrecht: Wonen en Zorg.

Vlaskamp F.J.M. (1992) 'From alarm systems to smart houses', in A.S. Dibner (ed) *Personal response systems: An international report of a new home care service*, Binghampton, IL: The Haworth Press, pp 105-22.

Vlaskamp F.J.M., van Dort W.J. and Quaedackers J.E.W. (1994) 'Integrated systems: towards modular and flexible control and communications systems for disabled persons', in A. Davies, H.M. Felix and H.A. Kamphuis (eds) *Research development knowledge-transfer in the field of rehabilitation and handicap*, Hoensbroek: IRV.

Walker A. (1993) 'Observing older Europeans', in G. Crosby (ed) *The European directory of older age*, London: Centre for Policy on Ageing, pp 3-5.

Walker R. (ed) (1991) *The future for community alarms*, London: National Housing and Town Planning Council.

Watzke J.R. (1994) 'Personal emergency response systems: Canadian data on subscribers and alarms', in G.M. Gutman and A.V. Wister (eds) *Progressive accommodation for seniors: Interfacing shelter and services*, Vancouver: Gerontology Research Centre, Simon Fraser University at Harbour Centre, pp 147-65.

Watzke J.R. and Birch G. (1994) 'Older adults response to automated environmental control devices', in G.M. Gutman and A.V. Wister (eds) *Progressive accommodation for seniors: Interfacing shelter and services*, Vancouver: Gerontology Research Centre, Simon Fraser University at Harbour Centre.

Weiller D. and Laumonier C. (1993) 'French case study: urban policy and social integration of elderly people in Niort', in G. Gottschalk and P. Potter (eds) *Better housing and living conditions for older people: Case studies from six European cities*, Hørsholm: Statens Byggeforskningsinstitut (SBI).

Wenger G.C. (1986) *Swedish services for the elderly: Report of a study visit*, Bangor: Centre for Social Policy Research and Development, University College of North Wales.

Wertheimer A. (1991) *Innovative community care projects*, London: National Federation of Housing Associations.

Wertheimer A. (1993) *Innovative older peoples housing projects*, London: National Federation of Housing Associations.

Westlake D. and Pearson M. (1995) *Maximising independence, minimising risk: Older peoples management of their health*, Working Paper 3, Liverpool: Health and Community Care Research Unit, University of Liverpool.

Wigley V., Fisk M., Gisby B. and Preston-Shoot M. (1998) *Older people in care homes: Consumer perspectives*, London: Office of Fair Trading.

Wild C. and Kirschner A. (eds) (1994) *Technology for the elderly: Safety alarm systems, technical aids and smart homes*, Akon series Ageing in the Contemporary Society, vol 8, Knegsel: Akontes Publishing.

Wilson G. (2000) *Understanding old age: Critical and global perspectives*, London: Sage Publications.

Wirz H. (1982) 'Sheltered housing', in E. Reinach (ed) *Developing services for the elderly: Research highlights no 3*, Aberdeen: Department of Social Work, University of Aberdeen.

Woolham J. and Frisby B. (2002) 'Building a local infrastructure that supports the use of assistive technology in the care of people with dementia', *Research Policy and Planning*, vol 20, no 1, paper 2.

Woolham J., Frisby B., Quinn S., Smart W. and Moore A. (2002) *The safe at home project: Using technology to support the care of people with dementia in their own home*, London: Hawker Publications.

Working Party on Services for the Elderly (1988) *The years ahead ... a policy for the elderly*, Dublin: The Stationery Office.

Wright D. (1998) 'Telemedicine and developing countries: a report of study group 2 of the ITU development sector', *Journal of Telemedicine and Telecare*, vol 4, suppl 2, appendix, pp 38-73.

Wylde M. and Valins M.S. (1996) 'The impact of technology', in M.S. Valins and D. Salter (eds) *Futurecare: New directions in planning health and care environments*, Oxford: Blackwell Science, pp 15-24.

Yatim L. (1997) 'An Israeli cardiac telenursing call center: home cardiac telemonitoring – revisiting Israel's Shahal', *Telemedicine Today*, December, pp 28-33.

Zhang Y., Bai J., Zhou X., Dai B., Cui Z., Lin J., Ding C., Zhang P., Yu B., Ye L., Shen D., Zhu Z., Zhang J., Ye D. and Zhou L. (1997) 'First trial of home ECG and blood pressure telemonitoring system in Macau', *Telemedicine Journal*, vol 3, no 1, pp 67-72.

Zoche P. (1994) 'Emergency aid: private alarm systems in a social and organisational environment, experiences and perspectives of the German Hausnotruf', in C. Wild and A. Kirschner (eds) *Technology for the elderly: Safety alarm systems, technical aids and smart homes*, Akon series Ageing in the Contemporary Society, vol 8, Knegsel: Akontes Publishing.

Index

Page references for tables and plates are in *italics*; those for notes are followed by n

Also available from The Policy Press

Assistive technology and telecare

Forging solutions for independent living

Simon Brownsell, Barnsley District General Hospital and University of Sheffield, **David Bradley**, University of Abertay Dundee. Edited by **Jeremy Porteus**, Office of the Deputy Prime Minister's Housing for Older People Working Group.

Paperback £14.99 ISBN 1 86134 462 7
297 x 210mm 100 pages January 2003

Telecare

New ideas for care and support @ home

Puay Tang, **David Gann** and **Richard Curry**
SPRU, Science and Technology Policy Research, University of Sussex; Richard Curry is an independent consultant

Paperback £12.99 ISBN 1 86134 216 0
297 x 210mm 64 pages May 2000

Social work and direct payments

Jon Glasby, Health Services Management Centre, University of Birmingham and **Rosemary Littlechild**, Department of Social Policy and Social Work, University of Birmingham

Paperback £17.99 ISBN 1 86134 385 X
Harback £50.00 ISBN 1 86134 386 8
234 x 156mm 184 pages July 2002

For further information about these and other titles published by The Policy Press, please visit our website at:
www.policypress.org.uk

To order titles, please contact:
Marston Book Services
PO Box 269 • Abingdon
Oxon OX14 4YN • UK
Tel: +44 (0)1235 465500
Fax: +44 (0)1235 465556
E-mail: direct.orders@marston.co.uk